Devil Take
The Youngest

DEVIL TAKE THE YOUNGEST:
The War on Childhood

by Winkie Pratney

HUNTINGTON HOUSE INC.

Shreveport ● Lafayette
Louisiana

*Huntington House, Inc.
1200 N. Market St., Shreveport, LA 71107*

*Library of Congress Catalog Card Number
85-80017*

ISBN Number 0-910311-29-3

Designed by Don Pierce

Printed in the United States of America

DEDICATED: To the LORD JESUS who made my part in the battle possible. To FAE, who makes my part of the battle worthwhile. And to BILLY-DAVID and all the children of his world who make my part of the battle so urgent.

THE SPIRIT OF MOLOCH
IN THE 1980s

This book is a challenge to war. This war is being fought now; like it or not, ready or not, and know it or not, YOU are in it. It is a battle of two rival kingdoms for the future of this generation; and the *winner names the age.*

This war is a war waged on *childhood.* Not just children, although children are really and quite literally being destroyed by it every day, but something even more basic: the whole idea of what childhood means to each generation of adults as well as children and the chance to be loved, safe and happy.

This book is in three parts. The first is about where this war began, and who began it. It is about the darkness of the past. It will show you the powerful patterns and ancient alien presences your spiritual ancestors fought to give their families and children a chance to survive. It will give you some of the keys to understanding the battle

7

and how you can join the fight yourself. It may shock you to see what went on in those days; it will shock you to know that it never stopped. In Part One, we show you where these occult powers began and why; you will learn to recognize the kind of world where civilizations kill their own children.

Part Two is a simple and single section. It is a look at this unique generation of children. It will tell you how and why and where they are different than any other generation before them. It will help you understand some of the reasons why they are under pressures no group of children in history has ever had to face. It may help you love them enough to fight for their lives.

Part Three is the saddest and ugliest part of the book. It details this war. It is a closer look at the web of destruction that threatens the children of our world. It looks at children, our children, that are being battered, raped, discarded, prostituted and murdered; the runaways, throwaways, and sacrifices of a culture that has enthroned again the spirit of Moloch in our time. It may make you angry; it may make you cry; but I hope to God it makes you do something.

This book is about a war but it is also a book about a victory. It is, in its own small way, a call to sign up in the only army that can make the ultimate difference for the future of our world.

Winkie Pratney
Manurewa N.Z. 1985

CONTENTS

PART I
The Occult Roots
of the War

Occult Roots of the War

Our search for the occult roots of the attack on childhood and the family must take us down some ancient and awful paths. It is a journey through "the dark side" of religious history; these roads to the past take us through the ugliest spiritual territories of deeply diverse cultures and nations. But as we go, we will notice one striking fact; much of this gathered darkness has a horrible similarity. At each crossroad we meet again and again the stuff of nightmares; another and another enthroned evil entity with names (as G. K. Chesterton put it) "that sound like laughter in hell" dealing out physical and spiritual death to children and parents alike. But time and time again, all these ghastly gods are the recurring image of just one original. The names seem changed, in this case, only to protect the guilty; the religion that kills children has its own "family tree" and its own "founding father." Each explored path invariably points back to the dawn of history and the mysterious story of one of the most significant figures of the ancient world. *His name was Nimrod.*

13

NIMROD

We first meet Nimrod in the Bible shortly after the great Flood of Judgment that first destroyed the world. Ancient Eden was gone, but the sin that led to its destruction was still abroad, in a world where both men and animals turned wild. Some territories became overrun with wild beasts, who in their fear and suspicion turned against their fallen earthly guardian, man. Into this battle between men and beasts came the son of Cush, a legendary hunter.

Nimrod was called a "mighty one," a "mighty hunter" before the Lord (Gen. 10: 8-10). Now the phrase "mighty one" is often used in the Bible to express heroism, greatness or grandeur. Cunningham Geikie thinks it likely that it means "the glorious" or "splendid" . . . "That his name filled the ear of the world in his own distant day is sufficiently proved by the fact that with those of Solomon and Alexander the Great it still has a mysterious grandeur among all the peoples of western Asia" (*Geike, Hours With The Bible,* Vol. 1, p. 272).

"Nimrod was a great ruler," says Matthew Henry. . . "Some way or other by art or by arms, he got power and so laid the foundations of a monarchy . . . other nations soon learned to incorporate under one head for their common safety and welfare" (*Commentary,* p. 24). Nimrod was by all accounts a very significant man in the ancient world. Alexander Hislop, whose fascinating study on this area in his book *The Two Babylons* is a detailed and important resource, comments: "The amazing extent of the worship of this man indicates something very extraordinary in his character; there is ample reason to believe that in his own day he was the object of high popularity. Though by setting up as king, Nimrod invaded the patriarchal system and abridged the liberties of mankind, yet he was held by many to have conferred benefits upon them that amply identified them for the loss of their liberties and covered him with glory and renown" (Hislop, *The Two Babylons,* p. 51).

Some commentators think that in this particular biblical passage the phrase "mighty one," in reference to Nimrod, implies not only a grandeur and greatness, but also a more hostile meaning; that Nimrod's meteoric rise to political power and fame gave rise to his rebellion against God. (The Septuagint translates Nimrod was a mighty hunter "before the Lord" as "AGAINST" the Lord). To set up a new government he seems to have set up a new religion of idolatry; perhaps he carried on his oppression and violence in defiance of God himself. Henry again comments:

"Nimrod was a great hunter; with this he began, and with this became famous to a proverb. 1. Some think he did good by ridding his country of wild beasts. 2. Others think that under the pretense of hunting he gathered men under his command in pursuit of another game he had to play, which was to make himself master of the country." Nimrod, greatest hunter in the world, began to hunger after global game—the domination of the world. "The same spirit that actuated the giants before the flood now revived in him. There are some in whom ambition and affectation of dominion seem to be bred in the bone. Nothing this side of hell will humble and break the proud spirits of some men" (*Commentary,* op. cit p. 24).

Hislop believes that the name "Nimrod" comes from "Nimr," a leopard, and "rada" or "rad," to subdue. Nimr-rod was "the Subduer of the Spotted One;" hence in his later worship (under other names) the Egyptian use of high priestly robes of leopard skins and later (in Greece) of a fawn (pp. 44-47). He comments, "The name Nimrod is commonly derived from Mered 'to rebel' but a difficulty has always been found in regard to this . . . it would make the name Nimrod properly passive, not 'the rebel' but 'he who was rebelled against.' There is no doubt that Nimrod WAS a rebel, and that his rebellion is celebrated in ancient myths; but his name in that character was not Nimrod, but MERODACH, or among the Romans 'Mars,' 'the rebel' " (Footnote: *The Two Babylons,* p. 44). And that he came to be called by many other names also, we shall presently see.

Nimrod's skill in hunting down the wild animals that threatened cities, and his great building ability, led to the next step; organizing all the cities into one united kingdom under, of course, his personal protection. Had it stopped there, history may have been significantly different; but it did not. "Had Nimrod gained renown only by delivering men from the fear of wild beasts it had been well. . . but he set to work also to emancipate them from that fear of the Lord which is the beginning of wisdom and in which alone true happiness can be found."

Nimrod began to perceive himself as a Savior, a Deliverer, if you like, a Messiah. "One of the titles men delighted to honor him with was 'Emancipator' or 'Deliverer'; he is probably also 'the Apostate' or Phoroneus who first 'gathered men together' and offered idolatrous sacrifice. In one form or another this title was handed down to his deified successors as a title of honor. All tradition from the earliest times bears testimony to the apostasy of Nimrod and to his success in leading men away from the patriarchal faith and 'delivering' their minds from that awe of God and fear of the judgments of heaven that must have rested on them while the memory of the Flood was yet recent. . . Men will rally around anyone who can give the least appearance of plausibility to any doctrine which will teach that they can be assured of happiness and heaven at last though their hearts and natures are unchanged and though they live without God in the world" (*Hislop,* op. cit. p. 52).

Nimrod the Hunter was the focus of legends, the kind of epic, evil figure around whom mythic stories arise. According to Jewish rabbinical legend, Nimrod's ancient reign was not only physical and military, but he actually gained rule in the ancient world by borrowed supernatural power. Without doubt exaggerated and fantastic, they nevertheless tell how that after Nimrod made himself invincible in battle he extended his rule continually "till by his cunning he made men regard him as the lord of the whole earth and persuaded them to look no longer to God but to trust only to their own powers." According to their story, Nimrod feared a new leader was shortly to be born who could turn the people back to God. Attempting to save his throne and his kingdom, (and significantly, like two other recorded power-mad kings in later biblical history) he put out the first mass contract on the children of his time:

"The longer Nimrod sat on his throne, the prouder he became. Having failed to kill the babe Abraham, as he desired, he slew 70,000 children in the hope that the dreaded child might be among them. He was full of forebodings that his empire would fall, and that a man should rise who would revive that of Him to whom alone all the glory and majesty of the earth rightly belong. To further prevent this, and to unite the people in his rebellion, he founded not only the first city of Babylon but the Tower" (*Geikie,* op. cit. p. 286).

FOUNDER OF BABYLON

"The beginning of his kingdom was Babel" (Gen. 10:10). Nimrod founded *Babylon.* He was a great builder. Possibly the architect in the building of Babel. "He (Nimrod) aimed at universal monarchy . . . under pretense of uniting for their common safety, he contrives to keep them in one body, that having them all under his eye, he might not fail to have them all under his power. It is God's prerogative to be universal monarch, Lord of all and King of Kings; the man that aims at it offers to step into the throne of God, who will not give his glory to another." Henry thinks that when his project to rule all the sons of Noah was baffled by the confusion of tongues "out of that land he went forth into Assyria (so the margin reads it, v.11) and built Ninevah, etc. (op. cit. p. 24) To him is ascribed the foundation of the great Babylonian empire and also the building of the cities which were afterwards combined together under the general name of Ninevah (after Ashur, one of the ancient capitals of Assyria). He therefore becomes also the founder of Assyria, and this country is called by the prophet Micah (5:6) 'the land of Nimrod' " (*Peoples Bible Encyclopaedia* p. 791).

Geikie, while pointing out that traditional Jewish views of Nimrod as an arch rebel against God and the prime mover in the building of the Tower of Babel (Josephus) are not established record, believes that history concurs: (1) That Nimrod was without doubt the *major military leader* of the world of his time, the founder of a "great empire" that absorbed the whole of west Asia, and one who was "the Caesar or Napoleon of the first races of men." (2) Nimrod was *worshipped as a god* at some time by his people; "There is at least very little doubt that the great king was deified after his death if not before it . . ." (*Geikie* op. cit. p. 280).

THE TOWER OF BABEL

What was this ancient wonder of the world? What was it like? And why did it draw such a drastic Divine intervention? We have a clue to its awesome size from discovered archaelogical ruins believed to be either the remains of the tower itself, or perhaps an attempt to duplicate something very much like it:

"It is at Borsippa... more than twelve miles in a straight line from the huge mound known as Babel that we find the most interesting trace of the earliest ages of Babylon, in the vast heap that has immemorially borne the name of Birs Nimrud, or the Tower of Nimrod. This great ruin, a bare hill of yellow sand and bricks near the left bank of the Euphrates reaches a height of 198 ft.; a vast mass of brickwork jutting from the mound to a further height... 235 ft. in all.

"If measurements given by ancient authorities are correct, the building must have indeed been immense, for the Great Pyramid itself is only 750 ft. square at its base, and rises to a height of only 480 ft.; whereas this tower from a square base of over 600 ft. rose 120 ft. higher... Alexander the Great employed 10,000 men for two months removing the rubbish which at his day had fallen from it" (*Geike* op. cit. pp. 275-276).

Despite its massive size, did the ancients really think they could "reach heaven" by building a skyscraper? No. Those who put that construct together may have been a lot smarter than we traditionally give them credit. This was no mere ladder of bricks to the sky. The tower was not just some stupid and ignorant attempt to physically invade "heaven" as if the actual sky was the realm of God's rulership. The phrase used in Genesis 11:4 is unclear; but it does not mean "to reach to heaven." The top of the tower was to be "in the heavens;" some think it had a much more dangerous significance. From the ancient records of its construction we find that it was built along religious and occult lines; a precise geometric shape, perhaps designed to focus and concentrate psychic power much like the supposed function of the pyramid or the pentagram; a center of astrological and occult research in which the combined might and mind of rebellious man might search out the structure of the universe, the nature of space and matter and time, and perhaps play God with the universe: "now nothing will be restrained from them which they have imagined to do" (Gen. 11:6).

"The original form of the whole structure (known to the Greeks as the 'Temple of Belus') was that of seven square towers, rising one above the other like gigantic steps; each smaller than the one below it and consecrated respectively to the seven planetary gods, to whom they formed distinct temples. (Saturn at the bottom; then ascending; Venus, Jupiter, Mercury, Mars, the moon and the sun; the colors assigned to the particular deity; black, white, orange, blue, scarlet, silver and gold distinguishing the respective storeys)" (*Geikie,* op. cit. pp. 275-276). In modern terms, it may have been the focal point of a demonically-inspired research project involving an ancient marriage of science and the supernatural, a combined humanistic attempt to lock into heaven's secrets. Combined with the secularized unity of man's communication and fallen imagination, the project was apparently so dangerous it drew a direct Divine intervention (Gen. 11:7-9).

The name Babel means "confusion;" the great project begun to unite mankind to seek the secrets of the universe was visited by Divine judgment. "Those that aim at a great name commonly come off with a BAD name," comments Henry wryly. "They would leave the monument of their pride and ambition and folly. We do not find in any history the name of so much as one of these Babel-builders. . . Yet the Tower of Babel did, in its own way, make its sorry mark in history; it marked the focal point of the first kingdom that was built outside of God. Babel is remembered in Babylon; and 'throughout the OT and NT, Babylon stands theologically for the community that is anti-God' " (*Int. Standard Bible Ency.* Vol. 1 p. 385).

Babylon is the Greek form of Babel, or in Semitic form, Babilu, "The Gate of God." The ancient city lay on the bank of the Euphrates in the land of Shinar (Gen. 10:10) in the northern area of Babylonia (now southern Iraq) called Accad or Akkad (as opposed to the southern area, called Sumer).

Ancient Babylon

What exactly is Babylon? The word is used both *historically* and *symbolically;* its rebel origins are transferred as a pattern to ANY ORGANIZED STRUCTURE THAT ATTEMPTS TO REPLACE GOD'S KINGDOM REIGN WITH HUMAN OR DEMONIC SUBSTITUTE. In the New Testament the word has been also thought a symbol for the *ruling religious-military power of the world.* As Hislop notes: "In Rev. 14:8; 16:19; 17:5; 18:2, Babylon is supposed to mean Rome, not considered as pagan, but as the promulgation of the ancient power in the papal form . . . The literal Babylon was the beginner and supporter of tyranny and idolatry . . . the city and its whole empire were taken by the Persians under Cyrus: the Persians were subdued by the Macedonians and the Macedonians by the Romans: so that Rome succeeded to the power of the old Babylon. And it was her method to adopt the worship of false deities she had conquered: so that by her own act she became the heiress and successor of all the Babylonian idolatry, and of all that was introduced into it by the immediate successors of Babylon, and consequently of all the idolatry of the earth."

*"As for my people, children are their oppressors
and women rule over them" (Isaiah 3:12).*

THE MYSTERY RELIGION
OF BABYLON

What was practiced in the ancient cults? And why does God call Babylon, "the mother of harlots, and of all the abominations of the earth?" What is the significance of Babylon?

Here we find the crux of the conflict, the dark heart of the occult war. While the Scriptures' primary concern is to deal practically and spiritually with the RESULTS of this evil, they do not inform us nor even require us to know of its roots and its origins. After all, nothing much need be said ABOUT evil in order to LEAVE it; and the Bible method of dealing with wrong is to surrender in faith and love to the right, embodied in the nature and person of God Himself in Christ.

But men and women of our amoral century do not now understand why Israel fought so fiercely against the pagan deities of their time, still less, when under the direct command of a loving and merciful God. Baal, Moloch, Chemosh, Astarte and Ashtoreth are bygone bogies from another time, archaic names without modern meaning. What possible relationship or significance can some ancient anti-family modes of pagan worship bear on the fact that our own 20th century families are falling apart, our own modern marriages are disintegrating, and our own children are dying?

Israel understood. They went to battle against something spawned in ancient Babylon for their lives and future. It was life or death, not with faceless and quaint religious concepts, but genuinely demonic realities that, left alone to infect others, would destroy everything beautiful and holy in the world. The war Nimrod's Babylon began so long ago and far away has come to our time, our place and our homes. In the old days, demons "wandered abroad like dragons." Did they leave then, in our enlightened age? Did reason and science and education exorcise them from our world? Not at all. *Moloch lives; Ashera still flaunts her power; Baal is exalted once again.* In our time, they have not passed away; they have but learned how to hide. What was the horror that moved so merciful a God to mobilize his chosen people to root that terrible stalk and branch out of the world? What it was, it began, at least on Earth, at Babylon.

THE VIOLENT
DEATH OF NIMROD

What happened to Nimrod? According to tradition, Nimrod's ambition and greed drove him further and further into the occult; he eventually became the high priest of devil-worship. Along the way he joined forces with *Semiramis,* a stunningly beautiful, clever, but patently immoral woman who became queen and may have helped build the battlements of his Tower. Then, without warnings, with the whole world at his feet, Nimrod was suddenly summoned to eternity. His end came swiftly, and in shrouded circumstances; there is some evidence it was an act of judgment.

"(As to) how Nimrod died Scripture is entirely silent. There was an ancient tradition that he came to a violent end. . . . profane history speaks darkly and mysteriously, though one account tells of his having met with a violent death . . ." (*Hislop*, p.55). It was represented symbolically as him being judicially TORN TO PIECES; in whatever way it must have shocked the world much more than the death of John Kennedy in the 1960s. This may have been the origin of the gruesome custom used by some as a national alarm and call for judgment in biblical days (Judges 19:29; I Sam. 11:7).

In the midst of his glorious career Nimrod is suddenly cut off by a horrible, violent death; when the shocking news spreads abroad, the "devotees of pleasure felt as if the best benefactor of mankind was gone, and the gaity of nations eclipsed. Thus began those 'weepings of Tammuz' in the guilt of which the daughters of ·Israel allowed themselves to be implicated, and the existence of which can be traced not merely in annals of classical antiquity but in the literature of the world from Ultima Thule to Japan" (*Hislop*, op. cit. p. 57).

Of all the concerned in the awful death of Nimrod none was more so than his wife, Semiramis, "who from an originally humble position had been raised to share with him the throne of Babylon." This was an emergency. All that she had was about to slip away, but she was a woman of great resolution and ambition. What could she do to retain her place on the throne? "In life her husband had been honored as a hero; in death she will have him worshipped as a god" (*Hislop*, op. cit. p. 58).

THE "SEED OF THE WOMAN" PROPHECY

The ancient world was familiar with the Edenic prophecy of the promised "seed of the woman" who would "bruise the serpent's head" and in so doing have his own heel bruised. They knew this implied the death of the Deliverer was the only thing that could remove the curse from the world. The idea of the Deliverer slaying the serpent runs through all the ancient traditions; Apollo slaying the serpent Pytho, Hercules strangling serpents while yet in his cradle, Horus piercing a snake's head with his spear, Calyia, the malignant serpent, slain by Vishnu in his avatar of Krishna, Thor bruising the head of the great serpent with his mace, Achilles, the only son of the goddess, invincible except in his heel.

Semiramis drew on her husband's initiation of magic and sorcery in Babel; she would make his death voluntary, mystical, for the benefit of the world. It was Semiramis that apparently initiated the secret mysteries; Nimrod's form of death would be covered up, made an act of devotion and greater power. And the facilities were there. Though carefully protected and kept secret, the initiations were fantastic, dramatic productions designed to awe and terrify, complete with the most advanced special effects.

The Babylonian mystery-initiation ceremonies were the SFX houses of their day. After candidates had passed through the confessional and sworn the required oaths, the historian Wilkerson says:

"Strange and amazing objects presented themselves. Sometimes the place they were in seemed to shake around them; sometimes it appeared bright and resplendent with light and radiant fire, and then again covered with black darkness; sometimes thunder and lightning, sometimes frightful noises and bellowings, sometimes terrible apparitions astonished the trembling spectators. Then at last the great god, the central object of their worship, Osiris, Tammuz, Nimrod or Adonis was revealed to them in a way most fitted to soothe their feelings and engage their blind affections." One ancient pagan guardedly gives a description of an apparent miracle, generated, it seems now, by an early ancestor of the movie, *The Magic Lantern;* "In a manifestation which one must not reveal . . . there is seen on a wall of the temple a mass of light, which appears at first at a very great distance. It is transformed, while unfolding itself into a visage evidently divine and supernatural of an aspect severe, but with a touch of sweetness. Following the teachings of a mysterious religion the Alexandrians honor it as Osiris or Adonis" (*Damascius, Bibliotheca cod.* 242, p. 343. Quoted by *Hislop,* p. 68).

TAMMUZ — THE GOD-CHILD

Somehow, Semiramis had to convey to the world that Nimrod had returned, that the "god" they loved had come back in a greater and more awesome display of his past glory. The obvious path, if you were going to claim something arrogantly significant, was the prophecy of the coming "seed of the woman" (Gen. 3:15). No doubt, with the full power of all the special effects she could muster, the die was cast. and she made her play to a waiting world. Rejoice: the dying god had risen again, in the form of her son.

Son? *What* son? Where did she get the child? A small detail for one like Semiramis to whom morality was power! That Semiramis was sexually immoral was a matter of record; the child she brazenly presented to the world was fair while Nimrod had been black! (*Hislop,* op. cit. 69). She may have become pregnant while Nimrod was away; now he is killed before he could return and she claims the baby as his. Perhaps even the most gullible of her kingdom would not put up with an unfaithful queen; maybe her life was on the line. The actual circumstances are unknown. But what she did was to lay the major occult foundations of demonic power in the world. To sanctify her adultery and justify her bastard child, she announces the Great Lie: she is the Virgin of Prophecy; the child she carries is the promised Messiah, the God-man, the Seed of Woman. Nimrod had "visited her in a flash of light" and the child she bears is the reincarnated king, elevated now to the status of a god.

If you hope to rule the world through a lie, better tell a *big* one. It catches on. It spreads like wildfire! The word goes around the world: "Nimrod is back; the ancient prophecy is fulfilled; who knows now what mankind can accomplish?" The people worship the child (Tammuz) as both their reincarnated king and their god (eventually to become known as Baal, the sun-god); and Semiramis moves smoothly, unobtrusively with the real power in her hands to direct worship from behind the throne. Thus the great launching of the mystery religion of Babylon, the worship of Rhea and Nin, the divine mother and child that spread from here, eventually to demonically affect the whole world.

To recap—Semiramis claims Nimrod is now the sun-god; the deified Nimrod thus becomes Baal, (the sun-god) with fire his earthly representation, and was thus later known also by sun- or life-symbols, fish, trees and erotic, phallic pillars. Her child Tammuz later becomes represented by symbols like the golden calf, as the son of the sun-god. Here are the three key figures in the pattern; Nimrod, Semiramis and Tammuz; a famous but sinful king who dies or is cut

off; an immoral queen who encourages false worship and who bears
a child that is elevated to the status of a god. The child, in all various
incarnations, is often seen as the husband/lover/consort as well as
the son of his mother.

This is the result of Hislop's detailed findings; track down the
deities of the ancient world and you will find a great majority
conform to the same pattern. "The Babylonians in their popular
religion, supremely worshipped a *goddess mother and a son* who
was represented in pictures and images as an infant or child in his
mother's arms. From Babylon this worship of the mother and child
spread across the whole earth. In Egypt, the mother and child were
worshipped under the names of ISIS and HORUS (OSIRIS=Nim-
rod); in India as ISI and ISWARA; in ancient Harrapan, SHAKTI
and SIVA; in Asia as CYBELE (SYBIL) and DEOIUS; in pagan
Rome as FORTUNA and Jupiter-pua, or JUPITER the boy. In
Greece she was CERES, the Great Mother with the babe at her
breast, or as IRENE, Goddess of Peace, with the boy PLUTUS in
her arms. Even in Tibet, China and Japan, Jesuit missionaries were
astonished to find the counterpart of the madonna and child as
SHING MOO, the holy mother represented with a child in her arms
and a glory around her exactly as if a Roman Catholic artist had
been employed to set her up" (*Hislop,* op. cit. p. 21).

There follows page after page of laborious analysis and comparison; Hislop draws from scores of diverse sources to nail down
his thesis, and finally concludes: "Thus from Assyria, Egypt and
Greece we have cumulative and overwhelming evidence all con-
spiring to demonstrate that the child worshipped in the areas of the
goddess-mother in all these countries . . . was Nimrod (reincarnated), the son of Cush. A feature here, or an incident there may
have been borrowed from some succeeding hero; but it seems impossible to doubt that . . . Nimrod was the prototype, the grand
original" (*Hislop,* p. 50).

The mother/child figure is, of course, an *ancient demonic counterpart to Mary and Christ.* Barbara Walker sees support for modern goddess worship in the Roman church: "Though Catholics still
worship the goddess under some of her old pagan titles, such as
"Mother of God," "Queen of Heaven," "Blessed Virgin" and so on,
their theologians refuse to admit she is the old goddess in a new

disguise, and paradoxically insist on her non-divinity" (*Womans' Encyclopaedia of Myths & Secrets,* p.viii). Of course, some don't; on one cross in modern Rome, Mary hangs on the other side of Jesus. In Babylon, both mother and child were treated as divine; at first the mother BECAUSE of the child; then later as equals. Finally, publically as well as privately, Semiramis calls the signals.

Hislop again observes: "While the mother derived her glory in the first instance from the divine character attributed to the child in her arms, the mother, in the long run, practically eclipsed her son" (p. 74). And why not? After all, Semiramis was the real power behind the poor puppet boy, brought up to believe the tragic lies about him were true. While the son was merely represented in art and sculpture without any particular focus of attention, the mother was something else again.

Semiramis (the original woman from which the Greek goddess of love APHRODITE and the Roman beauty VENUS were also derived) was apparently an absolutely (and quite literally) stunning beauty. Her sudden appearance among her subjects once actually quelled an uprising among them, and drew such admiration over the unforgettable memory of her in that incident, that they erected a statue to her in Babylon! She was "in point of fact the historical origin of the beauty goddess" and in the ancient world regarded as "the very embodiment of everything attractive in the female form and the perfection of female beauty." Semiramis, the mother, in fact became the favorite object of worship.

THE REINCARNATED GODDESS

In a book by *Aduleius,* a Roman writer of the second century A.D., the "Goddess" explains who she is:

"I am Nature, the universal Mother, mistress of all elements, primordial child of time, sovereign of all things spiritual, queen of the dead, queen also of the immortals, the single manifestation of all gods and goddesses that are. . . Though I am worshipped in many aspects, known by countless names and propitiated with all manner of different rites, yet the whole earth venerates me.

"The primeval Phyrigians call me PESSINUNTICA, mother of

the gods; the Athenians . . . CecropianARTEMIS; for the islanders of Cyprus, I am Paphian APHRODITE; for the archers of Crete, I am DICTYNNA; for the trilingual Silicians, Stygian PROSPER-INE, and for the Eleusians, their ancient Mother of Corn. Some know me as JUNO, some as BELLONA of the Battles; others as HECATE, RHAMNUBI . . . but both races of Aetheopians, whose lands the morning sun first shines upon and the Egyptians who excel in ancient learning and worship me with ceremonies proper to my godhead, call me by my true name, namely Queen ISIS" (*The Golden Ass; Robert Graves transl.* p. 22).

Look at the regions where the Goddess religion originally spread. They read like a summary of the world's major trouble-spots; areas now known as *Iran, Iraq, India, Saudi Arabia, Lebanon, Jordan, Israel* (Palestine), *Egypt, Sinai, Libya, Syria,* and *Turkey;* areas where powerful demonic princes still reign. *Greece* and *Italy* had entrenched goddess-worship as well as the large island cultures of *Crete* (of the Minotaur legend), *Cyprus, Malta, Sicily* and *Sardinia.* "The *Celts* . . . were known to have sent priests to a sacred festival for the goddess Cybele in Pessinus and Anatolia in the second century B.C. Carvings at Karnac and the Gallic shrines of Chartres and Mont-Saint-Michel in France suggests these sites were once devoted to the Goddess" (*When God Was A Woman,* Merlin Stone, p. 24).

Hislop continues in his detailed analysis to trace the development of the mother-son figure and related Babylonian mysteries to the Roman church and the more obvious deviations from biblical truth apparent in that structure. And it is certainly true that "at the fall of Babylon, the Babylonian priests fled to Pergamos (Rev. 2:12-17) where the symbol of the serpent representing concealed wisdom was introduced. From Pergamos, the cult spread to Etruscan plains of Italy where the priests adopted tall, pointed mitres in honor of the fish god Dagon . . ." (*"Sex Through The Looking Glass,"* Lambert Dolphin).

But Babylon as a pattern, Babylon as a structure, is much more widespread than the Church of Rome. Babylon is not just a city reincarnated in the past in Imperial Rome; Babylon is a *supernatural pattern,* a demonic structure that even now profoundly influences the entire world. Babylon, "the mother of harlots and the abominations of the earth," never died. *Babylon is here; and Babylon is now.*

SEMIRAMIS
IN THE 20th CENTURY

Before any other institution was ever introduced, God made the *home.* He established it before the church, before the school, before the government. Rich or poor, whatever our race, culture, or nationality, we once could call some place "home." It was to be the core of every country and very foundation of society. Because the home is also an earthly pattern of Divine spiritual reality, *the main target of evil is the home.* When God's pattern for the home is hurt, spiritual and moral destruction results. And there exists such an anti-Christian pattern. To understand it is to have the key to a vast number of home conflicts. We have seen this demonic pattern already at the dawn of civilization; the origin of occult worship in the first non-Christian kingdom of Babylon. Now we shall see the effect of the pattern superimposed on the home and the family.

THE BABYLONIAN PATTERN

As we have seen, ancient Babylon's religion became the foundation of all false and idolatrous worship. *Babylon is the prototype of all organized structures that rebel against God; Babylon is, in fact, a PATTERN OF SPIRITUAL DESTRUCTION.* Carl Jung, the psychologist, not a believer himself, nevertheless had some key insights when he studied the effects of what he thought of as powerful religious myths in the collective unconsciousness of mankind. His book, *Symbols of Transformation,* described and documented the strange and contradictory attributes of the goddess which he named "the loving and terrible mother." In his classic, *Four Archetypes,* he shows the psychological effect of the goddess pattern on the home, which he calls *"The Mother Archetype:"*

"The concept of the Great Mother belongs to the field of comparative religion and embraces widely varying types of mother-goddess . . . Like any other archetype it appears under an almost infinite variety of aspects" (pp. 9, 15).

He notes that its strengths are associated with a mother's care and sympathy; "the magic authority of the female; the wisdom and spiritual exaltation that transcend reason; any helpful instinct or impulse; all that is benign, all that cherishes or sustains, that fosters growth and fertility. The place of magic, transformation and rebirth together with the underworld and its inhabitants are presided over by the mother."

But, "on the *negative* side, the mother archetype may connote anything secret, hidden, dark, the abyss, the world of the dead, anything that devours, seduces and poisons, that is terrifying and inescapable like fate" (p. 16).

THE MOTHER AS A CARRIER

Jung claims that the powerful influences of the mother-figure exerted on the children in all personalistic psychologies "do not come from the mother *herself,* but rather from the *archetype projected upon her* which gives her a mythical background and invests her with authority and numinosity" (op. cit., p.18). In other words, a

mother has a spiritual pattern that can unconsciously weight her
influence over the home. Lambert Dolphin, in his exceptional little
book, *Sex Through The Looking-Glass,* points out the profound
insight an understanding of this goddess pattern brings to the pattern
of the home:

"Nimrod married Semiramis (a 'daughter of the goddess') who
bore a son named Tammuz. In the mystery religion of Babylon,
Semiramis and Tammuz were defied and worshipped as a divine
pair, Madonna and Child. This 'divine pair' is found in the pagan
fertility gods of the Canaanites who inhabited Palestine; they can be
identified as Isis and Osiris in Egyptian mythology, in Greece as
Venus and Cupid, in ancient Rome as Aphrodite and Eros. They are
also found in the pagan religions of national apostasy from Jehovah
as mentioned in Ezekiel 8. In Jeremiah (44:17.25), the Jews offered
cakes to the 'queen of heaven' (Semiramis or Ashtoreth), the virgin
mother of Tammuz. The worship of Tammuz in the O.T., the cult of
the mother and son with the missing father, is what modern psychology calls the Oedipus complex" (p. 22).

Dolphin notes that while the Babylonian pattern affects all visible
apostate organizations and that "during the end period, God will
call all believers to separate themselves," the *present battle is with
the pattern in ourselves.* ". . . God would have us recognize the
elements of apostasy in ourselves and the roots of incestuous ties
with the 'fallen' mother. It is an individual responsibility to break
free from all ties to our fallen parents through identification and faith
in the Second Adam, Jesus Christ. Rather than projecting our own
guilt upon others we are to let God handle the apostate church. We
are called upon to view ourselves in the complete truth which is
Jesus Christ (Matt. 10:34-39)," *(Dolphin* op. cit. p. 23).

PSYCHOLOGY'S INSIGHT
TO BABYLON

What Lambert Dolphin describes is a very significant insight; the
consequences of this ancient and darkly occult pattern even today in
a modern family. Today, psychologists that recognize the reality of
these pressures use clinical terms to label both the potential and the

problems; but the simple fact is, the biblical picture of the Church (the Bride) is the exact and direct opposite of what we can now see as Babylon (the Harlot). And the focus of both God the Father and Babylon the murderess, is the children.

Dolphin mentions how psychologists like Jung, (*Psychology of the Unconscious,* Dodd, Mead & Co. 1947), describe our psychic or emotional energy as "libido;" a word that means much more than mere sexual energy. "Jung discusses in great detail the child's initial investment of its libido in its mother as an object, and the lifelong process by which libido is transformed, detached from the mother, released from regressional processes and made available as love or creative, outgoing power to others." He sums up the essence then of commitment to God's pattern for us all: "Thus a child should . . . grow from helpless dependence on the mother, to marriage to a woman who no longer has the power to enslave and captivate him as his mother did" (p. 24).

LOSS OF A FATHER'S AUTHORITY

When a father is *not* a father, says Dolphin, i.e., when a father "abdicates his leadership responsibility to his wife, and fails to alleviate her deepest fears through love and strong guidance," serious problems in the home and family always result. The opposite of love is not *hate,* but *indifference,* so that indifference on the part of father to his wife or his children is serious indeed (I Jn. 3:15). Our tragic result of this Western abdication of fatherhood and strong male roles of community leadership is a *loss of a nation's creative spirit.* "National creative spirit fails because true creativity from the feminine element in society is dependent upon a strong masculine principle. Since all authority comes from God, the declining role of father in society reflects societies rejection of the authority of Jesus Christ and the Scriptures in his life. Jesus is called 'King of kings and Lord of lords' in the Bible because he intends that every man should be a king and a lord in his own life and home." But if a man rejects that biblical mandate, and attempts to establish some sort of kingship of self, he falls under the power of the Babylonian pattern. "When male authority is not derived from God, however, a man abdicates his rights to the 'feminine shadow' in his own unconcious, to his external wife or to the destructive forces of nature" (p. 25).

Thus a man is plunged under the power of darkness. Babylon arises; goddess worship is established; the hook goes in, and the journey downwards for the marriage, the family and the home begins. "The man who ignores God thinks he rules his own life, but actually his feminine 'shadow' does. He is a slave of the 'elemental spirits of the universe;' that is, he is a prisoner of culture, tradition, history, the family background, a conformist whether he likes it or not (Col. 2:8, 22-23; Gal. 4:1-3; Rom. 12:1-2). The man who commits sin is a slave to sin that is a prisoner within himself, held in the tresses of an internal harlot."

BIBLICAL FREEDOM
FROM BABYLON

To obey God by grace through faith, however, frees a person on all levels of their life, including those parts of the heart, mind and spirit that are not subject to direct counsel and reason. "Wisdom," says Dolphin, "is the *treasure of a redeemed subconcious,* a co-operative shadow of upwelling inner life. As a wife is man's helper and partner in life (Eph. 5:21-23), so the contrasexual components in the individual unconscious needs to be brought into subjection to Christ. A person thus becomes whole and balanced in himself. To be in union with Jesus means an inner marriage or fusion of the male and female elements in the personality which had previously not been integrated, or to put it another way, the 'land' which is found deep inside the 'kingdom of the heart' is free of its idols and its harlotries (Ex. 34:11-16). A Christian is complete or whole whether or not he or she marries" (op. cit. pp. 57-58).

CONSEQUENCES OF THE
MISSING FATHER

How does the initial breakdown in authority happen? When a person "gives in" to his wife in the garden rather than acknowledging God's revealed Word and following him by faith (Gen.

3:17-19). Shortly we shall see the awful and tragic results of our flippant abandonment of God's life-or-death warnings; the *destruction of childhood and children.* Dolphin notes: "Psychological studies of the generation under 25 show that many of our disillusioned youth come from upper middle-class homes where the father is for all purposes missing or ineffective. Fathers today provide economic and social status for their families, but usually destroy their sons and their daughters spiritually and psychologically in the process" (op. cit. p. 25).

Recently I spent an hour talking to a "rich and successful" wholly-materialistic businessman on the beach. His young son was playing in the water. He said he knew another Christian; it had really helped him, he said, but he was not interested in examining Jesus' claims for himself. He "knew the Bible was full of mistakes," although he confessed he had never read it. He told me he didn't believe in heaven, hell or God. "When you die, that's it," he said. "There's nothing." I looked at him. "Just a hole in the ground? Only 56 years, and nothing forever after? What about your son?" "Oh yes," he said. "My son. That's eternal life. He goes on after me." I looked again at the boy in the surf. "Are you willing to gamble his life as well as yours that you are right and Christ is wrong?" He hoped he was right. It was time to go. I hoped that something of what Jesus said would touch his Moloch-worshipping heart: "For what shall it profit a man," said Jesus, *"if he gain the whole world and lose his own soul?"* (Matt. 16:26). ". . . If a man offered for love all the wealth of his house it would be utterly scorned" (S/S 8:7).

THE OEDIPUS COMPLEX

Modern psychologists have observed that a boy's critical psychosexual development centers around his mother. "The mother," notes Jung, "is the first feminine being with whom the man-to-be comes in contact and she cannot help playing overtly or covertly, consciously or unconsciously, upon the son's masculinity just as the son in turn grows increasingly aware of his mother's femininity or unconsciously responds to it by instinct." Dolphin notes: "If a wife is not properly loved and made to feel secure by her husband, she usually becomes overprotective of her children and may project her unconscious wishes for a true lover on her son." This is what is called the OEDIPUS COMPLEX.

Jung says the typical effects of this mother-complex on the son are *"homosexuality, Don Juanism* and sometimes also *impotence.* In homosexuality it conditions the son's entire heterosexuality and Don Juanism; he unconsciously seeks his mother in every woman he meets." Dolphin observes that "the problem is compounded when the husband is missing (divorce, illegitimacy), because the boy does not have a physical father with which to identify— no one to model himself after unless it is an older friend, a brother or perhaps a Boy Scout leader. A boy is also deeply attached psychosexually to his mother at first, because of her warm unconditional protecting love; a mother is a boy's "first love." Although most boys have strongly repressed any incestuous desires felt toward the mother, the evidence of modern psychology seems to indicate incest is a deep problem in many families. . . A maturing boy has difficulty leaving the warm, sheltering love of his mother, especially if his father is cold, impersonal or non-existent. He may choose not to grow up rather than becoming like his unmanly dad, and secretly (i.e. unconsciously), he remains his mother's lover."

BABYLON AND HOMOSEXUALITY

Jung saw possible positive aspects in some sons' lives affected by a mother-complex; perhaps a great capacity for friendship even among men (although it may be also homosexual), good taste and aesthetic sense. He might be supremely gifted as a teacher because of his almost feminine insight and tact; he is "likely to have a feeling for history, cherish the values of the past and be conservative in the best sense." And he may often be endowed with "a wealth of religious feelings" and a "spiritual receptivity which makes him responsive to revelation." We could instead say that the true strengths of the mother's influence come when she derives her power, insight and authority from the heavenly pattern of the church under Christ, of which the goddess structure is only an occult perversion. Dolphin further notes:

"A healthy transition to adulthood involves an identification with the parent of the same sex followed by an internal synthesis of one's internal male/female heritage. Failure to overcome the Oedipal complex brings latent or overt homosexuality, or a bad marriage adjustment. The increasing gay population in the U.S. indicates fathers no longer exercise strong male roles of leadership in the home. Boys have no real men they can identify with. Dad is too busy making money, playing golf or watching television to love his son warmly and personally. Many men have partially resolved the Oedipal conflict in their own lives by marrying women who are just like their mother, and have thus actually returned to the bondage of the womb and infantile behavior patterns. Unless the original incestuous ties to the mother are broken, dependent ties to her are thus transmitted to the next generation and the culture deteriorates. The God-given order of relationships in marriage (I Cor. 11:3) thus breaks down and the entire society suffers disastrously from a lack of loving but strong male leadership" (pp. 21-22).

JESUS AND THE BABYLONIAN PATTERN

If *ever* a boy in the Bible had pressure put on him to conform to the Babylonian pattern, it was the *Lord Jesus Himself.* He not only had a mother who *wanted* him to be the Messiah; He WAS the Messiah! Joseph, Mary's husband, was in some way "cut off." He was not Christ's real father, and may have died early in Jesus' life; he is not mentioned after the early years. How powerful the ancient goddess pattern poised to twist the young Christ from his Father's purpose! Perhaps it was his profound spiritual sensitivity, whether He knew *then* all the underlying issues that drew out one of his first and most unusual responses to his mother, Mary.

Remember the first miracle? It was at a wedding in Cana of Galilee. The guests ran out of wine; and Mary and Jesus were there. So embarrassing! And Mary, bless her unsuspecting heart, makes the most innocent suggestion to her son, her loving, obedient son, the promised Messiah. It was only a simple hint: not even really a direct command, like; "Do me a miracle; make some wine." Just: "They have no wine." He would understand. Such a small thing. "I'm, after all, his mother." Jesus' reply sounds almost shocking: "Woman, what have I to do with you? My hour is not yet come" (John 2:4).

Woman? Not even "Mother?" And yet, in the light of what we have
seen, not shocking at all. The shadow of long-dead Semiramis hung
for a dark moment over Mary, and a tiny, controlling creeper slid
towards the boy that might be fitted into the mask of Tammuz. Not
all the most powerful temptations come in the wilderness. His
answer, strange at first to our ears, came like light. "My hour is not
yet come." (No, Mary. You are my mother, but you are not my
Father. And I move ultimately to his command.) And Mary somehow understood. Her answer is at once biblical and beautiful; she
defers to the highest authority. "Whatsoever he says to you, do it."
And the first miracle began. In such ways Jesus overcame, by faith,
the pressures of Babylon in his life, leaving for all of us the model and
the pattern of loving, continuous obedience to the Father. A woman
calls to him on his triumphal entry into Jerusalem something pa-
tronizing about how wonderful his mother must have been; Jesus
answers in what seems to be the basic content of any of his messages
on Mother's Day: "Yes, *rather* blessed are those that hear the word
of God and keep it!" Jesus loved his mother. But a son's love for his
mother is a lot different from surrender to Babylon. There is likewise
deep significance in the way he answered the woman at the well
(John 4, 19:26,27) and when his mother and his own brothers and
sisters came to see him, and couldn't get a good seat: Jesus points
directly back to the supreme importance of the Father; "Who is my
mother . . . ? Whoever does the will of My Father in heaven" (Matt.
12:46-59).

Dolphin further notes: "As the Second Adam, He overcame all
destructive forces in human life, including the Oedipus complex,
incest, self-centeredness and all the composite temptations which
came to the first Adam through fallen Eve. He made it possible for
men and women in His family of the redeemed to truly love one
another as mothers, fathers, sisters, brothers, husbands and wives
(Col.3:11)." (op. cit p.26).

THE ELECTRA COMPLEX

The female counterpart of the Oedipus is the ELECTRA COM-
PLEX. The daughter falls in love (unconsciously) with her father
and makes hims her chief idol. Jung says, "Only in the daughter is

the mother-complex clear and uncomplicated. Here we have to do with either an overdevelopment of feminine instincts indirectly caused by the mother, or with a weakening of them to the point of complete extinction . . . in the daughter, a mother-complex either unduly stimulates or else inhibits the feminine instinct, and in the son it injures the masculine instinct through an unnatural sexualization" (p.20).

EFFECT ON THE DAUGHTER

Jung noted three key effects of the mother-complex on the daughters: (1) *Intensified MATERNAL INSTINCT.* An exaggerated feminine side means intensification of all female instincts, and above all, the maternal. Here the daughter's only goal becomes childbirth and children, and her husband, to her, is obviously of secondary importance; merely an object to be looked after along with the children, poor relations, cats, dogs and household furniture. "Even her own personality is of secondary importance; she often remains entirely unconscious of it, for her life is lived in and through others, in more or less complete identification with all the objects of her care. First she gives birth to children, then clings to them, for without them she has no existence whatever . . . Women of this type, although continually living for others, are, as a matter of fact, unable to make any real sacrifice. Driven by a ruthless will to power and a fanatical insistence on their own maternal rights, they often succeed in annihilating not only their own personality but also the personal lives of their children. The less conscious such a mother is of her own personality, the greater and more violent is her unconscious will to power" (p.22).

(2) *OVERDEVELOPMENT OF EROS.* Not always does the maternal instinct intensify; sometimes the opposite happens. An overdeveloped Eros results as a substitute, and this almost always leads to an *unconscious incestuous relationship with the father.* An intensified Eros places an abnormal emphasis on the personality of others. Jealousy of the mother and desire to outdo her becomes the basis for all subsequent undertakings which are often disastrous. "A woman of this type loves romantic and sensational episodes for their own sake, and is interested in married men less for themselves

than for the fact they ARE married, and so give her an opportunity to
wreck the marriage . . . Once the goal is attained her interest e-
vaporates for lack of any maternal instinct; then it will be someone
else's turn. This type is known for remarkable unconsciousness;
they really seem utterly blind to what they are doing, which is
anything but advantageous for them or their victims."

   (3) *IDENTITY with the MOTHER* — A mother-complex in the
daughter can so lead to identifying with her that the daughter's
feminine initiative is paralyzed. "A complete projection of her
personality onto the mother takes place . . . everything which re-
minds her of motherhood, responsibility, personal relationships and
erotic demands, arouses feelings of inferiority and compels her to
run away—to her mother, naturally, who lives to perfection everything unattainable to the daughter. As a sort of Superwoman (admired involuntarily by the daughter) the mother lives out for her
beforehand all that the daughter might have lived for herself. She is
content to cling to her mother in selfless devotion, while at the same
time unconsciously striving almost against her will to tyrannize over
her, naturally under the mask of complete loyalty and devotion. The
daughter leads a shadow-existence often visibly sucked dry by her
mother; and she prolongs her mother's life by a sort of continuous
blood transfusion.

   Does this sort of woman ever marry? Yes, "she is not immune to
marriage; despite her shallowness and passivity, she is so empty, a
man is free to impute to her anything he fancies. She puts out constant feelers that suck up all masculine projections and please men
enormously. All that feminine indefiniteness is the longed-for counterpart of male decisiveness and single-mindedness; he can have it
only by getting rid of everything doubtful, vague or muddled, by
projecting it upon some charming example of female innocence. Her
notorious helplessness is a special attraction. . . she is so much an
appendage of her mother she can only flutter confusedly when a man
approaches. She doesn't know a thing, she is so terribly in need of
help that even the gentlest swain becomes a daring abductor who
brutally robs a loving mother of her daughter, a Pluto abducting
Perephone from the inconsolable Demeter. But by the decree of the
gods he had to surrender his wife every year to his mother-in-law for
the summer season. These legends do not come about by chance!"

(p. 24).

(4) *RESISTANCE To Mother.* These three extreme types are "linked together by many intermediate states; the most important being an overwhelming resistance to maternal supremacy often to the exclusion of all else." Jung called this kind of girl "the supreme example of a negative mother-complex: her motto is 'anything so long as it is not mother!' On one hand she has a fascination which never reaches a point of identification; on the other an intensification of Eros which exhausts itself in jealous resistance. This kind of daughter knows what she does NOT want; she is completely at sea over what she DOES. Should she marry, it will be to escape mother, or a diabolical fate will present her with a husband who shares all the essential traits of her mother's character. All instinctive mother-like processes meet with unexpected difficulties; sex doesn't function properly, the children are unwanted, maternal duties seem unbearable, or the demands of marital life are responded to with impatience or irritation." Jung believed it even effected her *physically:* "Resistence to the mother as 'uterus' often manifests itself in menstral disturbances, failure of conception, hatred of pregnancy, hemorrhages or excessive vomiting during pregnancy, miscarriages and so on." He felt the ancient identification of the mother as "materia," or the source and ground of all matter, "may be back of their impatience with objects, their clumsy handling of tools and crockery and bad taste in clothes; Resistance to mother can result in spontaneous development of the intellect; creating a sphere of interest in which the mother has no place. . . Its real purpose is to break the mother's power by intellectual criticism and superior knowledge so as to enumerate to her all her stupidities, mistakes in logic and educational shortcomings. Intellectual development is often accompanied by the emergence of masculine traits in general" (Jung, op. cit. p. 25).

There is much more that could be explored; the varieties of hurt are many. But thus from the Bible's light on the observations from the world of psychology, we have many insights as to the effects and consequences of the Babylonian pattern on the home and family. The *remedy,* though simple, is certainly not easy. Any family or home that hopes to survive this demonic attack launched in our time must determine to commit themselves in utter child-like faith to trust, love Christ the Lord, and model their entire lives on his commands. They are "not grievous;" they are life when all around is the death of everything lovely and beautiful a marriage, a home, and a family could be.

An outline on the *biblical versus the Babylonian pattern* is appended. To know and see the problem is to already have half the keys to becoming really free.

DEMONIC DEITIES

"Let not the wise man glory in his wisdom, neither let the mighty man glory in his might, let not the rich man glory in his riches: But let him that glorieth, glory in this; . . . that I am the LORD . . ." *(Jer. 9:23).*

What excites YOU most? *Knowledge, power and riches;* these, or him? Each civilization gets a choice; love and devote yourself to *things* or to *God* and in serving him, serve other people. Choose things and you get Moloch; choose him and you and your children both live. This was the choice that faced Israel; it is the choice we face today. *The attack on childhood in all its forms is simply a modern expression of a very ancient religious cult; a consciousness that worships sex and death; and a culture that deifies and glorifies education, power and riches.* Do you want to see what kind of culture kills its children? Then visit with me, through history, the horrors of these ancient pagan sanctuaries. How ugly and vicious can a people be? See for yourself in the image of their deities and the focus of their worship. WE BECOME LIKE THE GODS WE SERVE. In these times when empty-headed people seriously suggest a return to the "older religions" that exalt nature and pleasure above morality and responsibility, we had better look long at the kind of world these "nature" gods and goddesses created. And these are not "Trivia" questions. The awful records of this "hidden" history, the speciality of only a few scholars and archaeologists, are nevertheless clear. THESE GODS DESTROYED FAMILIES AND KILLED CHILDREN. The reality was worse than any Indiana Jones foray into a "Temple of Doom;" when the old gods rise once more the ancient war on childhood begins again.

BAAL: GENERATIVE POWER

Who were these demonic deities and what did they do? There were four main idols; *Baal, Ashera, Moloch* and *Ashtoreth.* Supreme god among the Phoenicians and Canaanites was the "sungod" BAAL. Babylonians called him BEL; the ZEUS and JUPITER of the Greeks and Romans. We have already looked at his ancient origins in Nimrod. Originally, BEL was more like the supreme God, the ruler of all; but as men began to depart further in heart from his knowledge their idea of him also began to change. By later biblical times, Bel was BAAL, a perverse and demonic deity that stole the glory and honor rightfully belonging to Jehovah.

The name BAAL meant "lord" or "ruler" for Baal governed the material universe. To his subjects or slaves, he was "the great father who gave wool, flax, bread and water, oil, corn and wine, and all else earth yielded for their wants and happiness" (*Geikie,* op. cit. p. 354).

People believed the local Baal of each area controlled FERTILITY in crops, beasts and people. Areas like Palestine had few natural streams or springs and uncertain rainfall, so idolators went to extremes to gain his favor including the practice of RITUAL PROSTITUTION (Jud. 2:17; Jer. 7:9; Amos 2:7) and CHILD-SACRIFICE (Jer. 9:5).

"High places" — summits of hills and mountains were especially

sacred to him, for the sun shone longest on them and they rose, as it were, into the midst of his full splendor . . . Baal was the symbol of creative power, for the sun was the great generative force in nature. At first worshipped without an image and typified only by an obscene phallic symbol of pointed stone pillars, he was ultimately represented as a horn-helmeted warrior in a short kilt with a thunderbolt as a spear, or riding a bull (his cult animal), bunches of grapes and pomegranates in his hands.

They gave him the loftiest names; "king of the universe," "light of the gods," their "creator" and "father." Each city had a "Baal," distinguished by adding the name of the city or place in which they were worshipped; like Baal of Lebanon or Tyre; there was little difference between them. "They were often represented by symbols taken from the animal world: bulls, lions, cows, doves and birds of prey in which the generative force of the consuming ardor of the sun was represented" (J.P. Peters, U. Pennsylvania, *The Religion Of The Hebrews*, pp. 112-113, Atheneum Press, 1940).

He also had various titles personifying particular powers of nature; like "Baal-zebub" (lord of the flies) — the "driver away of flies" and other similar pests; Baal-gad, the source of good luck; Baal-berith, the god of agreements and treaties. He was called Baal-shemesh, the sun god; Baal-shemaim, lord of the heavens; Baal-salah, god of the piercing rays; or Baal-zephnon, the god who conquers darkness and tames the fierce north wind, so dangerous to Phoenician sailors" (*Geikie*, op. cit. p. 356).

Two key myths were connected with Baal. In one, Baal is the storm-god in a critical fight as champion of the gods against some kind of water-monster or dragon, with the help of another deity (The Skillful and Percipient One). He finally defeats and confines this chaos-monster to his proper realm; the unruly waters are "dispersed and distributed so as to become a good servant instead of a bad master." Baal is then acclaimed "king of an everlasting kingdom;" apparently the Canaanite declaration of faith in Providence in nature, as "an assurance of faith and a means of influencing the course of nature by an articulate world and possibly an accompanying magic ritual" (*IDB* Vol. 1, p. 328).

The second is a "dying-rising god" motif that formed the basis of their fertility cult. At the height of summer drought (when vegetation was dying and the land was parched) Baal was deemed slain by Mot (sterility and drought). Anath or Astoreth(his sister consort) searches weeping for his body with the help of the sun-goddess Shapsh(as in Zech. 12:11, Ezek. 8:14). She finds it, and after slaughtering hundreds of animals in sacrifice (70 each of buffalo, small cattle, deer, mountain goats and roebucks), Baal (like Tammuz or Adonis) is "restored to life." Ashtoreth has vengeance on Mot; she "cuts him with a blade, winnows him with a shovel, parches him with fire, grinds him with a millstone and scatters him in a field;" rites acted out with the first or last sheaf of corn (*IDB* Vol. 1, p. 328). When Baal revives, (and after a seven-year battle) he reigns over Mot, assuring life and fertility for the time ahead.

"This," says Peters, "was acted out with a background of sympathetic magic at the Canaanite New Year Festival, doubtless the most important feature of the cultic year. It was attended by the appropriate response from the worshippers, culminating the grossly sensuous rites accompanying the sacred marriage in which ritual prostitution of both sexes was a prominent feature" (*J.P. Peters* op. cit.).

The Canaanites were farmers; their religion was a nature worship. "Nature's yearly revival and death were revival and death of a god." His worshippers took part in this rising and dying. To remember his dying (like Moloch and Ashtoreth) they mourned and mutilated themselves; to celebrate his reviving (with Ashera) they gave themselves over to the most unbridled merrymaking. Baal was giver of life and (as Moloch) the destroyer of life. As Moloch, men sought to appease his wrath by offerings, even of their children; as Baal, men reveled in his bounty with the wildest orgies. Because the life of nature appeared to them to rest on the mystical process of generation, sexual immorality was a central feature of their worship.

BAAL is thus associated with fertility, life and things; his worship the sexual celebration of the power of nature rising, glorifying the lust of the flesh. Do you recognize it today?

ASHERA: IMMORALITY

Along with the Baal was worshipped a BALLAT, or corresponding goddess. Baal's female counterpart was ASHERA; or ANAT

(ANATH); her symbol the rough trunk of a tree with some twigs on it, raised alongside the pointed stone pillars of her consort. Ashera (later the Greek ATHENE) was the female facet of focused immorality. "Sacrifices were offered to her in shady groves and on artificial mounds (representing her genital center, the "birthplace of all things"). Creatures sacred to her for their beauty, strength or fecundity were kept at her sanctuaries. Her temple grounds at Paphos in Cyprus had sacred goats, great flocks of sacred doves and ponds of sacred fish. Some trees and fruits were likewise consecrated to her for their fruitfulness, size, unfailing verdure or early budding; among others the terebinth, the pine, the cypress, the pomegranate and the almond which blossoms as early as January in some parts of Palestine. They held such trees as her visible embodiment and worshipped them as such: "They sacrificed upon the tops of the mountains (to Baal), and burned incense (to Ashera) upon the hills, under oaks and poplars and terebinths because their shadow was good" (Hos. 4:13) (*Geikie*, op. cit. p. 357).

Not only was fornication and adultery allowed in the worship of Ashera and Baal, it was *encouraged*, even *commanded!* Sodomy, lesbianism and bisexuality with both male and female prostitutes and transsexuals were part of the services. This sexual service was considered the very essence of holiness; Akkadian temple prostitutes, for instances, called themselves *quadishtu* — "sacred women" or "the undefiled." One Sumerian tablet mentions priestesses "who made love with strangers claiming they were incarnation of the holy spirit" (Merlin Stone, *When God Was A Woman*, p. 158). "Throughout the religion of the settled Semites, as we find it in Babylonia, Canaan and among the settled Arameans, there was a duality of sex and a tendency to worship the goddess with immoral rites. At her shrines and in her name, sexual license was permitted or commanded, and sometimes the sacrifice of female chastity was required in her service. At both places, strange and unnatural lust formed part of her worship; both male and female prostitutes inhabited her temples and served at her shrines" (*J. P. Peters*, op. cit.).

"The central idea of the worship of the Ashera was LEWDNESS. At the feasts of the goddess, and at that of the resurrection of Adonis (Tammuz), the high places, the sacred groves, the very roads became scenes of universal prostitution, its gains made over to temple treasuries. Every temple had at all times great bands of women and mutilated men consecrated to impurity. The Syrian Baal-Hercules, a hermaphrodite idol, was worshipped with an exchange of dress by the sexes; the men appearing as women, the women wearing men's clothes and weapons" (Geikie op. cit. p. 363). Primitive sacrificial rites to Ashera as ANAI or ANATH are described in the Ras Shamra texts. She was fertilized by male blood, not semen, and hecatombs of men seem to have been sacrificed to her. She hung the shorn penises of her victims on her aegis or goatskin apron" (*Gaster,* p. 416). Merlin Stone describes similar rites by a young male devotee of the goddess in Anatolia and Rome; he cut off his genitals, and "ran through the streets still holding the severed parts. He eventually flung these into a house along the way, custom decreeing that the inhabitants of the house should provide him with woman's clothing which he wore from then on" (*Stone,* op. cit. p. 150).

Small wonder then God jealously guarded his people from unhealthy fascination with the corrupted gay religions around them. Israel was like an unspoiled girl in love with God, surrounded by cities of worshipping pimps, hookers and perverts devoted to murder, lust and death. "Such was the worship universally practiced in Palestine at the time when Israel entered her promised home. Where these evil practices and devotees were not destroyed, but accommodated and allowed to continue, they corrupted the Hebrews. "Every generation from their settlement in Canaan to the Exile witnessed the old, yet ever-new struggle of Jehovah-worship against Baal. This was not a far-off, unreal imaginary evil, but was real, ever-present, alluring and challenging" (*The Heart Of Hebrew History* H.I. Hester p. 153, The Quality Press Inc. Liberty, Missouri, C. 1962 42nd Reprint 1979.)

MOLOCH: DESTRUCTION

If BAAL and ASHERA were the symbols of the quickening and producing powers of nature, MOLOCH and ASHTORETH were "the emblems of the destroying principle before which the bloom of nature withered and life in all its forms perished. They were hence the deities of war." We have seen how Baal and Moloch were once related as opposite incarnations of the same ultimate deity; in later times one sometimes became preferred above the other. "Moloch," says Matthew Henry, "was a deity of unnatural cruelty as others were of unnatural uncleanness (p. 430) to whom human sacrifice was made."

He was called by the Phoenicians and Carthaginians, MEL-KART, BAAL-MELECH, MALCOLM, and other such names; and was related to BAAL by the sacrifice of children" (*People's Bible Encyclopaedia*, p. 19). Moloch was the "sun-god" or a "star-deity" not quite identical with Baal, "but the tendency of one kind of worship was to pass over into the other. Moloch worship, at least in later times, may be characterized as the more intense and repulsive form of Baal worship" (*People's Bible Encyclopaedia*, p. 419).

Moloch — "the king" — was "the sun in his fierce summer heat, scorching the pastures, drying up the streams, smiting the land with unfruitfulness, pestilence, and poisonous winds. He was the consuming, destroying, but also the purifying fire; he was the winter cold just as fatal to vegetation. When the cloudless heat of summer parched the seed and burnt up the springing corn, when plagues desolated cities, when the calamities of war smote the land, it was his doing."

Moloch was known by different names in other places and times. In I Kings 11:7 he is Ammon's national god MILCOM. (Like BAAL, "MILCOM" is not a proper name but a title — "the king." In Amos 1:15; Jer. 49:1,3 the KJV reads "their king," in the LXX, it is "Milcom." Usually in the Old Testament, "Moloch" is written as "THE Moloch.") Jeptha's reply to the Ammonites (Judges 11:24) shows that Ammon's natural god was also CHEMOSH, the national god of Moab. Most Bible references to Moloch are on human sacrifice — specifically, making one's children "pass through the fire" (Lev. 18:21; 2 Kings 16:3; 23:10; Jer. 32:35). Some think this refers to a kind of "fire baptism" or "purification by fire" first without actual burning; but as the practice was always associated with what was cruel and abominable, it seems to have still ended with death.

The Moabites called their Moloch, CHEMOSH, the destroyer or, ARIEL, the fire-god; in Tyre he was BAAL-HAMMON — god

of the summer heat. His star was the planet MARS, from its appearing at different times fiery, clear or blood-red. He was honored
by stone fire-pillars in the form of an obelisk and his image carried
about in a golden shrine. A regular hierarchy of priests filled his
temples like those built by Ahab in Samaria; it boasted 450 priests
of Moloch and 400 of Ashtoreth (I Kings 18:19). Devotees were
circumcised and shaved off their hair so that only a round crown was
left; they had no whiskers or beard in violent contrast to the general
Oriental custom. Every first-born male was consecrated to him as a
human sacrifice or to enter his priesthood (*Geike,* Vol. 2, p. 358).

A backslidden Solomon allowed Moloch worship to accommo-
date his pagan wives and concubines (I Kings 11:7). He even built
high places for Moloch before Jerusalem on the Mount of Olives
which stood until Josiah's time (2 Kings 23:13). The Valley of
Hinnom (or that part of it called Tophet) was the scene of those
atrocities which signified Moloch worship of its princes (2 Kings
23:10; Is. 30:33; Jer. 7:31). This "worship of Moloch was punished
with death by stoning, as a desecration of the name of Jehovah and a
defiling of His sanctuary" (Lev. 20:3) (*People's Bible Encyclopaedia,* p. 419).

Israel fell under Moloch's spell during Ahaz's reign in Judah (2
Kings 17:17), and in Hosea's time (2 Kings 17:17). Though
Moloch is not named, the parallel passage in 2 Chron. 28:3 adds
that the scene of this abomination was the Valley of the "Son of
Hinnom" (specifically Tophet) associated with Moloch in Jer.
23:35. The Assyrians also practiced human sacrifice in Samaria
after 722 B.C. honoring ADRAMMELECH (lordship of the king)
and Anammelech. Adrammelech was probably MOLOCH (or
Malik); Anammelech a syncretism between Moloch, and Anu, the
supreme sky-god of Mesopotamian religion" (*Int. Dict. of the Bible*
Vol. 3, pp. 422-423).

MOLOCH captured the worship of the Ammonites, the Moabites, and the Assyrians, and later the Syro-Phoenician empire and
Carthage. We know him by the titles MILCOM "the king" (Ammonites), CHEMOSH (Moabites), and ADRAMMELECH "lordship of the king" (Assyrians), Moloch is associated with deadly,
war-like power and the triumph of such destructive power over all
living things, the "pride of life."

ASHTORETH: MUTILATION

ASHTORETH, (P1.) was the female counterpart of Moloch. Here is one of the horrible evolutions of Semiramis, the original goddess. The goddess of Sidon, Ashtoreth's other names are ASTARTE or Eastern horned moon-goddess; in Greece, APHRODITE; in Venice, VENUS the "Queen of the Sea." Her Carthaginian name was TANIT and she is sometimes also identified with the Egyptian ISIS. Astarte ruled "all the spirits of the dead" . . . who "lived in heaven wearing bodies of light," the moon surrounded by her ASTral-bodied star-bodied. She represented the passive principle in nature, the principal female deity. She was called "the *queen of heaven*" (Jer. 44:25).

Ashtoreth is mentioned in I Kings 11:5,33; 2 Kings 23:13; Israel became involved in her idolatrous worship in Judges 2:13; I Sam. 12:10, Solomon also in I Kings 11:5,33. She was the ISHTAR of the Assyrians and the ASTARTE of the Phoenicians and the Greeks (Jer. 44:17). There was a temple of this goddess among the Philistines in the time of Saul (I Sam. 31:10); Jezebel's 400 priests probably served her (I Kings 18:19). Ashtoreth worship generated insane acts of devotion; children were thrown by their mothers from the top of the temple walls during her feast to be afterwards burned on the altar.

But SELF-MUTILATION was the highest and most acceptable offering to Ashtoreth, like the priests of Baal-Melkarth who slashed themselves with swords and daggers at the sacrifice on Mount Carmel (I Kings 18:28). A historian describes such a group of Ashtoreth worshippers:

"On the days when the festival of the Syrian goddess is held a great crowd of priests and many Galli and Kadeshim take part in the rites, cutting their arms and lashing their backs as they circle the altar in wild religious dances, amidst the din of flutes, cymbals and songs to the god . . ." He says the Galli, "dressed in women's clothes, faces and eyes painted like women, and danced to the sound of 'wild music' making a 'hideous noise' " — "they howled, flew wildly past each other, dragging their hair in the dust. Presently they began to bite their bare arms, and next hack themselves with the two-edged swords they carried. . . . In the evening . . . they made up for the bloody chastisements of the day by a debauchery, and if the opportunity offered, gave themselves up to every abomination" (*Geikie*, p. 364). In Ashtoreth, sex, mutilation and death met in a perverse marriage.

THE RELIGION OF THE CANAANITES

Why did God tell Joshua to take the land of Canaan and send his people to *utterly destroy* its inhabitants as mortal enemies? Why is this warfare represented as the battle between light and darkness, and the account of their victories celebrated as a spiritual accomplishment?

When we understand the national devotion of Israel's enemies to Moloch and Baal, and the awful annual slaughter of pagan children as an act of worship and spirituality to "god," we can understand something of the great grief and anger of the Living God over the entrenched evil in Canaan.

The Canaanites, archaeologists now tell us, were a "cruel, fierce-fighting people" whose moral and religious practices were "exceptionally wicked and repulsive" (Lev. 18:22-30; Deut. 12:30-32). Their survivors and ancestors later became known as Phoenicians by the Greeks and the Poeni by the Romans; Tyre and Sidon their famous cities and centers of world trade and commerce. We shall later look briefly at what came from Tyre and Sidon; but the Bible record unhesitatingly condemns their worship and power-exalting culture as both demonic and destructive.

Archaeological discoveries have most impressively confirmed the biblical record; the work of a Dr. Macalister at ancient Gezer, a Canaanite city, was especially revealing. Uncovering this ancient mound layer by layer, he came upon the stratum belonging to Joshua's time. Here he found the "high place," a 150 by 120 foot area where the Canaanties carried out their awful religion. It contained 10 monoliths or upright pillars (made of local stone and without toolmarks) the tallest being 10 feet 9 inches and the lowest 5 feet 7 inches, running in a curved line north and south. The sacred stone (worn smooth by the rubbing and kissing of countless devotees) was of stone found around Jerusalem. The excavators believe they were erected about Abraham's times and used frequently each year until the time of the Exile in 587 B.C.

"The whole area of this high place was a cemetery for newborn babies. In all probability they were first-born children sacrificed to the deity. These were enclosed in jars with the body put in head first. Two or three small vessels, usually a bowl and a jug, were put in with them. That these were sacrifices is shown by the fact that they were children. It could not have been a burial place, since such was considered unclean and hence would not be near a place of worship. The gruesome discoveries of this high place make very real the horrible practices of the people just antedating the Israelites in Palestine.

"The large collection of suggestive images of ASTARTE found in this place bears convincing testimony to the immoral worship that went on here. All these images were designed to foster in the worshipper that type of service described in Is. 57:3ff". . . So many of these suggestive (pornographic) images and sketchings were found that Professor Macalister was led to say, "No one who was not at Gezer during the excavating can realize how demoralizing the whole atmosphere of such a worship must have been" (*Hester,* op. cit. p. 153).

CHILD SACRIFICE

Why on earth would an advanced people sacrifice their children? Where under heaven could a nation get the ghastly notion that any god required such a awful act of atonement or devotion? Every devilish practice of power has to borrow from the principles of the genuine and the good; and the growth of Moloch's power was no exception. What the beasts who passed for parents did in those days for their devilish deity was Satan's own parallel to Jehovah God's love-covenant with his chosen people — that every first-born son in a Hebrew household would be devoted to the Lord. That such a parental act of tender consecration and love for both the child and his future lord in life should be so maligned and perverted as to be turned into a regular ritual murder in the name of God, must have drawn down the full holy rage of heaven.

And Israel knew it. They had already seen such perversions in Eygpt; they had seen them in the dark practices of the pagan nations all around them. No wonder they were warned so strongly, and punished so severely, when they toyed with these strange adoptions of devotion! What God had in mind for his children and what Satan has in mind for them are directly opposed futures. No comparison of equivalence between them should ever be allowed. They were given again the first, the original revelation; the Word had come freshly to them to keep pure and unperverted. Hence, no Hebrew devotional practice was to be like that of other pagan nations; no suggestions made towards similarity or adaptation, no compromise. Israel knew, God had told them. There was no excuse.

"The claim of God to have the first-born child given to him to be redeemed only by a stipulated form showed in effect that what the heathen held to be due to Moloch was in reality due to Jehovah (Ex. 13:12; Lev. 4:5; 18:21; 20:2). These texts imply that already in Egypt, Israel had become familiar with human sacrifice — burning their first-born to the Asiatic Moloch" (*Geikie*, op. cit. Vol. 2 p. 358).

NIGHT SERVICES IN THE FIRST TEMPLE OF MOLOCH

What did he look like, this dark deity that ruled the pagan world by fear and frightful devotion? What was it like to grow up as a child in a Canaanite household, knowing that one day in church you would join in worship starring the first-born babies of your neighborhood in a once-only dramatic horror production? *Who was it that you saw, when you thought of "God" in Canaan?*

Moloch was a frightening metal Minotaur; a half-man, half-beast like some insane horned hybrid from "An American Werewolf in London" and the robot Gort from "The Day The Earth Stood Still." Geikie comments: "The ox in his fierce untamed strength was sacred to him and so was the wild boar which the glow of summer excited to madness. He was hence represented in the form of an ox, or as a human figure with a bull's head . . . represented by a towering metal human figure with a horned bull's head. Moloch had permanently-outstretched arms to receive the babies and children being sacrificed (Ezek. 16:20,21; 20:31; Jer. 32:5; 2 Kings 21:6). The sacrifices and surrounding flares that lit the night colored his brassy golden skin with dark shadows and flickering fire. You do not need a source book of ancient dieties to see a modern equivalent. There is a deity much like him in the jeweled-eyed god on the cover of the early ISR players manual for Advanced Dungeons and Dragons.

If you, as a first-born child, were taken to church that night it was better that you were too small to know the order of the service. It was better that you did not understand the real purpose of the intensely loud "music" and "hymns" sung frantically around you; better that you did not see the central focus of the meeting. A first-born child in his parent's arms on a service night had better hope they were either deeply religious or not religious at all. If they were deeply devoted, you might just get away with being enrolled as a future priest. If they were not that dedicated, perhaps they might leave you at home. But then of course, your neighbors would know. But what if your enrollment in the temple was unacceptable and they were unable or unwilling to do that? Then heaven help you on service night. You would not cry long during the awful music or the screaming that passed for singing. You would be too small to care how long the night's sermon was. For when the "invitation" was given, ready or not, you were going to the front. And after that, nothing mattered.

The huge brazen figure was hollow. Beneath its reaching arms of death was strategically placed either a deadly hollow lap redly glowing in the darkness by a fire kindled inside it, or sometimes a sacrificial bowl heated nearly white-hot by an external fire underneath. The newborn babies, or small children made suddenly and terrifyingly aware that they were to be made part of the nightmarish celebration, were laid in its arms to roll off into the fiery lap below. And all the while, their parents sang hymns and prayed.

This horrible devotion took place regularly once a year on a fixed day as an atonement for sins committed, before some great enterprise or after some great misfortune. The more bitter the sorrow for the loss of an only son, the more pleasing the sacrifice to the god and the greater the benefit. The demonic rite was celebrated particularly in the Valley of Hinnom. It geographically bounds Jerusalem on the southwest (2 Kings 23:10; Jer. 32:35) at a site known as "Tophet." This name may mean "firepit" as in Syriac, or alternately, derived from "toph" — "a drum," because they beat drums as they burned the children that their shrieks might not be heard. Parents stilled the cries of intended victims by fondling and kissing them — for their weeping would have been unlucky! Their dying shrieks as they smoked, charred and burned were drowned in the din of flutes and kettledrums. "Mothers," says Plutarch, "stood by restraining all signs of grief which would have lost them the honor of their sacrifice without saving their children" (De. Superst. 13).

Nor did the act involve just one or two children a year. The Carthaginians, for instance, later inheritors of the religion of Moloch, once lost a battle. Ascribing this loss to Moloch's anger over being offered boys brought up and fed for the purpose instead of boys from the noblest families as had formerly been given, they found that a number of parents had hidden their sons. *Two hundred boys* were offered up at once together; *three hundred others* voluntarily giving themselves up afterwards as freewill offerings for the good of their fatherland" (Diod. 10:14).

No wonder God was so angry with Israeli defectors to Canaanite religion! Cunningham Geikie describes this nightmarish worship in the time of Manasseh:

"The hideous image of Moloch, god of the Ammonites, once more rose in the Valley of Hinnom, and Manasseh himself led the way in consecrating his own children, not to Jehovah, but to the grisly idol, 'making him pass through the fire to the god' as if the flames burning away the impure earthly body let the freed soul pass through them cleansed from all taint of earth to unite with the Godhead. Human sacrifices became common at the 'high places of Tophet' in the Valley of Hinnom; the stately central mound on which the idol towered aloft rising 'deep and large' (Is. 30:33) in the midst . . ."

"Night seems to have been the special time for these awful immolations. The yells of the children bound to the altars or rolling into the fire from the brazen arms of the idol; the shouts and hymns of the frantic crowds; and the wild tumult of drums and shrill instruments by which the cries of the victims were sought to be drowned rose in awful discordance over the city, forming with the whole scene visible from the walls by the glow of the furnace and flames such an ideal of transcendent horror that the *name of the valley became and still continues in the form of Gehenna, the usual word for hell"* (*Geikie.* op. cit. Vol. 2 p. 34).

MODERN WITCHCRAFT

The worship of the goddess mother is certainly not merely an awful but ancient memory; it survives and thrives today in two key forms: *open witchcraft*, and the hidden spiritual power-base of the religious but anti-Christian section of the *feminist movement.*

Many Christians are not aware of the technical difference between *witchcraft* and *Satan worship.* Modern witchcraft is the demonic granddaughter of Babylon's Semiramis; the 20th century evolutionary product of the worship of the divine mother, "Witches do not believe the Christian devil, Satan, even exists, much less worship him," says Gordo Melton, author of the *Encyclopaedia of American Religion.* "Paganism represents a return to the 'Old Religion' that found the divine in nature and drew its self-image from the endless cycles of the seasons. Pagans with the self-conscious naivete', have re-entered the enchanted forest in which trees and animals are brothers and sisters. . . . This return to the enchanted forest includes a return to magic. . . mighty cosmological forces that magicians must control and subdue or to which they fall victim. . ." (J. Gordon Melton, Director Inst. Study of American Religion. *Christianity Today*, Oct. 21, 1983 pp. 22-25; *"Witchcraft — An Inside View"*).

Witchcraft is not only still alive, it is again widespread in much of the civilized world. Raymond Van Over says: "The ancient gods — Moloch, Osiris, Baal — did not cease to exist on the day of Christ's resurrection. Witchcraft as a 'religion' rose from the worship of pagan gods which predate history and very likely parallel in time the dawning of mystery and superstition within man's consciousness. As an 'organized religion,' however, the development of witchcraft has been sporadic. Indeed, its best period seems to be the present one" (*Witchcraft Today*, Martin Ebon Ed. New American Library 1971, p. 17). Like Babylon's original religion, witchcraft grows best in *advanced but godless civilizations.* It is a major underground movement in technically-sophisticated Western nations, like Germany, Great Britain and the United States. ". . . From Miami to Vancouver, from Houston to Toronto, from Bakersfield, California, to Farmington, Maine, over 30,000 children of the goddess gather to celebrate and call on her by one of her many names: Hecate, Isis, Cybele or Diana. On each Halloween after the little ones have finished their trick or treating, hung up their pointed hats or ghostly costumes. . . REAL witches congregate in their urban apartments, suburban homes and secluded rural groves to work REAL magic" (*Melton*, op cit. p. 23).

Many modern witches do not advertise their practice; understandable enough in a still uneasy, just, "post-Christian" society. Melton notes that "Like Jews, witches claim a special relationship to Christianity. They call paganism the 'Old Religion' and claim descent from pre-Christian religions of Europe. Long before the Holocaust, they claim, 'Christianity conducted its bloody conquest of the goddess worshippers.' They believe the church 'misidentified Pan with the devil' and 'turned the Inquisition upon innocent pagans.' Protestants carried on the tradition by misidentifying witches with 'ob' as in 'a man or woman who is an ob. . . must be put to death' " (Lev. 20:27) (op. cit. p. 25). Barbara G. Walker, author of *The Woman's Encyclopaedia of Myths & Secrets*, an occult pro-femi-

nist religious source-book, admits that the goddess religion with her
"sons and lovers, the old gods" was originally called by the church
"devil worship." She says these deities were "redefined as devils"
when they were not "adopted into the Christian canon as pseudo-

Religious people in the past have indeed put witches to death; but
the witches' protest that this was all simply a case of "mistaken
identity" is too glib. Not all real Christians behaved like the sometimes over-zealous Reformers and certainly not like the Inquisi-
tioners (who used the label "witch" for anyone they considered an
enemy, heretic, atheist, and Jews included). But Christians have
always understood with the *heart*, if not with the *head*, that there
was something nevertheless very *wrong* with real witchcraft. They
may not know the technical difference between a witch and a satanist; but those that love God, real life, and people, would certainly
give approval to neither, no matter how much they learned to dis-
tinguish their practices. Worship of any other deity than the one true
God was expressly forbidden in Israel; having now seen something
of the nature and character of these early "nature" gods and goddesses, we can much better appreciate the stern prohibition! The
early church did not "misidentify" witchcraft with devil worship;
witchcraft *WAS* a form of devil worship. Elijah, passing sentence on
the three hundred prophets of Baal was not a victim of poor communication or misinformation; he was a lone victor in a deadly war
for Israel's soul. True, in those days they did not call Moloch or
Ashtoreth "Satan" or "the devil"; but Moloch and Ashtoreth were
devilish nevertheless. The names were changed but it did *not* protect
the innocent. And as C. S. Lewis pointed out, the trial and execution
of a witch was not an insane thing for your village leadership to do, if
you really believed the deaths, disasters and sterility in your homes
were the direct result of the evil work of such a person.

Chesterton notes: "Certain anti-human antagonists seem to recur
in this tradition of black magic . . . running through it everywhere;
for instance, a mystical hatred of the idea of childhood. People
would understand better the popular fury against the witches if they
remembered that the malice most commonly attributed to them was
preventing the birth of children . . . This sense that the forces of evil
especially threaten childhood is found again in the enormous popu-

larity of the child martyr of the Middle Ages." He says that Chaucer simply restated a very national English legend when he conceived the "wickedest of all possible witches" as a "dark, alien woman watching behind her high lattice and hearing like the babble of a brook down the stony street the singing of little St. High" (*Chesterton: The Everlasting Man,* p. 138).

AN ANCIENT WARFARE WITH THE CHURCH

Witchcraft claims that goddess-worship, "the female holy trinity ruling all cycles of creation, birth, and death in her virgin mother and crone forms" is the oldest (hence "original and true") form, that "was destroyed by Christian's attacks on her temples, scriptures, rituals and followers." Barbara Walker correctly points out that "the church declared from the first that the great goddess 'whom Asia and the whole world worshippeth' must be despised and 'her magnificence destroyed' (Acts 19:27) and says this was 'virtually the only gospel tenet that churches followed through all their centuries with no deviation or contradiction.'" Although hardly a "gospel" tenet, the Church, for all its failures and tragic shortcomings, did recognize one thing: this witchcraft was no innocent religion.

Dr. Margaret Alice Murray (1863-1963), a British anthropologist, helped popularize the idea that there was nothing really wrong with witchcraft. She wrote a whole series of books on the theory that witchcraft had evolved from a harmless pre-Christian fertility cult. Though many scholars disputed her arguments, she helped change witchcraft's public image in Britain, leading to the repeal of the Witchcraft Law in 1961. Dr. Murray pictured witches as earnest seekers after eternal truths; "the craft" in her eyes was not only legally permissible but spiritually elevating. Understandably enough, a still somewhat secretive order, the CONCEPTS of real witchcraft have nevertheless been highly popularized: Gordon Melton notes the goddess takes her most complete embodiment in nature and "leads witches and pagans to *environment activism,* a love of *animals, advocacy of health foods* and a *healthy respect for the generative powers of nature*" (p. 24). It is an attractive, "high-touch" religion to high-tech civilizations, because it appears as a preserver of nature, environment and simplicity, all areas threatened by techno-cultures. Both pacifist and evolutionary, it claims to provide a balance to "Western society's proliferation of masculine images and values." Walker even claims that "if women's religion had continued, today's world might be less troubled by violence and alienation. Gods, including Yahweh, tended to order their followers to make war, whereas the great mother goddess advocated peaceful evolution of civilized skills." (No mention here, of course, of sacrificed followers or babies).

Occult themes have become banners for the disenchanted: *Led Zepplin's* mysterious song *"Stairway To Heaven,"* called by some the "greatest rock single of all time," appears to be a celebration of witchcraft and Druidic worship. Songwriter Jimmy Page (Led Zep's lead guitarist) who is deeply involved in the occult, not only owned the largest occult bookstore in Great Britain but also chose to live in Boleskin House near Loch Ness, the old mansion of *Aleister Crowley,* Europe's most infamous occult practioner of the 19th century. Crowley, a blatant satanist was so perversely evil he officially renamed himself "The Beast — 666." Those who see no connection between the innocent "nature worship" of witchcraft and satanism would not understand the purpose of what seems a clear reverse-masked message in the "Stairways" lyrics: *"Here's to my sweet Satan . . . whose power is Satan."*

Page is loath to talk about his beliefs or "involvement in magick" (sic) in any detail says Gary Herman, "merely hinting darkly at mysteries experienced and as yet unexperienced." Others associated with Crowley have been experimental film-maker *Kenneth Anger* (Lucifer Rising) for which Page wrote soundtrack music; *Robert Beausoleil* (one of the Charles Manson gang) imprisoned for torturing and murdering musician Gary Hinman; and *Graham Bond,* one of Britain's finest R&B musicians who once fronted a band called "Magick." Bond, believing somehow that he was Crowley's bastard son, became paranoid, and killed himself in 1974 by throwing himself under a train. It took police two days to identify his body. The Led Zepplins certainly had a "peculiarly tragic record of untimely death and severe accident associated with them and their entourage." *Keith Hardwood,* an early associate, died in mysterious circumstances; *Keith Relf* of the Yardbirds which formed Zep's nucleus committed suicide. Their road-manager *Richard Choles' wife* died; in 1977 *Robert Plant's five-year-old son* died of a virus infection during their American tour. In 1979 *Philip Hale*, a photographer friend of Page, fatally overdosed on morphine, cocaine and alcohol, and died in one of Page's homes; and in 1980 *John Bonham* topped off the list (Herman: *Hollywood Babylon* p. 161, Perigree; G.P. Putnam 1982).

The contemporary origins of modern wicca came from the fertile mind of one *Gerald Brousseau Gardner* (1884-1964). A small asthmatic man with a pointed beard, he was a British civil servant who spent most of his life in southern Asia. Melton notes that out of his amateur but serious anthropological and archaeological interests he wrote the definitive work on kris, the magical knife of the Malaysians and authored a novel on the goddess. Back in England in World War II, he assembled all his occult teaching to create a new synthesis, a pagan goddess faith. Gardner's changes both in the rituals and religious ideology hardly made it harmless. He adapted the kris which became the athame; from Asia he selected several magic practices to "blend with Freemasonry and Western ritual magic. He added a belief in reincarnation, tattooed his body with dragons, snakes and daggers, and organized the whole system under the goddess." Gardner had a Scottish ancestress *Grizzel Gardner* who was burned as a witch, and his grandfather Joseph was seduced away from his wife by another. In 1952 when Britain repealed its Witchcraft Law, he introduced his new form of goddess worship in "Witchcraft Today." Modern wicca, as the witches term their faith, grew from people who read it and requested initiation; like Raymond and Rosemary Buckland who took it back to America to spread (*Melton* op. cit. p. 24).

Twentieth-century witchcraft still involves spells and the invoking of supernatural deities: "I conjure thee, o circle of power" ... Athame (ritual knife) in hand she inscribes an imaginary circle around the 12 green-robed figures facing the central round altar. "... that thou become a boundary between the world of men and the realm of the Mighty Ones."

"The priestess raises her ritual knife and invokes the prime deity, the Great Mother Diana ... the priest, who had played only a superficial role to this point, intones the invocation to the horned god, Pan. A young woman begins a song, 'we all come to the goddess, and to her we shall return, like a drop of rain.' One song leads to another. Soon the whole coven is dancing within the circle. The dance is simple but brisk and raises the cone of power, the magical intensity experienced as a sense of oneness and a high level of emotional energy." The linking of sex and worship becomes simple in witchcraft; as "Goddess worship usually entailed frank acceptance of the natural cycles of sexuality, birth, death . . . love was not the abstract principle that 'love of God' was to become. In the very process of worship it could be directly, intimately and physically experienced" (*Walker*, op. cit. p.x).

FEMINISTS & WITCHCRAFT

There is a deliberate attempt by some sections of the Feminist movement to introduce witchcraft as a spiritual power-base and as a substitute for Christianity. In a number of women's forums, special classes are offered, purportedly teaching "Spiritual Consciousness-raising" or the "History of Feminist Thought," that are actually various forms of introduction to the concepts and practice of witchcraft. Since many of the goals of the Feminist movement are so statedly anti-family, and anti-Christian, the Christian church is rightfully looked upon as one of the chief opponents to Feminist ideals and goals. It is impossible for any movement to survive without some kind of provision for the spiritual; witchcraft under various non-threatening names has become the offered substitute for Christianity.

This theme is presently being popularized by feminist writers and activists. Erica Jong's 1981 book *Witches*, a lavishly-illustrated and colorful sympathetic treatment of the witch, is a case in point. We can expect corresponding vilification of the church's role in opposing witchcraft, and more specifically, slander of the Lord Jesus, the Son of God; the ancient battle from Babylon is joined again, and the prize is the heart, mind and soul of our generation. Barbara Walker, in the introduction to her *Encyclopaedia*, refers to this so-called *"hidden history,"* the Feminist movement, as attempting to reintroduce the True Church for the woman of the

1980s.

"Among the secrets in this book are many surprising historical secrets that were covered up, whitewashed or otherwise falsified through 1500 years when the church maintained a monopoly of literate records and virtually wrote its own history to its own order." . . . "The unremitting warfare of the church against followers of the Goddess is a large part of what feminists now call our hidden history. Even though Christianity itself grew out of the once-universal religion of the Goddess, it was a matricidal son whose bigotry tinged every thought and feeling with women-hatred" (p. xi).

Beware the movements that pose as life-celebrating, peace-loving and nature-exalting. Behind the green, green trees are graves filled with little bodies; *Moloch and Ashera wear garlands of flowers fertilized with the blood of innocents.*

SANTA, THE TOOTH FAIRY AND THE EASTER BUNNY

G.K. Chesterton's brilliant book, *The Everlasting Man* (Dodd-Mead 1943), is a reconstruction of important ideas in history leading up to the birth of the Lord Jesus. The book is in two parts: the first about men and the second about Christ. Three of the earlier chapters deal with early pagan religious ideas, and, in these chapters, Chesterton gives what I consider one of the most profound insights into the nature of the demonic and occult world in print.

PAGAN IDEAS OF DIVINITY

Chesteron says there are *TWO KINDS of paganism*. First, there is *MYTH*, which at its best is an attempt to reach divine reality through the imagination alone. Myth has always had power through the centuries, because it directly touches the human spirit. "The most simple people have the most subtle ideas. Everybody ought to know that, for everybody has been a child. Ignorant as a child is, he knows more than he can say . . ." The best myth draws on spiritual reality: "Imaginative does not mean imaginary. Because behind nature is the creative and sustaining hand of God, real myth has both power and a measure of truth. Every true artist does feel consciously or unconsciously that he is touching transcendental truth; that his images are shadows of things seen through the veil. In other words, the natural mystic knows there IS something there, something behind the clouds or within the trees, but he believes that the pursuit of beauty is the way to find it; that imagination is a sort of incantation to call it up. Such fairy-story images can directly bypass our reason, making their appeal to those 'very deep things in our nature, some dim sense of the dependence of great things upon small, some dark suggestion that the things nearest us stretch far beyond our power.' (p. 114). Beauty and terror are both very real and related to the spiritual world; and 'to touch them at all, even in doubt or fancy is to stir the deep things of the soul' " (p. 118).

MYTH AND THE HOMEY GODS

Myth in its simplest and most innocent form gives rise to the fairy story, the patron saint, a Santa Claus or the Easter Bunny. For all its pagan origins, it usually has a good deal of *nice nonsense* about it; in the "happy or hilarious sense in which we talk of the Jabber-wocky." These homey gods were for special days and special times, something for parties and festive occasions and important events. Fairies or nymphs were not expected to be real; it was rather something LIKE the real thing, never thought "true" in the concrete sense. This sort of imaginative paganism crowded the early world with temples. "In a word," says Chesterton, "mythology is a SEARCH; it is something that combines a recurrent desire with a recurrent doubt, mixing a most hungry sincerity in the idea of seeking for a place with a most dark and deep and mysterious levity about all the places found." This is where all these things differed from religion or the reality . . . not in what they looked like but what they were. They did not profess to be realities; they were fore-shadowings, shadows; something LIKE the real thing; and to say they were LIKE is to say they were different. They were never meant to be true in the sense Christianity is.

Mythology is pagan man's attempt to *seek God through imagination*, or "truth through beauty in the sense in which beauty includes much of the most grotesque ugliness." In myth, daydreams are made into persons or objects of power and significance. Even in modern times, people wear "local images almost concentrated into idols;" like good-luck charms, a fetish or talisman. But what did pagans get out of myth? Man found it natural to worship even when he worshiped unnatural things. He felt partly fulfilled and good even if he knew what he worshiped was probably not the reality. When he made the gesture of salutation or sacrifice, poured out a libation, or lifted up a sword, he knew he was doing a worthy and noble thing; he was doing something for which man was made. His imaginative experiment was therefore justified. But precisely because it began with imagination, the object of his worship was less real than the act of worship itself. Myth never claims to BE the reality; just to suggest it. "And," says Chesterton, "pagan and primitive myths are infinitely suggestive, as long as we are wise enough not to enquire WHAT they suggest."

THE DARK SIDE OF THE MIRROR

But there was a DARKER side of paganism. If mythology was like the daydream, the second was like the *nightmare*. "This sort of paganism had an early collision with another sort of paganism; and the issue of that essentially spiritual struggle really determined the history of the world."

First, despite the confident predictions of men like H. G. Wells in the last century, belief in the supernatural has not gone away. As a matter of fact, the most high-tech cultures of our world also lead the world in psychic and occult experimentation. We believe in UFOs, E. T., and Atlantis; in pyramid power, astrology and magic. Isn't it strange that such high-tech civilizations like ours are still superstitious? Surprisingly enough, superstition especially appears in rationalistic cultures. An agnostic age finally doubts its own rationality; being skeptical of anything, it becomes superstitious about everything. Why should we be surprised if our modern world begins

to accept and practice pagan ideas? Our modern culture IS pagan.
And Chesterton says superstition rests on TWO IDEAS: (1) We
really do not know all the laws of the universe; and (2) they might be
very different from all we call reason. "Such men realize the real
truth that enormous things do often turn upon tiny things . . . that one
particular tiny thing is the key or the clue, something deep and not al-
together senseless tells them it is not unlikely. This feeling exists in
both forms of paganism; but when we come to the second darker side
of paganism, we find it "transformed and filled with another and
more terrible spirit."

Could spirits actually COME when they were called? Popular
superstition is as frivolous as any popular mythology; a sort of "airy
agnosticism about the possibilities of so strange a world." But
"there is another kind of superstition that does definitely look for
results; what might be called a REALISTIC superstition. And with
that, the question of whether spirits do answer or do appear becomes
much more serious."

DEALS WITH DARKNESS

Here Chesterton touches on the heart of the occult world. Perhaps "the Fall has really brought men nearer to less desirable
neighbors in the spiritual world" or merely that "eager or greedy
men find it easier to imagine evil;" but "the black magic in witchcraft has been much more practical and much less poetical than the
white magic of mythology." . . . Some impulse, perhaps a sort of
desperate impulse, drove men to the darker powers when dealing
with practical problems. There was a sort of secret and perverse
feeling that the darker powers would really DO things; that unlike
myth, they had no nonsense about them. . . . The man consulting a
demon felt as many a man consulting a private detective; it was dirty
work, but it would really be done . . . The devil really kept his
appointments and even in one sense kept his promises; even if
sometimes afterwards, like Macbeth, a man wished he had broken
them."

In his radical missionary study *Eternity In Their Hearts,* Don
Richardson speaks of what he calls "The Melchizedek Factor;" that
early men, cut off from the West, nevertheless had revelations of the

one true God without any contact from Judeo-Christian civilization. Flying in the face of evolutionary anthropological theory, Richardson shows that early pictures of God are the exact opposite of that touted by Darwinian and Marxist theorists who claim monotheism is the end-product of an evolutionary process that began with primitive ideas of demons or multiple gods and gradually developed into the "myth" of one God. Chesterton concurs. He says, "In the accounts given us of many rude and savage races, the cult of demons often came after the cult of deities and even after the cult of one supreme deity. Perhaps they thought the higher deity was too far off for appeal in certain petty matters, and men invoke the spirits because they are, in a more literal sense, familiar spirits."

FIT FOR DEMONIC SOCIETY

"But," he goes on, "with the idea of employing the demons who get things done, a new idea appears . . . of BEING WORTHY of the demons; of making oneself fit for their fastidious and exacting society . . . With the appeal to the lower spirits comes the horrible notion that the gesture that triggers the mysterious machinery of the world must not only be small but very LOW; a monkey trick of an utterly ugly and unworthy sort. *Sooner or later a man deliberately sets himself to do the most disgusting thing he can think of.* It is felt that the extreme of evil will extort a sort of attention or answer from the evil powers under the surface of the world" (p. 133).

This is the meaning of most of the *cannibalism* in the world; it is not a primitive habit. It is done deliberately, not innocently; "Men do not do it because they do NOT think it horrible; but on the contrary because they DO think it horrible." They wish, in the most literal sense, to feed on horror. Rude, primitive races are often not cannibals; more refined and intelligent races often are. The *Maoris,* cited by Chesterton as an example of the latter race who occasionally practiced cannibalism, attacked and ate an entire crew of a British whaling boat at Marsden Point. It sent a message of fear and horror to the British government, as a deliberate warning to the whalers who had previously take Maori men and women as slaves on their boats. The *Australian aborigines* mentioned by Chesterton as an example of a more primitive race are certainly not cannibals;

but when the tribes in what is now Cairns were overrun by Chinese, imported by the British to work the area, the Abos began to catch, kill and eat them, hanging them up alive on trees by their pigtails. "They are not doing it because they do not think it wrong, but precisely because they DO think it wrong. They are acting like a Parisian decadent at a Black Mass . . . As a matter of fact, some of the very highest civilizations of the world were the very places where the horns of Satan were exalted, not only to the 'stars' (in the darkness, in secret) 'but in the face of the sun' (publicly, openly)" (p. 134).

AZTEC SEARCH FOR OCCULT POWER

The Aztecs and American Indians of the ancient empires of Mexico and Peru had civilizations "at least as elaborate as Egypt or China;" they were not primitive cultures. And those advance civilizations were certainly NOT innocent; . . . We know that the sinless priests of this sinless people worshiped sinless gods who accepted as the nectar and ambrosia of their sunny paradise nothing but incessant human sacrifice accompanied by horrible torments." And here is where Chesterton touches on the *fundamental secret of the occult drive for power;* he mentions, almost in passing, the SINGLE ELEMENT that describes and defines most of the ugly and irrational things that characterize genuine devotion in the demonic world.

"We may note," says Chesterton, again speaking of the Aztecs or Toltecs, "in the mythology of this American civilization *that element of REVERSAL or violence against instinct of which Dante wrote; which runs backwards everywhere through the unnatural religion of the demons.* It is notable not only in ethics (right and wrong) but in aesthetics (order and beauty). A South American idol was made as ugly as possible, as a Greek image was made as beautiful as possible. They were SEEKING THE SECRET POWER BY WORKING BACKWARDS AGAINST THEIR OWN NATURE AND THE NATURE OF THINGS" (Emphasis mine). "There was always a sort of yearning to carve at last, in gold or granite, or the dark red timber of the forests, a face at which the sky itself would break like a cracked mirror" (p. 135).

REVERSAL

What is it that runs through the occult world like a dark thread, that connects all their rites and supplications and results? Satan takes beauty and makes it ugly; music and makes it noise; turns harmony into dissonance, truth into lie and life into death. Those who seek him and follow him do likewise. And why? Because life, true and genuine life, spontaneous, growing, God-ordained life, always grows OUT from the center where God holds creation by the word of his command; and the idea of the one who seeks power from the darkness is that the way to find the secret of true power is to go AGAINST it. The more deeply you go against the natural, the more closely you approach the source of power. *And this REVERSAL is the law of the satanic world.* It is the mark of all its works. It is the badge of darkness. It is the one fundamental principle of the occult world.

Sometime ago I had supper with a young lady heading up an anti-abortion movement. We were discussing this idea of reversal in the war against children and I glanced at her own little baby peacefully sleeping beside us. "Why couldn't you kill her?" I asked. I glanced at the table knife. "Why couldn't you just pick up this and stab her to death?" Shocked, she blurted out the essential truth: "I just couldn't." Then I asked, "Why not?" "It wouldn't be natural," she said. *"It just wouldn't be natural."*

And that is the fact. All the works of darkness are unnatural. Satan must go against the normal, the natural, the instinctual in order to seek power. Evil is PARASITICAL; it cannot rest until it has sought out the heart of life and sucked it dry. Evil is ALIEN. It is the opposite of all that would bring harmony, happiness, and normality to mankind. It takes innocence and turns it into prostitution. It takes beauty and turns it into punk ugliness. It turns trust into fear, love into selfishness, joy into hurt and happiness into agony. REVERSAL. Look for it and you will almost always find the activity of the darkness.

Aleister Crowley, later mentioned in this book as one of the most evil men of the past century, wrote a book in which he described his methods of what he called "magick." One of the keys he advocated was REVERSAL in everything. He wrote backwards, attempted to think backwards, even entered doors walking backwards! To live a life of reversal is to turn against everything normal; to have, in God's words, "Turned their back to Me, and not their face: though I taught them, rising up early and teaching them; yet they have not received my instruction" (Jer. 32:33). Sin is not only rebellion against God, it is a violation of nature. "For this cause God gave them up to vile affections; for even their women did change the natural use into that which is against nature" (Rom 1:26).

"This inverted imagination," continues Chesterton, "produces things of which it is better not to speak. Some of them indeed might almost be named without being known; for they are of that extreme evil which seems innocent. They are too inhuman even to be indecent" (p. 138).

THE WHEEL VERSUS THE CROSS

As the ancients all knew, some symbols have power. Think for instance of the occult *pentagram*, the eastern *mandala* and the *swastika*. If a man's life in the Kingdom of God in symbolic form was set side by side with the symbol of a man's life in Satan's kingdom, at first glance both may look initially alike. Both kingdoms could be represented at first glance as *spirals* and in a sense they are; but the Kingdom of God has at its heart a cross, and the kingdom of darkness has at its heart nothing but a "black hole." The spiral of God's Kingdom frees, EXPANDS, grows ever outwards to eternity; the spiral of the devil's realm SHRINKS ever smaller, becoming irrevocably more self-centered and meaner. Like a whirlpool, the victim's circles speed up as they near the suction death center; life in the fast lane results in acceleration to burnout. That is why Chesterton, analyzing the major difference between other religions and systems of man and Christianity, points to their embodiment in the ENDLESS WHEEL (or disk or swastika) of all those founded in falsity; and the CROSS of Christ as the exact opposite. The wheel, "the great Asiatic symbol of a serpent with its tail in its mouth," is "really a very perfect image of a certain idea of unity and recurrence that does indeed belong to Eastern philosophies and religions. It is really a curve that in one sense includes everything and in another sense comes to nothing. In that sense it does confess or rather boast that all argument is argument in a circle . . . The cross is a thing at right angles pointing boldly in opposite directions; but the swastika is the same thing in the very act of returning to the recurrent curve. That crooked cross is in fact a cross turning into a wheel. Before we dismiss even these symbols as if they were arbitrary, we must remember how intense was the imaginative instinct that produced or selected them both in the East and the West. The cross has become something more than a historical memory; it does convey almost by a mathematical diagram the truth about the real point at issue; the idea of a conflict stretching outwards to eternity . . . In other words, the cross in fact, as well as figure, does really stand for the idea of breaking out of the circle that is everything and nothing" (pp. 154-155).

WAR OF THE GODS AND THE DEMONS

If all that was not enough insight for a whole book, Chesterton turns next to another deeply significant observation. He speaks of the conflict which we now know as the Punic wars; when a small growing empire called Rome came into violent confrontation with an older, advanced civilization based in a city called Carthage. He calls it the War of the Gods and the Demons. He believes it was *a war which decided the future of the world.*

Rome was a city built on eternal revolution; "From the first Plebian riots to the last Servile Wars, the state that imposed peace on the world was never really at peace. The rulers were themselves rebels" (p. 167). Rome was in constant political turmoil because to the Roman the family unit was supreme; "The truth is that only men to whom the family is sacred will ever have a standard or a status by which to criticize the state." Rome's local gods were of the fairy-tale kind; where "Grecian deities radiated outwards into the morning sky," the Italian gods were local and domestic in character. "We gain the impression of divinities swarming about the house like flies . . . we have a vision of a god of roofs, and a god of gate-posts, a god of doors and even a god of drains . . . The old household gods of the Italian peasants seem to have been great, featureless, clumsy, wooden images. The religion of the home was very homely; if mythology personified the forces of nature, their mythology personified nature AS TRANSFORMED BY THE FORCES OF MAN. It was a god of corn and not the grass, of cattle, not the wild things of the forest; in short, the cult was literally a culture; as when we speak of it as agriculture" (p.164-166).

RELIGION OF CARTHAGE

Carthage, on the other hand, was the center of a powerful and advanced civilization. "The civilization that centered in Tyre and Sidon was above all things practical. It has left little in the way of art and nothing in the way of poetry. But it prided itself on being very efficient; and it followed in its philosophy and religion that strange and sometimes secret train of thought which we have already noted in those who look for immediate effects. There is always in such a mentality an idea that there is a short cut to the secret of all success; something that would shock the world by this sort of shameless thoroughness. They believed, in the appropriate modern phrase, in 'people who delivered the goods.' In their dealings with their god Moloch they themselves were always careful to deliver the goods .. It is enough to say here that it involved the theory I have suggested about a certain attitude toward children. This is what called up against it in simultaneous fury the servant of the one God in Palestine and the guardians of all the household gods in Rome. That is what challenged two things naturally so much divided by every sort of distance and disunion, whose union was to save the world."

There was only one thing where Rome and Israel agreed; and that is hatred of the horror that marched ahead of the armies of Carthage. Carthage or New Town was an outpost or settlement of the energy and expansion of the great commercial cities of Tyre and Sidon. "There was a note of the new countries and colonies about it; a confident and commercial outlook. It was fond of saving things that rang with a certain metallic assurance; as that nobody could wash his hands in the sea without the leave of New Town. It depended almost entirely on the greatness of its ships . . . it brought from Tyre and Sidon a prodigious talent for trade and considerable experience of travel. It brought other things as well. . . ."

In the psychology that lies behind a certain type of religion there was a tendency in those hungry for practical (apart from poetical) results to call upon spirits of terror and compulsion . . . In the interior psychology of the Punic peoples this strange sort of pessimistic practicality had grown to great proportions. In the New Town which the Romans called Carthage, the god who got things done bore the name of *Moloch,* who was perhaps identical with the other deity whom we know as Baal the lord. The Romans at first did not know what to make of him or what to call him; they had to go back to the grossest myth of Greek or Roman origins and compare him to Saturn devouring his children. But the worshippers of Moloch were not gross or primitive. They were members of a mature and polished civilization abounding in refinement and luxuries; they were probably far more civilized than the Romans. And Moloch was not a myth; or at any rate his meal was not a myth. These highly-civilized people really met together to invoke the blessings of heaven on their empire by throwing hundreds of their infants into a large furnace" (p.169). We can only realize the combination by imagining a group of high-tech Silicon Valley executives going to church every morning at 11 o'clock to see a baby roasted alive. And it was with this civilization that Rome had got herself into a life-or-death war.

HANNIBAL

Rome set herself to do battle with one of history's all-time military genuises; a man who had pledged his life and future as a nine-year-old before the idol Moloch to destroy the Imperial City. At the worst crisis of the war, Rome learned that Italy itself, by a military miracle, was invaded from the north. "Hannibal, the 'Grace of Baal' as his name ran in his own tongue, had dragged a ponderous chain of armaments over the starry solitude of the Alps; and pointed southwards to the city which he had been pledged by all his dreadful gods to destroy." Something awful happened in Rome that hour; her soothsayers spoke of unearthly prodigies, that a child had been born with the head of an elephant, that the stars fell down like hailstones; that nature herself was being invaded, upended, overturned by something alien. This was no mere commercial confrontation, or military rivalry: "Something far different was felt at the time and on the spot . . . that filled the Roman imagination with such hideous omens of nature herself becoming unnatural. It was Moloch upon the mountains of the Latins, looking with his appalling face across the plain; it was Baal who trampled the vineyards with his feet of stone; it was the voice of Tanit the invisible, behind her trailing veils whispering of a love that is more horrible than hate ...

"Hannibal marched down the road towards Rome and the Romans who rushed to war with him felt as if they were fighting with a magician. Two great armies sank to the right and the left of him into the swamps of the Trebia; more and more were sucked into the horrible whirlpool of Cannae; more and more went forth only to fall in ruin at his touch. The supreme sign of all disasters, which is treason, turned tribe after tribe against the falling cause of Rome, and still the unconquerable enemy rolled nearer and nearer to the city; and following their great leader, the swelling cosmopolitan army of Carthage passed like a pageant of the whole world; the elephants shaking the earth like marching mountains, and the gigantic Gauls with their barbaric panoply, and the dark Spaniards girt in gold, and the brown Numidians on their unbridled desert horses wheeling and darting like hawks, and whole mobs of deserters and mercenaries and miscellaneous peoples; and the grace of Baal went before them (pp. 170-171) ...

"The burning of the Italian cornfields, the ruin of the Italian vines, were something more than actual; they were allegorical. They were the destruction of domestic and fruitful things, the withering of what was human before that inhumanity that is far beyond the human thing called cruelty. The household gods bowed low in darkness under their lowly roofs and above them went the demons upon a wind from beyond all walls ... The door of the Alps was broken down, and in no vulgar, but a very solemn sense, it was hell let loose. The war of the gods and the demons seemed already to have ended; and the gods were dead. The eagles were lost, the legions were broken; and in Rome nothing remained but honor and the cold courage of despair."

Rome was lost; Hannibal was within sight of the city. All Rome had left was its fierce loyalty to its families; and its only motive for refusal to surrender was hatred for all that Carthage stood for. "Whatever starts wars, the thing that sustains wars is something in the soul; something akin to religion. It was what men feel about life and about death. A man near death is dealing directly with an absolute . . . if he is sustained by certain loyalties they must be loyalties as simple as death. He has generally two ideas, or two sides of one idea. The first is he loves something thought threatened if he only vaguely knows it as 'home;' second, his dislike and defiance of some strange thing that threatens it . . . Men fight hardest when they feel the foe is at once an old enemy and an eternal stranger, that his atmosphere is alien and antagonistic . . . Men can think of this difference even at the point of death; for it is a difference about the meaning of life. Men are moved in these things by something far higher and holier than policy; by hatred."

WHEN WORLDS COLLIDE

"There is a religious war when two worlds meet; that is, when two moral atmospheres meet." Only one thing still threatened Carthage; and that was Carthage itself. Hannibal himself realized it; these Romans were fundamentally different from the good old Moloch-worshipping, practical, business-like Syrophoenician empire. Rome was beaten; Rome was not only dying, but dead; it was obviously impossible for the Italian city to resist any longer, inconceivable that anybody should still resist when it was hopeless. Wars cost money; this one was over, and it was time for peace and economy. Then why was Hannibal asking for more troops?

So argued the shrewd financial experts, the business-minded Carthaginian Empire, as they tossed aside more and more letters filled with strange alarmist reports. "For them, as for all men, the first fact is their notion of the nature of things; their idea about what world they are living in. And their faith was that the only ultimate thing is fear and therefore the very heart of the world is evil. They believed that death was stronger than life, and that therefore dead things must be stronger than living things; whether those dead things are gold or iron and machinery or rocks and rivers and forces of nature. It may sound fanciful to say that men we meet at lunchtables or talk to at garden parties are secret worshippers of Moloch. But this sort of commercial mind has its own cosmic vision and it is the vision of Carthage. The Punic power fell, because there is in this materialism a mad indifference to real thought. Disbelieving in the soul, it comes to disbelieving in the mind. It fancies that money will

fight when men will no longer fight. So it was with the Punic mer-
chant princes. Their religion was a religion of despair even when
their fortunes were hopeful. How could they understand that the
Romans could hope even when their fortunes were hopeless? Their
religion was a religion of force and fear; how could they understand
that men can still despise fear even when they submit to force? Their
philosophy of the world had weariness in its very heart; above all
they were weary of warfare; how should they understand those who
still wage war even when they are weary of it?"

But Hannibal knew. He knew he could not take Rome unless he
killed every man, woman, and child on the way and in her streets; he
knew he had to have more men, because Rome was not at all like
Carthage. They would fight when there was no reason to fight, they
would resist because they loved life and their families and children
more than power and things and money. And out of the ashes Rome
rose to take back the world. "Before the very gates of the city,
Hannibal fought his last fight for it and lost; and Carthage fell as
nothing has fallen since Satan . . . Only men digging in its deep
foundations centuries after found a heap of hundreds of little skeletons, the holy relics of that religion. For Carthage fell because she
was faithful to her own philosophy and had followed, out to its
logical conclusion, her own vision of the universe. Moloch had eaten
his children.

"Nobody understands the romance of Rome and why she rose
afterwards to a representative leadership that seemed almost fated
and fundamentally natural . . . Men knew in their hearts she had
been representative of mankind even when she was rejected of men.
And there fell on her the shadow of a shining and as yet invisible light
and the burden of things to be. The struggle which established
Christendom would have been very different if there had been an
Empire of Carthage instead of an Empire of Rome. Divine things
descended at least upon human things and not on inhuman . . . Can
any man in his senses compare the great wooden doll whom the
children expected to eat a little bit of the dinner with the great idol
who would have been expected to eat the children?"

PART II
Welcome to the
Nightmare

"Come mothers & fathers throughout the land
And don't criticize what you can't understand
Your sons and your daughters are beyond your
command
Your old road is rapidly agin'
Please get out on a new one if you can't lend a hand
For the times, they are a-changin"

(Bob Dylan 1960)

Something is happening in our world . . .
Something so terribly profound it is changing the face to
the earth.
Something is happening in our century that has never
happened before.
What is happening does not have much to do with a
"generation gap" because the gulf that is widening in
our world includes many ages.

Charles Reich said a decade ago in *The Greening Of America:* "There is a revolution coming. It will not be like the revolutions of the past. It will originate with the individual and with culture and it will change the political structure only as its final act. It will not require violence to succeed and it cannot be successfully resisted by violence. This is the revolution of the new generation."

For better or worse that revolution is here. And it is time we had some people who profess to belong to Jesus aware of it. It was, after all, of a generation like this that the prophet Joel spoke—"It shall come to pass in the last days that I shall pour out My Spirit on all flesh; and your sons and daughters shall prophesy; your old men shall dream dreams, your young men shall see visions."

Joel told us the signs of those days—"And I will show wonders in the heavens and in the earth blood and fire." (Then the Hebrew uses a very unusual word—) "Palm trees" of smoke" (Joel 2:30). The King James translators came to this verse and said: "You can't have a palm tree of smoke. Smoke either looks like a pillar or a puff, but it doesn't look like a palm tree."

Not so many years ago, a white silk parachute blossomed out over a city called Hiroshima. The anti-aircraft crew on duty that day saw only one plane eighteen thousand feet from the ground and the white dot of a parachute. Those two things were the last two things they ever saw. Then hell was reborn in the skies. Their bodies were literally cooked by streamers of radiation. Brain cells seared, their eyeballs melted and ran down their cheeks. *The age of terror had begun.*

On the ruins of that city, Mr. Ripley, of Ripley's "Believe It Or Not" series, recorded: *"I am standing at the spot where the end of the world began."*

This is your generation.

This is my generation.

This is the generation marked by the "palm tree of smoke."

And it could well be the last one, the one in which Jesus will return.

WHY ARE KIDS WORSE TODAY?

"There is little doubt that the present generation of college young men and women is in serious moral difficulty. Compared with generations preceding, they have shunned discipline and a willingness to excel in their studies. Many give little or no thought to the serious issues of life. Common decency and modesty in manners and dress apparently are things of the past. The fact that evil is called good while good is called evil seems to be of small concern to them. Student groups indulge in wild orgies of self-gratification while coeds dress and walk in a manner deliberately intended to arouse sexual desire. Both young men and women in their actions and conversations make sexual overtures in the most shameless fashion . . ."

Sound like a fair description of kids today? That was written by a man called *Aristophanes*—some 500 years before Christ.

Another philosopher comments:

"Our youth today love luxury. They have bad manners, contempt for authority, and disrespect for older people. Children today are tyrants. They no longer rise when their elders enter the room. They contradict their parents, chatter before visitors, gobble their food and tyrannize their teachers." And that was *Socrates,* in the fifth century before Christ.

There are some things about being young that has always been "the pits." But history shows this generation is no more righteous OR rotten than any other generation of young people before; the same problems recur in each era. Young people are no worse than before, or better; but unfortunately *just as bad.*

Yet there are some things *uniquely different* about this generation of young people that have NEVER been true about kids at any time in history. They face pressures and problems that no other generation has ever had to face; and they face them at a time unlike any other generation.

PARENTS: YOU NEVER WERE
THEIR AGE

Perhaps no single adult phrase in the world can turn a teenager off faster than this one; *"When I was your age . . ."* *usually followed by* "I had to" ——— *(fill in your own blanks, like ". . . walk through*

the snow in bare feet five miles to go to school," etc.) Want to lose a
kid? Compare one generation's present benefits (his) with another's
previous hardships (yours). But as one Youth for Christ writer
points out "when I was your age" is not only a turnoff; it is *untrue.* In
a number of key ways, the two generations born since World War II
are absolutely different from any other generation of kids before.

(1) First with a TOTAL MEDIA EXPOSURE. We are only
beginning to understand the profound effect the communications
revolution has had on society in the past three decades. It has not
only changed WHAT people know about their world; it has changed
the very WAY they perceive. Grandparents who can still remember
days with no TV, when radios had "valves" or tubes, a hit song
could stay popular for a year and there were no walkmans, watch-
mans, or video players, do not even THINK the same way as their
grandchildren. This is the first generation growing up in the Information Age; and for better or worse, no children have ever been
exposed to so much so fast before.

A Christian psychiatrist commented: "I believe we have the most
serious-minded generation of youth today that the church has ever
had. Kids know more than their parents knew at a comparable age.
They are exposed from an early age to all the great issues of life; war,
crime, sex—they can sit and watch it all on TV. And in a way, I'm
sorry.

"There used to be a stage called *adolescence*— a time where you
could sort of live in neutral. God really designed it for kids; to give
you those few years between childhood and adulthood; a beautiful
time in your life. Here is a time when you can sort out things. You
can make some identifications; you can find out who you are and
hopefully, with guidance and prayer, you can find out the kind of
person you want to be" (Dave Irwin).

That time of adolescence—the "teenager"—is *relatively recent*
in civilized history. (Before this you were apparently a child, then
suddenly, boom—an adult.) Although people as far back as the 17th
century used the word "teen" (to refer to anyone whose age ended in
a "teen"), the word "teenager" itself was popularized by marketing
people in the early '40s. Here was this huge group of people in the
world, neither adults nor children, but with lots of "disposable
income" — money not needed for food, rent or transport. U.S.

teenagers DO have some awesome buying power; 60 percent hold full-time jobs, especially during the summer, bringing in weekly earnings of $600 million. Another 40 percent get some kind of weekly allowance. This adds up to some $35 BILLION dollars a year of "disposable income"—money to spend on clothes, food, movies, records, games and "zit" creams. As a result, kids have become a prime advertising target (See *War on the Mind*).

But children and teenagers do need this transition and adjustment time, when adults can give them learning space as the generation who will one day take their place. It was not always like this. As a matter of fact, *it was the effect of genuine Christianity in society that gave children back their childhood.* In the "Dark Ages," children were treated no differently than adults; from a very early age they were expected to work full, adult jobs on the farms as well as in the later Industrial Era mines and factories. Children then had no protection from abuse, from sexual molestation for adult pleasure, from the rigors of child labor and the horrors of child prostitution. They were forced into an adult world, made part of adult activity and entertainment, and even punished, sentenced and executed like adults when things went wrong. Children were imprisoned, beheaded or hung each week in the Middle Ages, some for such trifling offenses as stealing a loaf of bread to stay alive. The Christian spiritual awakenings of the early 1800s brought them their first freedom; the Booths, and men like Shaftesbury, Mueller, and Barnardo were raised up by God to give children back some of the shelter and protections of childhood.

But now, as Neil Postman points out in his trenchant book, *The Disappearance Of Childhood,* the media have broken down most of the distinctions between children and adults. There is now a new attack on the time of childhood; and it has come not from the people their parents work for, but the programs they and their parents watch (See *War On The Mind*).

(2) *The first GROWING UP WITHOUT A POTENTIAL FUTURE:* The first whose parents have lived with the constant consciousness of "The Bomb."

"And what do you want to be when you grow up, little girl?"

"Alive." (The Singer: Calvin Miller)

Of course, the idea that there may be no future is certainly not new with children or teenagers. "They were long-haired and young and wore wild, brightly colored clothes. Sometimes they frolicked nude in the streets, chanted obscentities at their elders and consumed generous amounts of dope . . . They were protesting the materialism of their parents generation."

Sound familiar? But they weren't hippies. They were the Bouzingos, a remarkably similar French youth movement in the 1830s. Similar movements have occurred through history during the fall of Rome, the French Revolution, the Napoleonic wars. William Moore, researcher of this article says:

"The belief in the inevitability of the future serves as a gyroscope to stabilize behavior. The loss of a future makes . . . an immersion in sensory experience a necessary adjustment" *(California's Health Magazine;* State Dept. Health).

But this is the first generation which has grown up with the constant subliminal reminder *that there may be no future for ANYONE, ANYWHERE, FOREVER.* In a 1960s Swedish rock opera, a group of young people hijack the first interplanetary star ship to escape the pollution, tension and conflict of Earth. Meaningless "music" from their home planet drifts from the speakers as they prepare for the "warp jump." Suddenly there is a brilliant blue-white flower of light outside the portholes, rapidly fading to yellow, orange, and then a reddening darkness. Moments later the music from the speakers is suddenly interrupted by one sharp, short report, then silence. Someone back home pushed the button. Earth is gone— and because this is a modern play, EVERYTHING is gone. There is no heaven, no hell—just gas, dust and ashes. Seconds later, the actual explosion wave rocks the ship; somehow everything holds. They gaze at each other in shock, realizing that they are the last human beings left alive in the universe; on their success hangs the fate of the human race. Someone bravely starts to sing; they all join in. Then the captain comes back from the control room. He is not singing and he is not smiling. "The explosion has destroyed our guidance systems," he says. "We are out of control. We are heading into the sun. *This is the end of the human race."* And then the curtain comes down. It is the end of the play and the audience goes home.

So I ask you—how do you feel? Get that in your gut and you will understand the difference between all other generations with a sense of no future and this generation.

No wonder *Barry McGuire's* song made such an impact on those who became the parents of today's inheritors of fear.

"But you tell me over and over again my friend
Ah, you don't believe we're on the Eve of Destruction"

(3) Maturing PHYSICALLY Earlier.

For some reason, children are actually *growing up faster.* (Fluorescent lights? Fluorocarbons in the ozone layer?) Put an early physical maturity with a teenager's roller-coaster emotions in a sexually-saturated society and you have a moral hand grenade with the pin pulled:

"Among teenage girls, part of the explanation for the early sexual trend is biological. In the past century, the age of first menstruation has dropped from about 17 years to 12.5 (For boys, puberty usually begins at 13)." This has pressured many kids toward early experiments in immorality. "Sexual adventurism among young girls has risen to an astonishing degree. A Johns Hopkins University study indicates that nearly 50% of the nation's 10.3 million young women (ages 15 to 19) have had premarital sex. The percentage has nearly doubled since the survey began in 1971.

" 'I'd say half the girls in my graduating class are virgins,' says 18-year-old Sharon Bernard, a high-school senior . . . 'but you wouldn't believe those freshmen and sophomores. By the time they graduate there aren't going to be any virgins left.' . . . Statistics in a 1977 study show that 600,000 unwed teenagers were giving birth each year with the sharpest increase among those under 14. Venereal disease is rampart among adolescents, accounting for 25% of the 1 million reported gonorrhea cases every year" (*Newsweek,* Sept. 1, 1980, P. 48).

And despite the wholesale spread of abortion, this has not greatly diminished the age-old problem of TEEN PREGNANCY:

"More than a million teenagers—one out of every 10 girls, ages 15-19, become pregnant every year, most out of wedlock. More than half of them decide to have their babies. Teenage sexual activity is increasing even though young people's knowledge about sex is often limited. Surveys show 80% of boys and 70% of girls have had sexual intercourse before they are out of school (p. 42).

"An estimated 80% of the countries' five million sexually-active teenagers fail to use birth control because of unwillingness, ignorance, or the unavailability of contraceptive devices. . . . Some see it as fallout from the decades great social upheavals; women's liberation, the exploding divorce rate, the decline of parental and institutional authority, the widespread acceptance of 'living together' and the swift media reflection of those trends. . . . The message everywhere is sex" (*Newsweek*, Sept. 1, 1980).

(4) Having To Make MAJOR DECISIONS EARLIER:

TOO FAST TOO SOON

"For these kids, life in the fast lane isn't just a cliche'. It's a fact." (Stanford University social scientist).

Davis is a 16-year-old hustler who sells sex to men and women near Times Square in New York—one of a million runaway and unwanted youth who roam big-city streets. His advice: "Stay home and be a child for as long as you can. Don't grow up too quick and don't try" (*U.S. News and World Report*, Dec. 14, 1981 p. 40).

What would you do if you were a kid who lived in a world where adults forced you into ugly, violent, and sexual situations before you could possibly have time to handle them? No wonder that virginal, moral, and even vegetarian *Michael Jackson*, the "boy who never grew up" and the best internationally-known example of the Peter Pan syndrome, was voted in 1984 the Number One singer of the decade.

"We dress our children in miniature adult costumes with designer labels, we expose them to gratuitous sex and violence, and we expect them to cope with an increasingly bewildering social environment—divorce, single parenthood, homosexuality" . . . "Many adolescents feel betrayed by a society that tells them to grow up fast but also to remain childlike" (Elkind, *U.S. News and World Report*, Dec. 14, 1981).

CROWD PRESSURE

Kids have always been deeply influenced by their peers; it is far worse when your friends themselves are pushed into things they find they cannot emotionally handle. Mary, a 15-year-old sophomore from Newton, Massachusetts, recalls how she was swept up into the brave, sometimes bewildering new world of adult hedonism. "I wasn't able to handle pressure," she says. "I was part of a group in junior high that was into partying, hanging out and drinking. I started to have sex with my boyfriend, and it was a real downer. It was totally against what I was, but it was important to be part of a group. Everybody was having sex."

Culture Club's *Boy George* is a gentle example to kids of the willingness to stick up for the right to be different; his asexuality, like Michael Jackson's, is a non-threatening stance in a world where the sexually abusive may come from either sex. "While adolescents are traditionally rebellious, within their own circles they tend to be fiercely conformist. Perhaps at no other stage of life is the behavior of one's peers so strong an influence . . . one of the most important reasons for taking the sexual plunge.

"A guy will say, 'Everybody's doing it, what's the matter with you?' " reports Dana, a 16-year-old San Francisco high-school junior. "You just tell him, 'Well if everyone's doing it, find someone else to do it with.' " But not every girl will risk a flippant reply. "All they think about is that they really want this guy to like them," says a 14-year-old, "and so they're going to do it." Some feel caught in a double bind: scorned if you do, and damned if you don't. "If you say 'no,' you're a tease, and if you say 'yes,' you're a slut." Sexually-aggressive girls "brag about which jock laid them where. It's as if now we can be equal, we're going to be equally tacky" (*Newsweek*, op. cit., p. 51).

The pressure to be immoral is enormous, and moves continually down in age. "The only place where being 'hard to get' is really admired these days is on *Laverne and Shirley* said one girl. . . . Once, chastity was something to be guarded—or lied about when lost. Now an uncommonly virtuous teenager lies to protect the 'dirty little secret' that she is still a virgin" (*Newsweek*, p. 49 op. cit).

(5) Loss of the FAMILY STRUCTURE:

Alvin Toffler (*Future Shock; The Third Wave*) gives an astonishing statistic in answer to the question: What percentage of the
U.S.A. are left that are still the "typical family"—Dad out working
for mother who is at home to take care of the two children? And the
answer is: *Only 7.3 percent.* The "typical family" no longer exists
except as a tiny minority. *Ninety-three percent of American homes
no longer fit the pattern.*

"We move now," says Toffler, "from the *Agricultural Age* and
the *Industrial Era* to the *Third Wave—the Information Age. Yet
for all our improvements in communication,* the one area we have
not rescued with the rest of the community closeness of the Agricultural Age is *communication within the family.*" Husbands and
wives "don't talk anymore;" Dusty Springfield sang in the early
'70s "If you let me make love to you, they why can't I touch you?" In
the 1980s it's *Missing Persons* with *"Words"*:

> *What are words for*
> *When no one listens anymore?*
> *. . . Media overload bombarding you with action*
> *it's getting near impossible to cause any distraction*
> *Someone answer me before I pull out the plug.*
>
> (*Spring Session* 1983)

Kids especially spattered with uncomfortable adult sexual-con-
sciousness are often completely unable to talk to their parents
anymore about their own important sexual battles:

"For a girl to talk to her mother about sex is to talk about the
husband and father . . . It's a very difficult situation for mother and
daughter." . . . "I'd rather pick a name out of a phone book and talk
to a stranger than talk to my mother about sex," says Janice, a 13-
year-old from Pleasant Hill, California. It's too embarrassing" (*Newsweek,* Sept 1, 1980, p. 51).

(6) Too much UNSUPERVISED FREE TIME:

All the working parents out there hustling to make the extra buck in a Moloch society find themselves hard-pressed to be fathers and mothers as well; the feminist movement's influence on the culture has successfully made many mothers feel unfulfilled and useless in being a "mere housewife." As a result again, where education, wealth, and power become the dominant gods of a society, the children are laid on the altar. In this case, the *sacrifice is quality, and quantity, time.*

Five million American children under the age of 10 have no one to look after them when they come home in the afternoon; some 500,000 preschoolers under the age of six are in a similar predicament. These days most parents of young children work outside the home; two-job parents have become the RULE rather than the exception, and the number of single parents has DOUBLED in the past decade.

Children by the millions are being left in a home without proper adult care for long periods of the day; children who are supposed to somehow care for, feed, and supervise themselves day after day, week after week and year after year. In a dubious justification that this will teach them "independence" they are often left prone to all the temptations facing abandoned children in an adult culture.

"Something has happened to those endearing young charmers who used to wobble around playing grownup in Mom's high heels. They are reaching puberty earlier, finding new freedom from parental restraint, taking cues from a pleasure-bent culture and playing precocious sex games in the bedroom—often while Mom and Dad are at work. The sexual revolution of the '60s has filtered down to high schools and junior high schools" (*Newsweek,* Sept. 1, 1980, p. 48—*The Games Teenagers Play*). The Latchkey phenomenon is looked at in more detail in *War In The Street.*

(7) NO MORAL GLUE IN SOCIETY:

The Western world has been called the "Post-Christian society." Not only do the young have little or no moral example in the home; for many there is none left in society either. Each year they are bombarded with more news of crooked judges, corrupted police, pornographer teachers and homosexual gym instructors, fornicating ministers, and pedophile nursery-school directors. Where are they going to get an example of goodness and quality in character? Glorify wealth, power and knowledge long enough and even the young get the message; the world is a jungle, all people are animals and only the strongest, toughest, and the most cunning survive. Villains and crooks become the heroes; they are the ones with the knowledge, money and power.

Rebellion among the young increasingly takes violent forms. In Amarillo, Texas, a 17-year-old was charged with the strangulation and rape of a 76-year-old Franciscan nun. In Maryland, an 18-year-old woman hired a gunman and participated with four young men in the murder of her husband of two months. Teenagers account for nearly one-third (31 percent) of all violent crime arrests, including those for arson and 54 percent of property crimes . . . Increasingly, the victims are the young themselves. In Los Angeles, in 1980, 453 teenagers were murdered by other teenagers . . . Hunter Hurst, Director of the National Center for Juvenile Justice points out, "There is often more violence in a given crime. Instead of just robbing a supermarket, a youth may also shoot the manager and pistol-whip the clerk. It's not an increase in the QUANTITY of violence but the QUALITY of it" (*U. S. News and World Report* Dec. 14, 1981).

One-third of major crimes are committed by people under 20 years of age. A 16-year-old in Santa Clara County took 12 classmates to look at the body of his ex-girlfriend. None of them told police. Later the boy was charged with murder . . . One of the most significant and disturbing trends in recent years is "a new generation of teenagers," deeply troubled, unable to cope with the pressures of growing up in what they perceive as a world that is hostile or indifferent to them. Among thousands of teenagers . . . alienation and a lack of clear moral standards now prevail where individual lives, families and, in some cases, whole communities are threatened.

In John Whitehead's challenging analysis, *The Stealing Of America*, he points out the staggering rise in child crime, as the distinction between adult and child crime vanishes. In 1950 (the year TV was introduced to America) only 170 people in the whole nation were arrested for what the FBI calls "serious crimes" (murder, rape, robbery, aggravated assault). Statistically then, children's serious crime was 215 times less than adult crime: only .0004 percent of the under-15 population of the U.S. But by 1960, the figure for child crime had jumped shockingly; it was now only eight times less. By 1979, (and while adult crime had itself increased to three times its 1950 rate) child crime was only 5.5 times that of adults. So what does this mean? "Between 1950 and 1979" — in a little over a generation — "the rate of serious crime committed by children increased *11,000 percent!* The rate of less serious child crime (burglary, larceny and auto theft) increased 8,300 percent" (*Whitehead,* p. 68.)

Why this incredible explosion of violence? There are no simple answers. Let's look at some of the terrible pressures children face.

"Many suffer from stress and depression at being bounced from parent to parent after divorce. Youth from middle- and upper-income families often wilt under constant urgings to excel in sports or academics, to become popular, win acceptance to good colleges, or to aim for high-paying professional careers. Inner city kids remain largely jobless and feel trapped in despair . . . One side effect: a rise in what experts call 'sociopathic' subcultures, ranging from membership in far-out cults and extremist groups like the Ku Klux Klan, to the demented punk-rock underground" (*U.S. News & World Report,* Dec. 14, 1981, p. 40 "*Troubled Teenagers—A Special Report.*")

One of the most alarming trends involves teenagers who turn violently on their own parents. "Parent Abuse" is becoming evident in courts where parents seek restraining orders on their belligerent children. Deputy Inspector Thomas Gallagher of the New York Police Department's Youth Services Department—himself a father of seven—says flatly, "Some parents are afraid of their own children" (p. 41).

John Whitehead observes: "The solution suggested by many authorities is a *tougher stance by society.* Some states have attempted to drop the legal age at which minors become adults to as low as 12 years of age, and some experts say juveniles who commit 'adult crimes' should be treated as adults."

This leads to *new state laws;* in New York, for instance, children between 13 and 15 charged with serious crimes can be tried in adult courts and, if convicted, receive long prison terms (*Whitehead,* op.

cit. p.8).

"Society's mixed message to the young has left them with a mixed blessing. They have more choices than their elders ever had, but no guarantees they will choose wisely. As one reflective 16-year-old summed it up, 'It must have been a lot easier when society set the standards for you. It can get awfully complicated. I guess that's the price we have to pay for freedom.' " (*Newsweek* Sept. 1, 1980, p. 53).

(8) *INABILITY TO COPE with pain, delay, disillusionment, discouragement, depression.*

All these have led to a sad consequence; kids who cannot handle the disappointments and delays of life.

As many as one-third of the nation's 27 million teenagers seem unable to roll with life's punches," says one sociologist. "They grow up lacking the internal controls needed to stay on course." (*U.S. News & World Report*, Dec. 14, 1981, p. 40 "Troubled Teen- agers—A Special Report")

The answer of the 1980s is threefold among kids: (1) *With- drawal;* the most common method, that of fantasy in music, film, comics and video. (2) *Numbing;* the use of drugs like glue, pot, or coke are especially used to null out the painful reality. The Na- tional Institute on Alcohol Abuse and Alcoholism says alcohol is the number one youth drug problem."About 15 percent of 10-12th graders and 11 percent of 7-9th graders are classified as problem drinkers . . . Many teenagers also drink while using other drugs or sniffing glue . . . the combination can be lethal . . . and they don't even know it." Drunkenness is the chief cause of auto accidents among young people (*U.S. News and World Report* Dec. 14, 1981). There is a very high correlation between drunkenness and suicide; an estimated one-fifth of all drunks end their life by suicide. Many people drink heavily prior to killing themselves. (3) *Suicide;* the plug is pulled. This is such a major problem we have devoted a whole chapter to it (See "War To The Death").

SO IS THERE ANY ANSWER?

Yes, but when in one direction; the way of him who said he is

Way, the Truth and the Life." None of these pressures need stack up impossible odds against us." Children, teenagers and parents alike can be gripped by the love and reality of the risen Christ. With him, most of today's unique pressures can be transformed into *unique opportunities.* Fear of the future is put into the hands of someone who is in final charge of history, who said, "Lo, I am with you even to the end of the world." Media exposure can be activated into a sensitivity to a hurting world. Early physical maturity and responsibility can be made a challenge to lay aside childish things and become a man or woman of God. The collapse of family and society can be a call to establish a new world order under his lordship; and incapability to handle pressure an open door of invitation to find power, security, and love in his arms. Dave Irwin said it so well:

"Yet you have an ability to be more concerned about your world than we were. We have no reason to expect anyone to share what another generation shared; but for many kids there has been no happy time—for millions of kids in the world today, the birds don't sing.

"I don't deny there are more evil people in the world. But nearly half of all the people who have ever been born are alive today. And what you and I do for Jesus Christ in this century will determine whether heaven has a greater population than hell."

PART III
Suffer Little Children

STRANDED IN SPACE AND TIME

You are a 20th century time-traveler, lost somewhere in the spatiotemporal matrix. When your machine finally stops you get out to discover *you have arrived in a very frightening world.* At first, everything looks so normal, so ordinary. It is not very long before you realize just how *inhuman* the human-type creatures here really are.

This is an alien world indeed of much mindless violence, one that seems somehow utterly careless and conditioned to the murder of its weak, its small, and its helpless. You discover you are on a planet where even the best parents routinely kill their children; a world where, for instance, a man may plan to have a child so he can kill it later for a kidney transplant he needs himself.

This gruesome conditioning is planet-wide. In some high-tech cities of this alien world, couples are forbidden more than one child. Most girl babies there are unwanted, so are usually thrown away or drowned. In the nation you have landed in alone, you find to your horror that each year *over a million and a half people* — the population of a large city back home— are routinely, efficiently and "compassionately" killed, with the full support of the government, the media, the medical and the legal professions. Bodies here are treated like recycled junk; some of their grisly desk decorations are dead babies, tiny brains or feet or hands set in plastic.

Bewildered and sickened, you go for a sedative in what seems to be a drugstore, to find in shock that even the *skin cream* sold there is made from the fresh-frozen intestines and other organs of dead babies! The alien women who buy it for "refreshing their skin cells," either don't seem to know or care. Doctors in this place kill children every day at their mothers' whim, preference and insistence, and they do it without regard for the terrible torture they inflict on their helpless victims. While the mothers are made as comfortable as possible during the kill, the doctors matter-of-factly burn their children alive with skin-searing poison solutions, or if they are too old, chop them up with special instruments. Then they either vacuum up the pieces for garbage disposal or collect them in ice-cream containers to sell for sideline industries. Public centers for family planning actually counsel people how to NOT have families, and have attached rooms where unwanted or inconvenient children can be brought to be quickly and profitably disposed of. One in every three children are killed like this every day. Yet the people here don't seem to correlate the killings to the diminishing number of children in the land.

Shaken now, and thoroughly afraid, you look for someone more rational who can help you try to make sense of such an inhuman culture; you are directed to a medical lab. But there it is even worse. The researchers in this horrible place actually *homogenize living babies in meat-grinders* to make biological cultures, and use their tiny lungs and tissues to make vaccines! But what is that? For just a moment, from behind that closed door you heard a little cry. You go over and open the door. And you never forget what you see. Your eyes widen, you nearly faint. You run retching to your time machine. It is hard to believe that any planet of any time would do what you have just seen with your own eyes. *A row of little severed heads, all kept alive by tubes pumping blood into them. A row of little living, disconnected human baby heads.*

If a planet does that to its *babies,* what will it do to its *older citizens?* You barely make it back to your machine. Wild-eyed with fear and horror, you punch the computer to take you safely back to your own time and your own planet. The machine energizes, shimmers—*but nothing happens.* Desperate, you recalibrate the controls—but something is still wrong. The machine won't move! Something is terribly wrong. You cannot get back. You are stuck here in this awful world. Shaking, you scan the controls one more time.

Then your eyes fall on the chronometer and you realize the awful truth. *You cannot get back because you ARE back.* This is no other planet. This is no future time. This is Earth—*your* Earth. And it is 1985.

WAR ON THE WOMB: ABORTION

"I have set before you life and death . . . therefore choose life, that you and your descendants may live" (Deut. 30:19).

Our time-traveler story is fictional. The horrors he encountered unfortunately are not. Moloch has risen again to challenge Jehovah's care for the families and the children. Abortion has been rightfully called the 20th Century Holocaust.

Let's examine some various statistical issues on this subject.

★ Communist China: Planned Parenthood rules permit only one child per urban couple, two for rural. Since a son is seen as a worker and provider for aged parents, female babies, generally unwanted, are abandoned or drowned.

★ By April 1983, the abortion toll in the United States was 10,000,000 (*The National Educator,* April 1983 p. 14). We destroy one of our own children every 20 seconds, at least 4,500 every day.

"Hitler and his henchmen were condemned by American judges at Nuremberg because they encouraged the killing of the unborn. Hitler was wrong even though most of the men today on the Supreme Court defend what he did" (Dan Lyons: *Christian Crusade Weekly*).

BEAUTY FROM MURDER

★ Since 1981, a cosmetic firm in Paris, France, has been making a skin-care product "designed to rejuvenate skin" using the youthful cells of aborted babies, specifically the spleen, liver, thymus and intestinal membranes. The use of aborted children in cosmetics came to light when guards at the French-Swiss border encountered a truckload of frozen human fetuses destined for a French cosmetic laboratory (Nick Thimmesch; Fetuses & Cosmetics: The French Connection *Los Angeles Times,* 1982).

★ Human embryos and other organs have been enclosed in plastic and sold as paperweight novelty items. The Nazis were not the last to think of uses for discarded humans; the soap they made from human fat, and lampshades made from human skin, were considered trendy then too.

ANOTHER JOB FOR MARY SHELLEY

Mary's famous book needs an update today; the horror story she wrote has stepped outside fiction into the realm of reality (She was, of course, the author of *"Frankenstein").*

★ A young couple wanted to conceive a child to be aborted so the father-to-be could use the baby's kidneys for a transplant he needed for himself.

★ In California, babies aborted at six months were submerged alive in jars of liquid with a high oxygen content to see if they could breathe through their skin. They couldn't.

★ The Diabetes Treatment Project at UCLA depends for its existence on the availability of pancreases from late-term aborted fetuses.

★ A rabies vaccine is produced from viruses grown in the lungs of aborted children. A polio vaccine is also grown with cells from aborted babies.

★ Brain cells would be "harvested" from aborted babies for transplant.

★ Tissue cultures are obtained by dropping still-living babies into meat grinders and homogenizing them, according to the prestigious *New England Journal of Medicine.*

★ *Dr. Peter A.J. Adam,* Associate Professor of Pediatrics at Case Western Reserve University, reports to the American Pediatric Research Society on studies he and his associates had conducted on 12 babies born alive by hysterectomy abortion. They cut off the little heads alive, much as the Russians kept dogs' heads alive in the 1950s (*Medical World News,* June 8, 1973 p. 21).

★ *Dr. Martin Kekomaki,* a Finnish researcher, and his associates conducting research on aborted babies, took a living baby boy, still moving and even secreting urine out of the incubator, and without anesthetic, cut open his belly. The shocked nurse said, "They said they wanted its liver." Asked to explain the implications of his research, Dr. Kekomaki said, "An aborted baby is just garbage" (*International Life Times;* Nov. 7, 1980 p. 9).

ABORTION AS BUSINESS

★ A hysterectomy-aborted fetus in the seventh, eighth and ninth months is removed intact. (*Translation: the baby is alive.*) The trade in fetal tissue is about $1,000,000 annually. The high prices may encourage unnecessary abortions on welfare patients as the surest way of getting "saleable tissue."

★ Another abortionist is needed at a large abortion center. The ad reads:

"Salary and fringe benefits extremely attractive. Imagine the opportunity to make at least $80,000 a year for no more than ten hours work each week" (J.T. Burtchaell, *"The Holocaust and Abortion," Catholic League Newsletter* Supplement Vol. 9 #11).

★ In an Albany, New York, speech (March 17, 1981) Bernard Nathanson pointed out that with over 1.3 million abortions in the U.S. each year carried out at the average cost of $350 per abortion, the baby-killing business could be ranked in the Top Ten of *Fortune Magazine's* industries—over FIVE HUNDRED MILLION DOLLORS a year (*Lecture,* Legislative Bldg. Albany New York).

LESS THAN CRIMINAL

A few years ago on an international flight, I found myself sitting next to a doctor based in New York City who was heading for an international medical conference on abortion techniques. This doctor had developed some new and improved techniques and tools to kill babies more effectively, and was proud of the slides and instruments he had with him to show the conference, at which he was a key speaker. During the course of the convention, it turned out that he was also deeply against the death penalty. Hiding my astonishment, I asked him *why.* "Because," he said indignantly, "people have their life taken from them in a plain violation of the most basis human right." All I could do was shake my head. He who would nobly save the guilty, mercilessly murders the innocent. *The most dangerous place in America is a mother's womb.*

This is certainly a tragic war on children.

THE UNBORN BABY
IS A REAL PERSON

Dr. Bernard Nathanson, co-founder with Betty Friedan of the National Abortion Rights League once personally performed thousands of abortions; he was director of America's largest abortion clinic. *The Center for Reproductive and Sexual Health* performed 120 abortions a day and a total of 60,000 during Nathanson's tenure. He helped formulate the catchy slogan "A woman's right to her body." *He is now a vocal and determined opponent of abortions.* He actively campaigns against abortions worldwide.

What caused the about-face? New technology; including ultrasound monitors which enable doctors for the first time to look at the fetus. "It was like a window," says Nathanson. "We could see through the abdominal and uterine walls of the pregnant woman. We could see directly into the womb at any stage of pregnancy. We could examine the fetus on a TV screen . . . treat it with injections, blood transfusions; we could diagnose its illnesses, determine its physiology. We knew how its sleep cycles went, we knew its reactions to pain, drugs, and even maternal smoking."

"I realized it was a human being I was looking at," he said.

The film which he has since produced, *Silent Scream,* is not a pretty sight. A needle is shown, inserted into the woman's body. The child appears to pull back, attempting to avoid the probing needle. Its mouth is open and makes movements which Nathanson calls "a silent scream.' The needle makes contact and a violent struggle begins. The body is torn from the head by suction, crushed and pulled out. Nathanson considers the film conclusive and told TV viewers in Sydney, Australia, recently, "this is a human being. Prenatality is a part of life, just as infancy or old age" (Allan Gill: *Challenge Weekly,* Sept. 21, 1984).

THE AMBIGUITY OF ABORTION

Many expectant mothers do not relish the idea of an abortion; but for some it seems the only way out of an impossible situation, and they are aided and encouraged to do this wrong by well-meaning Moloch-worshippers and the popular media. Most mothers faced with the prospect of their first abortion really suffer terrible pangs of guilt, fear and apprehension. It is never an easy decision, especially the first time. The clash between the internal protest of a still-unseared conscience and popular opinion produces some very strange tensions and feelings.

John Powell, author of *Abortion: The Silent Holocaust,* whose writings have sold over six million copies, talked to a Minneapolis gathering about a young woman who came to see him. She said, "I'm pregnant. Since it has been confirmed . . . I have not smoked, because you know, nicotine can harm a developing baby. I have not drunk alcohol because of the fetal alcohol syndrome we hear so much about."

"Then she looked down almost as if she could not believe her own words. She said softly, 'But I have an appointment to kill this baby next Thursday morning.'

"I could hardly believe the same mind and mouth were thinking and saying these three statements . . . I felt somehow I had to plead for the child's life. 'This baby, this baby you are carrying inside you, is an innocent, living human being.' I kept talking about the baby, the baby. 'Please give your baby a chance at life.' After a short while she looked up at me pleadingly. 'I know you love my baby. Do you also love me?' " (*Challenge,* Dec. 24, 1983 Reprinted from *Humanity*).

Where did she get those three messages? From the media. TV and radio warn about the dangers of smoking and drinking. And they reassure that it is all right to "terminate pregnancy." That's what they call killing a baby.

DANGERS OF BEING
ACTIVELY PRO-LIFE

Powell warns of the *two temptations* facing those who fight abortion:

(1) *Discouragement.* The pro-life movement is only a voice crying in the wilderness. But something is happening. The message is being heard. There is still a long way to go, but for the first time since Roe vs. Wade in 1973 (when the Supreme Court gave America the "dubious distinction of having the most permissive abortion laws of any nation in the Western world") the tide is beginning to turn. In 1984, more than a decade after the fatal, fateful decision, *for the first time in more than a decade,* abortions went *down.* Something is beginning to happen.

(2) *Over-responsibility.* The Messiah complex: to take on all the problems of everyone around; all the problems of the world. Especially we must beware of the trap of falling into sinful methods and motives of bitterness, revenge and a desire to harm back in order to make the world understand. We are not God. We must not pretend to be.

Meanwhile, the "slaughter of the innocents" goes on. Many have pointed out the parallels between what is happening in this issue and others today and the rise to power of Hitler and the Nazi movement in Germany. Others have shown the close resemblances of the abortion issue in the 1980s with the slavery issue a century before. In both cases, in each time and nation, there was some kind of Christian witness; there were some who professed to "seek first the Kingdom of God and his righteousness."

So what of the church in our time? What of *her* voice? one of the tragedies of today is that the church has not sounded a clear and unmistakable warning. As it has been in times past, the church is not wholly the Church; the chaff and the wheat grow side by side until the day of the Reaper. A church entranced by the same powers that rule the world is a powerless, gutless, and useless appendage. When the spirit of Moloch is abroad even there, money, power and status become the dominant rule; *dead things celebrated over life.* Some clergy who ought to know and do better do not speak out against abortion because of ignorance, fear or unwillingness to face the consequences of a possible loss of congregation, popularity or financial support from pro-death members of the congregation.

John Powell speaks of his disappointment in one so-called "minister" who was also the head of the National Abortion Rights League. This man's argument for supporting abortion was "a legal abortion for a woman on welfare now costs the state $150; but if the abortion were not performed, the state would pay out over $60,000 over an 18-year span to support the mother and child." Obvious which is best, isn't it? Powell asks, "How does such a minister . . . come face to face in prayer with the Lord who said, 'Whatever you do to the least of my children . . .' "? (*Abortion: The Silent Holocaust* p. 102).

ALTERNATIVES TO ABORTION

What can we do to stop this thing?

Scott Reed sums up the basic alternatives of attempting to help inner-city mothers facing the possibility of unwanted children:

(1) *Teach young people abstinence.* But this is a gospel task and not likely broadly successful, except in times of spiritual awakening.

(2) *Provide contraceptive information and advice.* But this is already being done by secular agencies with only mild success. Many who are past self-esteem still go ahead and say, "Who cares?" Despite the first two provisions, 1.25 million women annually still abort.

(3) *Support abortion.* But believing this is the moral equivalent to murder, we reject it. Unwanted children WILL be born and those born to the poor will suffer a double setback of poverty and rejection. Here we must face the consequences of our position.

(4) Either we *take care of these children AFTER* they become rejected, abused, antagonistic or perhaps criminals,

(5) OR we take care of the *mother and child so as to prevent this kind of result.* (Medically, educationally and nutritionally). "We want to join right-to-birth with right-to-life meaning quality of life."

(*"If Not Abortion, What Then?"* Scott Reed with Paul Fromer, *Christianity Today* May 20, 1983, p.19).

CHRISTIAN RESPONSE

The Christian response to the national sin of abortion can and should be four-fold:

(1) *Prayer* for those in authority, especially those who influence or affect national legislation. Pray for leaders in church, law and government.

(2) Seek in whatever legal means possible to *influence public opinion against abortion*; by letters, tract distribution, screening pro-life films and video. A list of materials and organizations is given at the end of this chapter. If you run into legal problems in seeking to oppose abortion in your area, you can contact *The Rutherford Institute*, Box 510, Manassas, Virginia 22110, (703) 491-5411.

(3) *Picketing* of the abortion clinics and hospitals; the kind and loving offer of alternatives to girls entering such places. Many clinics have closed down because of this. This must be done wisely and *within the confines of local law*. Seek God as to the content of your signs. Remember, your goal is to *win people to Christ's side* and *save babies*, not just make people mad.

We must also not forget the MAN's side of this. Often they too suffer from guilt, and rarely will a girl still decide to kill her child if the father is against it. One Christian relates a particularly effective way of getting through to a boyfriend or husband who may be with the girl heading into the clinic for an abortion. He takes with him a disarming picture of his young sons. When he meets the husband or boyfriend with the girl intent on having the abortion, he introduces himself, and shows the guy his family with the following words: 'Hi, Dad." (He calls him Dad.) "I'm _____, I want to show you a picture of my children. This is what they look like." (Shows his smiling children). "Now I want to show you a picture of *your* son." (Pulls out a color picture of a dismembered aborted baby from underneath the other two shots.) "That's what he'll look like after she goes in there. You'll never laugh and play with him because they'll kill him."

(4) *The Alternative Offers:* Many Christian groups have begun to mobilize across the nation to provide alternative counsel, help, and ongoing concern for the girl who needs another way. *Melody Green* of *Last Days Ministries* (Box 40, Lindale, Texas 75771-0040) not only has authored and distributed pro-life Christian posters and tracts number in the millions like "*Children—Things We Throw Away?*" but has been active in providing an adoption service for parents who *do* want the children, and counsel and shelter for girls who decide to have their children. Concerned missionary groups like *Youth With A Mission* offer materials and helps to teach people how to set up a "*Crisis Pregnancy Center*" in their cities. These offer free pregnancy tests, individual counsel and referral service for pregnant mothers to help them not go through with an intended abortion. (For information write *Living Alternatives;* Box 4600, Tyler, Texas 75712. 214-592-3448). College and campus outreach groups like *Maranathá Ministries* not only actively lobby on campus against liberal and pro-abortion groups, and seek to put pro-life leaders in key positions of office, they also, through their campus churches, provide support and ministry and shelter to expectant and single mothers. Write them at: P.O. Box 1799, Gainesville, Florida 32602, 904-378-6000. There are many pro-life health organizations and groups through the U.S. now—that provide alternatives to the clinics and hospitals that practice abortion.

Here is *National Communications Service's* list of groups active in one way or another in the fight to end abortion:

Alternatives To Abortion International
46 N. Broadway
Yonkers, N.Y. 10701
(914) 423-8580

Birthright
686 N. Broad St.
Woodbury, N.J. 08096
(609) 848-1819

Christian Action Council
442 "C" St. N.E.
Washington, D.C. 20002
(202) 544-1720

National Right To Life Committee
419-7th St. N.W. Suite 402
Washington, D.C. 20004
(202) 626-8800

One Nation Under God
Box 62524
Virginia Beach, VA 23462
(804) 495-1905

Women Exploited By Abortion
Rt. 5, Box 54-A
Columbia, MO 65202
(314) 445-6567

WAR ON THE FAMILY — DIVORCE, CHILD KIDNAPPING AND WHITE SLAVERY

"Kramer vs. Kramer" is an academy-award-winning film that powerfully and poignantly portrays the agony, hurt and struggle that both parents go through in a divorce or separation involving a child. Dustin Hoffman plays a father who pursues a business career and promotion over his wife's happiness and security. Meryl Streep is the mother, on a woman's liberation road to her own independence and career. Their little boy Billy is the small and innocent victim of the resulting angry and hurtful breakup. The film asks all the right questions. But like most secular films, cannot provide any answers. *Divorce* is one of the major ways the Babylonian pattern destroys a home.

CONSEQUENCE OF DIVORCE

Failure in school, a problem that frequently plagues suicidal children, is more common among children whose parents are divorced. Children from one-parent families are more likely to be discipline problems, three times more likely to be suspended from school and twice as likely to drop out (*A Cry for Help* op. cit. Footnote p.152).

And what kids are afraid of has changed significantly over the last two generations. Some fears, of course, stay the same. Kids worry about how they look, whether other kids will like them, and if they will be able to get a boyfriend, a girlfriend, or a job.

But 40 years ago, some of their chief fears were about failing in school, not finding a job or having enough money. *Now,* says Ruth Formanek, an educator, author and child psychologist, *the main fears of children are of robbers, kidnappers, rapists and strangers.* Once death in the family ranked very low. Now it is *fourth* on the fears list, and rising right along with nuclear war is *family break-up.*

A 10-year-old girl in treatment for depression wrote this poem:

> *Divorce shakes you off the ground*
> *Divorce whirls you all around*
> *Divorce makes you all confused.*
> *Divorce forces you to choose*
> *Divorce makes you feel all sad.*
> *Divorce pushes you to be mad*
> *Divorce makes you wonder who cares*
>
> *Divorce leaves you thoroughly scared*
> *Divorce makes a silent home*
> *Divorce leaves you all alone*
>
> *Divorce is supposed to be the answer*
> *Divorce in fact, is emotional cancer*
> *(A Cry For Help* op. cit. p.153)

There are, of course, new factors behind the new fears. *Families* today are more unstable, the *divorce rate* is much higher, and the *varieties of alternative lifestyles* bandied about, produce a lot of insecurity. Also *news about crime* is more widespread. TV and newspapers play up murders and other tragedies and give sensational treatment to the horrible and frightening. Some basic fears remain altered to fit the times. Children and youth who once feared that parents might die now fear they will get a divorce. Other family fears are loss of love, abandonment, and physical harm. (Ruth Formanek: *U. S. News and World Report* Aug. 22, 1983)

Children have good reason to be afraid. A child abduction occurs every THREE MINUTES in the United States and only a small percentage of those children will ever be found alive. An estimated 150,000 children are abducted each year, 100,000 by parents in custody disputes and 50,000 by strangers. Of the children kidnapped by strangers 10 percent are found alive, 10 percent are found dead and the rest simply vanish.

ABDUCTIONS ON THE INCREASE

Michael Meredith, founder of Child Industries, said that two major factors are contributing to the escalating problem of child abduction—the increasing demand for "black market" babies and the thriving underground business of child pornography. "Legalized abortion has resulted in a dearth of babies available for adoption," he said', "and that supply-demand gap is frequently filled with abducted children. Catalogs are now widely available through the gay community and others which show children for sale for as little as $400." They are for sale for "any purpose—and these catalogs include color photographs of every part of the children's bodies." No child is immune from abduction (*Savannah Morning News* Oct. 11, 1983).

Many stolen children are NEVER found. Doris Freed of the Committee on Custody of the American Bar Association estimates that SIX to SEVEN out of every 10 children stolen are never returned. Senator Alan Cranston, co-sponsor of a federal bill to help stop the problem, says only 10 percent of the stolen children are ever recovered. And the problem grows with over a MILLION DIVORCES a year. More than 10 million children under the age of 18 live in families headed by a single parent, eight million headed by women, two million headed by men. "With escalating divorce and an increasingly mobile society these figures are on the rise," Senator Charles Mathias of Maryland says. "The American family and American society are in flux. We are in a whole new ball game where old rules no longer apply and new rules haven't been written. Small wonder that custody disputes have been called potential inter-state nightmares" (John Edward Gill "Stolen Children" p.15)

PARENTAL CHILD-STEALING

A friend of mine who had some difficulties in his marriage re-turned home from work one day to an empty house. No wife, no children, no furniture, no note. *Gone.* Frantic, he began to call and check all around. It was like some kind of nightmare. Finally, after some sleepless days and nights he was able to trace what had happened. His wife had abandoned the marriage, sold the furniture, and moved in on a permanent live-in basis with a lawyer in another state. Eventually he discovered the children with relatives. He was lucky. Many parents, unable to cope with what they feel are in-tolerable pressures from their mate or ex-mate, simply take the children and vanish.

Another husband I counseled once had a child by a previous marriage. With his new wife and daughter he was deeply involved in Eastern and occult thought. His previous wife, into the occult her-self and now remarried to a well-known rock star, seemed dis-interested in her daughter until the little girl, with her daddy and new mother, gave their lives to the Lord. Then the new Christian family began to get some strange communications from this world-famous couple that culminated in their actually threatening to take the child away from them and out of the country forever. Told that if they got her even for a visit, he would never see her again, the husband became afraid enough to resist even the legal writs the couple obtained for visitation rights. One day while the girl was in school, some men even tried to *kidnap* her right out of the classroom. Her daddy freaked out. After spending one Christmas in jail because he refused a court order requiring him to surrender his daughter for the weekend to the couple, he and his whole family went underground.

Now years have passed. The musician that was after his daughter was murdered. But here is a Christian family that had to spend years on the run and in hiding from the threat of kidnap. In this case with the full support of U.S. law.

"The Child Stealer," a 1979 movie starring Beau Bridges and Christina Raines, is about an ex-husband who kidnaps his divorced wife's two daughters. It explores very well some of the feelings, fears and struggles of a parent who has had their children stolen. Bridges says he wanted this role because he believes it tells a worthwhile story about love and its pressures, and he found that the importance of children in his own life was reaffirmed. "I love kids," he said, "and I love working with them. . . . All of us have a little bit of a child still within us and being with children, laughing, and pretending, allows us to be a child again" (*Listener* Dec. 22, 1984 p. 16).

John Edward Gill's compassionate study on parental child-snatching gives much practical and legal advice. The extent of the problem is alarming. "The government says child-stealing, where a parent involved in a divorce or separation hides with the children, happens about 250,000 times a year. Private groups feel it can happen as many as 100,000 times a year." Michael Agopian, Los Angeles, a criminologist, says, "If you include children who are not returned after a visit to a non-custodial parent, the figure may be as high as 400,000 cases a year" (*Gill,* op. cit, p.16).

Parents who steal children don't break Federal Law. ". . . the Lindbergh Law (Title 18 of the United States Code) makes kidnapping a federal crime, but excludes parents who take and conceal their own children." Local laws differ from state to state. In some places a child stealer is a felon. They can be arrested in another state, sent home, and carry a year or more in jail as punishment. Other states, New York, or Pennsylvania, treat concealing children as a minor offense, a misdemeanor. An abducting parent who leaves those states will not be tracked down by either the F.B.I. or the state police of the state they've moved into (*Gill;* op. cit. p.17).

There is little that law or government can or will do when a parent steals their own children. "Both civil and criminal approaches only recover children; they don't find them. And locating the children is 75 percent of the problem," according to Gill. Parents who try to recover children sometimes run great risks (one mother was shot to death trying to stop her ex-husband from stealing their daughter) and pay huge sums both personally or to private investigators trying to track down their missing spouse and family. Some live on the road in vans and motels, migrants who abandon homes and jobs in their search; others hire self-proclaimed "civil rights workers" who, for profit, travel the country looking for stolen children. "There are no laws against stealing children for profit or recovering children for profit as long as a natural parent hires and goes with them," Gill points out. Stolen children themselves can suffer terribly and the scars may last a lifetime. Who do you love when both parents try to hide you from the other one?

The best way to stop this, says Gill, is to prevent it before it happens. Most of the best advice boils down to a few basic things. If you suspect your partner or ex-partner is the kind of person who might take your children, you need to know as much as you can about them, including the kind of jobs they may take, close friends they have, identification, like bank or Social Security numbers, and to stay in good communication with their relatives. If it happens, your best path apparently is to try to find them yourself, while carrying on with the business of living.

There are at least *two groups* in the U.S. that can give free counsel and help: *"The Stolen Children Information Exchange,"* an organization begun by two sisters, Laurie Cancellara and Barbara Freeman, provides a parent's hotline and counsel.

Children's Rights of New York, Inc. is affiliated with the American Society for the Prevention of Cruelty to Children, a national organization involved in the legal and practical aspects of child protection.

All these things are just one more sad result of the attack on the family. *No wonder God hates divorce and dissension.* The problem comes squarely back to the pressures on marriage, the home and the family. When Babylon reigns in a household, the family is already under attack, and child-stealing is just one of her trophies. Gill says, "There could be more human rights for children in divorce which would mean a change of attitude for government officials, courts, judges, lawyers, police. Human life should come before money or property in divorce settlements. *Stolen children should come before stolen cars"* (p.258). Again, children are sacrificed on the altar of money, knowledge or power. Moloch lives, and love dies.

CHILD ABDUCTION RING
UNCOVERED BY THE FBI

The war on the womb, and the growing disease of child pornography, has led to even more bizarre criminal organizations. In New York, the FBI uncovered a *national kidnapping ring* that specializes in abducting children, primarily young boys, and selling them here and abroad for the purposes of sex and pornography. The ring accepts orders from "customers" based on height, weight and hair color, then steals children as young as three-years-old who fit that description. Several suspects are affluent, well-educated professionals. During one of 50 current investigations an undercover agent arranged for the purchase of three 13-year-old boys.

A mother in New Zealand waited for her junior high-school daughter outside a public restroom. The wait seemed abnormally long. Just as she was about to go down to hurry up her daughter, she saw her at the foot of the stairs apparently unconscious, being half-carried up between a man and a woman. Shocked, she blurted out, "What's wrong with her?" "Oh," said the woman, "She'll be all right. My daughter has just fainted." "YOUR daughter!" raged the mother, "That's MY daughter!" The couple dropped the girl, and rushed past the woman to escape in a waiting car. White slavery exists today, just as it has in past centuries.

Investigators believe other children and babies are being stolen solely to satisfy the needs of a separate black market for adoption. "We have identified individuals who have the ability to order children for the purpose of having sex with adults and a system involved in systematic kidnapping and transporting here, and internationally, of children," according to James F. Murphy, in charge of the special task force composed of agents from the FBI, U.S. Customs Service, postal inspectors and detectives. He said the theft of children and their subsequent sexual exploitation is a "well-established" fact of life in the U.S. that has been relatively unrecognized and undetected (*Arizona Republic,* Dec. 22, 1983).

WHITE SLAVE TRAFFIC IN AMERICA

Child prostitution. Child selling. Child kidnapping. The murder of children. *What on earth is happening to the West?* But this is not new. It has gone on before in other towns and at other times. It goes on all around the world. You see it in Thailand, where little 12-year-old girls dance in numbered swimsuits before tourists who select them sexually. You see it in India with the *devasi*, the temple child prostitutes. You see it in Iran and Iraq where children are sent out to fight with real guns almost as big as they are, and given potions of "invincibility" to drink. We only react with shock or horror when we have some kind of moral code or memory left other than the single purpose to please ourselves. In the Western world, the basis of that morality once established British and American law. Now the erosion of that same morality is challenging it.

Horrible, yes; but new, no. Child prostitution, kidnapping, slavery and murder has been fought before. William Booth of the Salvation Army took the war against child slavery and prostitution to England and broke its back. The battle against child prostitution, abduction and white slavery has been waged in America before. Ernest A. Bell, for instance, wrote a book at the turn of the century. It was called *Fighting the Traffic in Young Girls* or *War On The White Slave Trade—The Greatest Crime In the World's History.* (1910 G. S. Ball/1911 by L. H. Walter) Here are excerpts:

From the Frontispage:

DEDICATED
"To the Army of Loyal Workers
who, in the name of God, and
Humanity, have enlisted in this
Holy war for the Safety and
Purity of Womanhood."

Bell apparently faced the same ignorance that exists towards the traffic in children and young people in his time. He said:

"There are some things so far removed from the lives of normal decent people as to be *simply unbelievable* by them. The white slave trade of today is one of these incredible things. The calmest, simplest statements of its facts are almost beyond the comprehension or belief of men and women who are mercifully spared from contact with the dark and hideous secrets of the 'underworld' of the big cities ... Things are being done every day in New York, Philadelphia, Chicago and other large cities of this country ... which would by contrast make the Congo slave traders of the old days appear like Good Samaritans" (p.47).

"The characteristic which distinguishes the white slave traffic from immorality in general is that the women who are victims of the traffic are forced unwillingly to live an immoral life. . . . The white slave trade may be said to be in the business of securing white women and of selling them or exploiting them for immoral purposes" (p.14).

HISTORY OF THE WHITE SLAVE TRADE

Bell points out that these sorry practices are not new, but were a secret part of most of the early "civilizations," especially when allied to religious worship. He says:

"Most of its history cannot be written for two reasons; these crimes are *kept secret* as far as possible, and they are *so revolting that their details cannot be published* and ought not to be read anywhere outside of the bottomless pit."

BABYLON

Bell also traces the genesis of the attack on innocence to the Babylonian pattern. He points out that "in ancient Babylon the dishonoring of girlhood was a part of the temple services, as it is to this day in many temples of India. Dr. Grau believes they probably derived their hideous custom from Babylon which the book of Revelation calls 'the mother of harlots and of the abominations of the earth.' . . . Up the valley of the Euphrates from Babylon and westward among the Canaanites and Phoenicians the horrible alliance of religion and lust extended until it reached Asis Minor and

Greece.

GREECE

The Apostle Paul clearly warned the Corinthian Christians about the dangers of their immoral culture. Some in the church there had been converted from such backgrounds. We may not remember now that the word "lesbian" was coined from these times, nor that every form of sexual perversion known was practiced in those days. "At Corinth," Bell notes, "a great commercial city and seaport, business shrewdness was linked with sensuality and profanation. A great temple of Venus was built, with one thousand priestesses required to lead a life of religious infamy to make money for their despicable masters. There were constant importations of new girls from Lesbos and other Grecian Isles. . . . At Athens the lawgiver Solon established houses of shame by statute, and filled them with slave girls for whom there was no possible escape. But whichever man or woman caused a freeborn Athenian girl to enter one of the houses incurred the penalty of death."

ROME

What of the Imperial City herself? "In Rome, immoral women were enrolled by police in a public register . . . many bakers, barbers and barkeepers were also traders in women," Bell writes. "Key government figures, even the emperors themselves were involved in deep sexual immorality and perversion: Augustus, even in his old age, sent out men to bring him women and girls." The beautiful Mallonia stabbed herself to death rather than yield to the Emperor Tiberius. Marcus Aurelius Antoninus who was very "virtuous, religious and wise" according to Roman ideals, persecuted Christians to the extent of legally condemning Christian girls to houses of infamy. Young women were seized and required to sacrifice to idols. Upon refusing they were dragged through the streets and given to a white slaver (Bell, op. cit. pp. 19-23).

POSTER:
WANTED—60,000 GIRLS To Take The Place of
60,000 White Slaves Who Will Die This Year (p. 50)

Bell's warning to the mothers of girls heading out to the big cities has an oddly familiar ring despite the passage of more than three generations.

"There is. . . a remarkable and impressive sameness in the stories related by these wretched girls. . . . Some man of their acquaintance had offered to 'help' them to a good position in the city to 'look after them' and to 'take an interest in them.' After listening to this confession from one girl after another, hour after hour until you have heard it repeated perhaps fifty times, you feel like saying to every mother in the country: 'Do not trust any man who pretends to take an interest in your girl if that interest involves her leaving her own roof. Keep her with you. She is far safer in the country than in the city, but if go to the city she must, then go with her yourself; if that is impossible, place her with some woman who is your friend, not hers; no girl can safely go to a great city to make her own way who is not under the eye of a trustworthy woman who knows the ways and dangers of the city life.' Above all, distrust the 'protection' the 'good offices' of any man who is not a family friend known to be clean and honorable and above all suspicion."

White slavery continues today in the West. We are not talking about the East or Asia. We are talking about good old modern, high-tech, laid-back America. You can buy a child in New York City today for $5,000. They seem to be on special in San Diego; where they only cost $500.

The AUCTIONEER OF SOULS

"How much will you give for a human being—body and soul?"
"What is the soul worth?"
"Nothing. I throw that in with the sale of the body." (P. 163)

So what are you going to do about it? What can the average, ordinary citizen DO about this? You can care. You can dig around. You can go out and see for yourself what is happening in your town. And if you are a Christian you can do more. You can pray. You can get behind others who have the vision, the call, and the courage to fight it in the cities, the streets and in courts of law. But if you love God at all, you must do whatever you can.

One man who loved children, especially street children, did not merely agree there was a problem. He put an army together to help and reach those streets, and those who came were his greatest and best soldiers. He had a word to say when Bell asked him for a message to those who read his book. And here is what he said:

"FOR GOD'S SAKE DO SOMETHING. IT WILL COST YOU TIME, IT WILL COST YOU MONEY, IT MAY COST YOU REPUTATION, BUT FOR GOD'S SAKE DO SOMETHING." *(General William Booth)*

For Help in *preventing kidnap see Appendix.*
For *initial help when a child has been kidnapped,* contact:

The Stolen Children Information Exchange
P. O. Box 465, Anaheim, CA 92805
(714) 847-2676

Children's Rights of New York Inc.
19 Maple Ave. Stony Brook, NY 11790
(516) 751-7840

WAR IN THE HOME—
CHILD ABUSE & INCEST

"Be it ever so humble
There's no place like home."

For thousands of children the old song has an ominously different meaning. Home is a dream that only happens in fairy tales; the place where they live, the house they have to stay in is called hell.

PHYSICAL ABUSE

Every 60 seconds in the U.S.A. a child is abused; more than 50,000 a year. The actual total may be much higher because many incidents go unreported. Estimates run between 1,000,000 and 4,000,000 children being mistreated in some way by adults. Two thousand children are killed each year by their own parents. The average age of the abusing mother is 26, the father 30. Alcohol plays a role in more than 50 percent of the cases. Frustrated parents (many of them teenagers) have beaten infants whose only offense was crying or fussing from colic.

Francis Schaeffer observed how crime against children has increased dramatically since abortion-on-demand became legal. Dr. Harold Brown says legalized abortions may have caused some parents to reason, "I didn't want him before he was born. I could have killed him before he was born. So, if I want to knock him around, isn't that my right?"

> "Beat the brat, beat the brat
> Beat the brat with a baseball bat"
>
> *(The Ramones)*

"It is a sad day for our society when a court must intervene to protect a child from its own parents," Circuit Judge Frank DePond said in sentencing two members of Stonegate, a West Virginia religious community. They spanked their two-year-old son for two hours with a wooden paddle for disobedience. He died of shock.

Some animals fare better than children. A wounded American eagle found in Maryland was rushed too late to an emergency hospital. It died. A $5,000 reward was offered for the arrest of its killer. It is also illegal to ship pregnant lobsters to market. There's a $1,000 fine and a year's jail term as a penalty. Perhaps we should get future help for endangered children from the S.P.C.A.

A RECENT PROTECTION

The protection of children has only become acknowledged in fairly recent legal history. In 1869, New York opened the Foundling Hospital to cope with an alarming rise of murdered or abandoned babies. They placed a crib on the front steps where mothers could quietly leave their children. Over the next 90 years they saved over 100,000 children. Then in 1874, a woman reporting a boy being pitifully abused found there was no legal protection. She actually DID appeal to the Society for the Prevention of Cruelty to Animals! The courts ruled in her favor. A year later the first Society for the Prevention of Cruelty to Children was organized. (*The Smallest War: Child Abuse JPUSA* 4707 N. Malden Chicago, IL 60640).

LEGAL DEFINITION

In July 1975, the state of Virginia made some major and model amendments to their Child Abuse and Neglect Law, and established a *Unit of Child Protective Services* (8007 Discovery Drive, Richmond, VA 23229-8699 with a 24-hour Hotline (1-800-552-7096). "Emphasis was placed on protecting the child and treating the parents rather than removing the child and punishing the parents." Their code of law defines child abuse and neglect like this:

"Abused or neglected" child shall mean any child less than 18 years of age whose parents or other persons responsible for his care:

1. Creates or inflicts, threatens to create or inflict, or allows to be created or inflicted upon such a child a physical or mental injury by other than accidental means, or creates a substantial risk of death, disfigurement, impairment of bodily or mental functions;

2. Neglects or refuses to provide care necessary for his health; provided however, that no child who in good faith is under treatment solely by spiritual means through prayer in accordance with the tenets and practices of a recognized church or religious denomination shall for that reason alone be considered to be an abused or neglected child.

3. Abandons such a child; or

4. Commits, or allows to be committed, any act of sexual exploitation or any sexual act upon a child in violation of the law. (*Child Protective Services Annual Report*, 1982-83)

OTHER FORMS OF CHILD ABUSE

Perhaps as many as one-third of the population have experienced some form of assault, rape or molestation when they were children. (U.S. Senate Committee: "Protection of Children Against Sexual Exploitation Act of 1977" Report on S. 1585 Washington, D.C., U.S. Gvt. Printing Office, Sept. 16, 1977 p. 5). The problem of *the missing* or *throw-away children* is also increasing. According to THE FBI, 50,000 children disappear from their homes and families each year. Why do they leave? They give many reasons but one thing is clear: parents *neglect* their children much more than beating or harming them. Listen to this first-hand account of neglect:

"My mother would come to visit us on weekends... My father's visits were a highlight too. He would come and take Bud and me out to dinner and buy us little hats and stuff. For a short while it would be like God Himself had come to take us for a walk and we'd think we were in heaven. I loved my father despite his faults and I just couldn't understand why we couldn't be together more. And when he had to go it was almost more than I could stand." (Gary Fisher "The Abusers" Mott Media 1975 p. 8)

> "We gave her most of our lives
> Sacrificed all of our lives
> (She's leaving home after living alone for so many years)
> (The Beatles— She's Leaving Home)

WARNING SIGNALS

Parents who physically abuse children rarely do so with deliberate intent. It happens when pressures or stress build up and become too much to handle. They lose control. Parents who have a history of being abused or neglected themselves, brought up in very strict families, or who wanted an abortion but did not go through with it or waited until it was too late, are potential child abusers. One report says: "Abusive parents keep to themselves, move from place to place and are usually young. They pick a mate who is of little help to them, who is rather passive. The mate almost always knows about the abuse, ignores it, even may participate in it." A child victim may bear bruises, welts and sores on the back, thighs, face, buttocks or back of the legs, be chronically unclean, wary of physical contact with adults, show extremes in behavior, be habitually truant or late for school. Usually only one child in the family is abused. Handicapped children, adopted children and those under six are more likely to be abused, as are hyperactive or emotionally disturbed children.

After a fire, a nine-year-old boy was found locked in his mother's basement. He had been there *eight or nine months*. He had only been allowed out once, on his birthday. Her live-in boyfriend did not like the child and threatened to leave her if she let him out. The boy's only companion was a parakeet, which had died in the fire. After the child was discovered, authorities asked the mother how she could ignore her nine-year-old son for such a long time and if, during his imprisonment, she ever heard him crying, asking for help or making any sounds whatsoever. "I'd just hear him singing to himself sometimes," she said.

Not all those abused as children die or withdraw. Some take revenge by "showing the world." A young man from Minneapolis is locked in his room for six weeks by his stepfather with only a bed and a piano for company. He learns music. His teachers say he will never amount to anything. Driven to practice obsessively sometimes five-six hours straight, he becomes a rock star whose theme on his first major-selling album "Dirty Mind" is oral sex, lesbianism and incest. He calls himself *"Prince."*

THE WORST KIND OF CHILD ABUSE

Children are becoming easy prey for a rising new breed of child abuser that "extends much further than a mother whacking a kid or a father putting a child in a tub of scalding water," said State Police Supt. Col. Clinton L. Pagano. "There are people who will exploit children who escape from their homes to avoid abuse; escape to only a life of prostitution in Atlantic City or New York . . ."

Detective Sgt. James Koeller says, "The real disturbing statistics we have show better than 75 percent of all our youthful offenders have a background in which they themselves were abused, either physically, sexually or emotionally." Recent cases: a teenage boy sexually assaulting a preschool girl, and a seven-year-old raped by her mother's boyfriend. Since a lot of sexual abuse cases are not reported, abuse may go on for years. Sexual abuse tends to make deeper psychological scars on a kid impacting further into their adult years. A broken arm on a kid will heal . . . the other will last a long time."

Sgt. Harold Kauffman of the Atlantic County Prosecutors Office, investigating 62 cases of child abuse referred by state social workers, says most cases involved "the physical abuse of a child by the mother or her paramour—the live-in boyfriend." About one-third of the cases actually involved sexual assault of a juvenile. Gloria Murphy, (who is in charge of the Essex County Sexual Assault Rape Analysis Unit and handles some 400 cases a year of sexual abuse) says, ". . . half those cases invariably involve children." She agrees the problem appears to be looming larger than ever and "There is no question that most runaway girls have been usually sexually abused at home; that is why they have run away and that makes them fair game to become prostitutes" (Linda Lamindol; *Star Ledger,* Newark, N.J., June 19, 1983).

The problem is growing and the victims are getting smaller. According to an American Humane Society survey, child abuse increased 90 percent between 1976 and 1980. Younger and younger children are becoming involved in sexual abuse. Findings from projects by the National Center on Child Abuse indicate that 21 percent of children treated for sexual abuse were under the age of 12, with at least one study showing 51 percent of its child client population as 11 years old or younger and one-third of its population under the age of SIX (p. 7 op cit.). Now, one in every six children are sexually molested before they celebrate their 16th birthday *(U. S. Dept. Health & Human Services).*

WHAT IS CHILD SEXUAL ABUSE?

Child Sexual Abuse is defined by the Federal Child Abuse Prevention and Treatment Act of 1974 as:

"The obscene or pornographic photographing, filming or depiction of children for commercial purposes; or the rape, molestation incest, prostitution, or other such forms of sexual exploitation of children under circumstances which indicate that the child's health or welfare is harmed or threatened thereby."

The National Center on Child Abuse has adopted this definition:

"Contacts or interactions between a child and an adult when the child is being used for the sexual stimulation of that adult or another person. Sexual abuse may also be committed by a person under the age of 18 when that person is either significantly older than the victim or when the abuser is in a position of power or control over another child." (pp. 4-5)

WHO ARE THE ABUSERS

We teach "Don't go with strangers" but most sexual assaults on children (as high as 80 percent in some studies) are committed by *someone known* to either the child or the family. A child is far more likely to be involved in child pornography by a teacher, coach, or youth leader than the "dirty old man" we often picture for our children. Besides the *other* names that may spring to mind for child abusers, here are the legal terms:

PERPETRATOR: One who commits a crime against a child victim.

PEDOPHILIAC (pee-doe-FILL-ee-ack): one with a strong sexual interest in children; one with an erotic craving for a child.

PEDERAST: A male over 18, erotically attracted to boys between the ages of 10 and 16. Pederasty is sexual experience or involvement by one with boys that age, called "chickenhawk" on the streets. Child pornography is usually an integral part of the chickenhawk-chicken seduction, playing an important part in breaking down the child's inhibitions or reserves. They often take pictures of sexual activity with one victim to use to seduce others.

PORNOGRAPHER: (a) collector who builds up a large file of pictures of children in sexually explicit poses; (b) a photographer who actually takes such pictures to sell for profit. They also engage in sexual activity with children.

PIMP: A male or female go-between or agent for illicit sexual affairs. He usually provides house, food and clothing, in exchange for money offered to children for sexual services rendered. It is estimated that as many as 600,000 children under the age of 18 may be involved in prostitution each year. So the pimp is a significant contributor to child abuse" (*We Can Combat Child Sexual Abuse* Shirley J. O'Brien; College of Agriculture, University of Arizona Tucson, AZ 85721, Sept. 1982).

LEADS TO CHILD PROSTITUTION

What happens to the *one million children* between 11 and 17 (documented by Senator Birch Bayh's Juvenile Delinquency Subcommittee) around the country who run away each year? "Every city has them; homeless teenagers who use only their first names to hide their identities . . a new generation of runaway and abandoned children struggling to survive on their own." More than half are girls and the *majority are never reported missing* by their apparently indifferent families. They have to find some way to live. Available and seeking friendship, they become easy targets of pornography dealers and pimps. Some estimate that about 50 percent of these one million runaways have been abused in some way.

In 1978, Judianne Densen-Gerber, founder of *Odyssey House* in New York, estimated there were about 300,000 girls involved in prostitution in the nation. After three years of extensive underground investigative reporting, Robin Lloyd also estimated there were more than 300,000 male prostitutes under the age of 16 (*For Money or Love: Boy Prostitution In America*, New York, Vanguard Press 1976). Some of the children were runaways; some from broken families where they did not feel loved or needed. Still others had foster parents, natural parents, or guardians addicted to drugs or alcohol. Some of them had introduced the child to prostitution to support their addiction.

In 1977, Lloyd Martin, officer in charge of the Sexually Exploited Child Unit (Los Angeles Police Department), testified before the Arizona House Hearings on *"Pornography, Child Pornography and Child Prostitution."* His estimates were that between 40,000 and 120,000 children are involved each year in pornography and prostitution; child exploitation is a thriving, multimillion dollar business. (In 1982, the child sex industry made over five BILLION dollars). See *War Of The Street: Child Runaways & Prostitution.*

CHILD MOLESTERS: DANGER SIGNS

What kind of children fall prey to the pederast and pervert? A convicted child molester said that he looked for a boy rather late in his development, and in conversation tried to find the answers to these four questions:

(1) Did the boy lack any close *church affiliation?* (2) Was there a *weak or absent father* figure? (3) What was the child's *income level;* did he want money? (4) Had the child recently gone through a *traumatic situation* like a move, a death or divorce in the family?

Generally speaking, child victims do not have strong moral or religious values. They have not been taught the difference between right and wrong, good and bad. With little self-esteem they lack inner strength to resist sexual exploitation. Often child-sexual-abuse victims are passive in nature (*O'Brien,* op. cit. p. 16).

SIGNS OF SEXUAL ABUSE

(1) Sudden rather abrupt changes of behavior; overnight becoming moody, quiet, withdrawn, or belligerent, quarrelsome and contrary.

(2) Depression—may not want to eat, go to school, go outside and play, try new experiences or show any interest in activities previously found exciting. May begin drug/alcohol abuse.

(3) Drastic behavior changes in the classroom or playground.

(4) An air of secrecy: the child may stop in mid-sentence in describing an experience, become selective in talking about certain friends' activities or relationships, conceal photographs or other materials, or may become indirect, vague and devious.

(5) May try to manipulate or control adults as in sexual relationship with victimizing adult.

(6) May use language or terms to describe parts of body, sexual acts or deviant behavior not appropriate for the child's age or development.

(7) Obsessive talk of a person unknown to family or others. Though perpetrators may be well-known to the family, a child's obsession with a particular individual may signal something wrong. Doesn't want to be alone with an adult friend or relative.

(8) Appearance of material goods. Sudden money, clothes, toys, or talk about trips and other gifts that parents did not provide. However, when sexual abuse occurs within the family, gifts are not part of the bargain; coercion, power, bribery or threats are the usual

avenues.

Shirley O'Brien emphasizes that the basic problem stems from the collapse of a happy family. "There is considerable evidence," she says, "that the QUALITY OF FAMILY LIFE is extremely important to emotional well-being, happiness and mental health. Poor relationships within the family are very strongly related to many of the problems in society. Obviously strengthening family life should be one of the nation's top priorities. Unfortunately it has not been a top priority in the past" (op. cit. p. 39).

In 1982, approximately 1.6 million children ran away from home. Of these, 35 percent left home because of sexual abuse or incest. Ten percent of these runaways never return and over 70 percent are forced into child prostitution. The average starting age for child prostitution is 14 years; 51 percent are boys and 49 percent, girls. The average age of the sexually-molested child is FIVE (Carole Pytel: Executive Director of Paul & Lisa, Inc.; *Youthletter* May 1984 p. 39).

Our motto is "Childhood ends . . . when sexual abuse begins" (Carole Pytel).

INCEST

Perhaps the most awful sexual abuse of children—INCEST (rape by immediate relatives like father, brother, stepfather)—is also increasing. Forms of incest include genital fondling, oral-genital and genital-genital contact up to and including sexual intercourse. It can involve exhibitionism and indecent suggestion. One study indicates the true incidence could be as high as 800 to 1,000 per million people. *Dr. Karen Zelas,* a New Zealand child and family psychiatrist puts the ratio of abuse of boys to girls as 1:25 in the United States and 1:6 in the United Kingdom; 42 percent of the abused are 11-15 years old; 46 percent of those abused are 10 years old or under; 18 percent are only five years old or less. Seventy-five percent of these molestations are from offenders known to the child. Almost half of these are family members. Thirty-five percent of these take place in the child's own home. A large percentage (42 percent) of molesters are adolescents who commonly do this while babysitting and half of these adolescent molesters were themselves sexually abused.

The U.S. National Center on Child Abuse estimates in 1976 alone, at least one percent of over 1,000,000 child abuse cases were sexual abuse. Most child sexual abuse comes from within the family. (A child is more likely to be sexually molested by a member of his or her family than by anyone else.) Most of the abused children are girls. The largest single group of offenders are fathers and step-fathers; 88 percent of molesters are male and only 12 percent female. "The consensus is that these figures based only on reported instances are way, way low. Some estimates suggest there are 25,000,000 women in this country who have been sexually abused by their fathers (*Kiss Daddy Goodnight*: Louise Armstrong, Simon & Schuster 1978 p. 7). Older brothers, exposed to pornography and forms of sexual immorality, also involve their younger sisters in forms of incest.

BECKY was always running—running, hiding, trying to get away from someone. Sometimes in her dreams she was kicking, scream-ing, hitting—always against that same person. With the help of Dr. Alice Murray, a Christian psychiatrist, Becky begins a long and painful journey to her past; through the layers of memory scar-tissue under which this straight-A college student has buried her hurt, fear and anger. As a child, Becky was raped by the one who haunts her sleep. That person was her father. (Ruth Senter: *"Becky: An Untold Story," Campus Life* April 1981, p. 51).

JENNY (not her real name, but a real girl) wins a long and terrible struggle with bitterness towards her father; incest, from when she was a little girl, all the way into her teenage years. Her mother didn't believe her. She finally ran away from home. Now many years and many tears later she is a young woman, learning to love a young man who cares very much for her. Finally, after much counsel she gets the courage to forgive her dad for his immorality. He is deeply moved, sorrowful, repentant. Mom is dead; he is alone now. She agrees to one day return home to visit him. Months later, while in her old home city, she becomes ill and is hospitalized. Calls dad. He comes to the hospital to visit her. And there, in the hospital, he does it again.

"Rape by a stranger is quick and brutal. It allows for a straight-forward reaction—anger, hate. But the seduction or coercion of a child by a needed and trusted parent is far more complex. It's not amazing that some run away, that some turn to drugs, that some, having been called slut by their fathers, become promiscuous prostitutes. What's amazing is that many (no one knows how many) do not" (*Armstrong,* op. cit. p. 40).

I lead a church camp. Mostly junior high school kids. In one of the sessions, I speak about what a real father is supposed to be like; about God. I talk about hurt in homes, about forgiveness. After the session, there are a whole lot of girls who ask for some help with a problem that is obviously very personal and painful. I see each one individually, and none knows what the other has asked. I did not mention nor allude to incest during the talk. EVERY ONE of the girls has a dad or a brother who has or now is involving them in incest. Every single one. We do another camp in another part of the country at another time. I comment on the radiance of some of the newly-converted kids in attendance. "And yet," their senior leader tells me, "over 80 percent of these kids come from homes where there is incest in the family."

THE FEMINIST VERSION

Some more radical feminists try to blame incest ultimately on the Christian revelation about God's creation of the first man and woman. "Father-Daughter sexual union is implicitly sanctioned," says Elizabeth Ward, "from the Bible to the latest movie-star marriage." Movie-star marriage perhaps; but hardly the Bible! Elizabeth, who is to be otherwise commended for a concern deep enough to work and write on the subject (*Father-Daughter Rape* The Woman's Press 1984) thanks "the goddess or my stars or the lines on my palm daily" that she was born in a time and place enabling her to be part of the woman's liberation movement.

She need not look so far back as the Creation story to find the sin of incest; the symbol of it is an integral part and practice of the "goddess" pattern she blithely espouses, and incest is a major consequence of its imposition on the family. In this feminist version of the roots of the justification of incest, God created Adam as "brother" as well as "husband" to Eve. Because Eve was taken from Adam's body, she is somehow also Adam's daughter! This sort of reasoning might also allege that Adam, (made from the dust of the ground) is a son and brother to dirt and sexually sanctions mud. It is also nonsense. Incest is a consequence of violating God's standards. Modern secular society has almost no record of support for any sexual purity. It approves almost everything that God explicitly forbids as sexual immorality. When the consequences of that immorality begins to hurt women and children one need not be a Christian to feel shock and anger, but that is a direct testimony to the wisdom and counsel of God. Attempts to blame violations of one of the last of society's remaining taboos on the Christian teaching that expressly forbids it is nonsense indeed.

BIBLICAL LAW & INCEST

But as much as they differ, radical feminists and true Christians here at least should have a common concern; both must be deeply opposed to sexual mistreatment of woman and children. Incest is never sanctioned nor allowed in the Bible. On the contrary, Scripture imposes the heaviest penalties against it. INCEST COMES FROM IMMORALITY; the Bible is clearly and fundamentally "dead set" against all immorality, and especially sexual intercourse among near relatives in all its forms:

"None of you shall marry a near relative; for I am the Lord. A girl may not marry her father, nor a son his mother, nor any other of his father's wives, nor his sister, or half-sister whether the daughter of his father or his mother, whether born in the same house or elsewhere."

Under biblical law you cannot marry your *granddaughter*—the daughter of either your son or your daughter—for she is a close relative. You may not marry a *half-sister*—your father's wife's daughter; nor your aunt—your father or mother's sister or the wife of your father's brother. It covers a lot more ground than secular society ever penalizes. You are forbidden to marry your *daughter-in-law* (your son's wife) or your brother's wife. God says you cannot marry both a woman and her daughter or granddaughter for they are both near relatives; he calls this a "horrible wickedness" (Lev. 18:6-17). The penalty for incest or any kind of sexual cooperation and consort between parents and children in early Israel was *death* (Lev. 20:11,12). Paul called a man who was living in sin with his father's wife a " terrible thing, something so evil that even the heathen don't do it" (1 Cor. 5:1).

THE CAUSES & CONSEQUENCES OF INCEST

Incest is the end product of a family where *adult immorality, pornography and sexual fantasy have not been dealt with:*

"I remember like hiding behind things and him just saying 'Pamela, come here', and I would say, 'No, I don't want to.' And he'd say, 'Pamela, come HERE!' He'd say, 'You don't want your brothers to hear do you?' And I used to say, 'I hate you. I want to kill you!' But for a long time he just wouldn't listen . . . all my crying, my saying 'I hate you' was meaningless. It didn't matter if I hated him. It didn't stop him from chasing me. . .. He wasn't like mean, nasty, hitting. But obsessed. Like that's the only thing he saw . . ."

Incest is also a byproduct of a *society that glorifies success and beauty.* The spirit of Moloch exalts things at the expense of life-quality. Bill Gothard points out that the development of the "Strange Woman" (the prostitute of Proverbs 2:16, 5:3-6, 20; 6:24-26) results from her parent's focus on APPEARANCE rather than CHARACTER in a child. A daughter models her attractiveness to men by her father's response to her; when this is perverted through his sexual immorality, the girl's own self-image is shattered and defiled:

"I remember before it all happened. I really liked my body. . . . But there was my father telling me how much he loved me. How beautiful he thought I was. How he couldn't resist me. And as a result I used to think I was really ugly. Because I didn't want my father attracted to me. And so if he told me I was beautiful I didn't want to be beautiful. If being beautiful attracts you, I don't want to be that way" (*Armstrong* op cit. p. 47, 50).

Incest on a child often opens the door to a *whole life of sexual immorality;* it is devastating to happy and normal friendship relationships between the sexes:

MAGGIE was only four when her father returned from the war. Maggie is much older now. She has been through three marriages, all disasters. Her teenage years were even worse, a whole cycle of meaningless, rebellious sexual affairs. In her words: "I felt that the only way I could have relationships with men was on a sexual basis. That was the only way I could be accepted—if I 'put out.' That was the only tool I had. Nothing else. They called me a whore; so therefore I am. Therefore I can go to bed with anybody." When did Maggie's lonely, ugly picture of herself begin? When she was four. When her newly returned soldier father began to sexually molest her.

"I thought, 'My God, what is wrong with me? What is it that I do to people? What is wrong with me?' And feeling dirty, feeling guilty. As a kid I felt that it was my fault, I was unclean. I was dirty. I was guilty. I didn't fit in. A sense of being tainted somehow. You're keeping so many secrets to yourself. So many skeletons in your closet. You hear other children say 'my father this and my father that.' But you're so guilt-stricken and so guarded you can't say anything about your father" (*Armstrong,* op. cit. p. 105).

MAIN MYTHS ON INCEST

There are some widely held misconceptions about incest. Because it is rarely spoken about, still more rarely, uncovered or reported, people don't realize how much pain, fear and terror some children must live with every year. When a choked confession comes to light, some adults simply don't believe the child. They think it is some kind of fantasy, and if a child talks about it, it is probably made up. But what child knows enough to make up a story like that? If they tell you something about sexual abuse, BELIEVE IT. It is almost never a lie. Others think the child has promoted or encouraged it. But it takes a perverted father to think a small daughter's snuggles are an invitation to incest. "The responsibility for incest always lies squarely on the adult," says Dr. Alice Murray. "The child is always the victim, never the cause. Becky's love for her father as a small child did not cause him to rape her. . . . She has the innocent victim of her father's uncontrolled sexual desires. Incest is the result of a sick parent, not a sick child" (op cit. p. 52).

Then again, the mother rarely knows or colludes in the relationship. "I remember loneliness," says Becky. "Who could I tell about the way my daddy treated me? Who would understand? . . . I didn't dare tell my mother. I was afraid it would destroy her, her marriage and our home. I couldn't tell someone my age. They probably wouldn't even know what I was talking about. I didn't want anyone to know. If I felt I was getting too close to friends I would suddenly drop them. If they got too close, they might find out. And if they knew, I was sure they'd drop me. So I carried my hurt alone."

The situation where a mother or daughter commits incest with a son or brother is rarer. But in a society where morals have collapsed and the image of an older woman seducing a boy *(Class)* or two child innocents thrown together away from civilization *(Blue Lagoon)* are popular movie themes, even these are occurring more frequently. The rise of lesbianism and sodomy among "parents" in society has affected the family at its roots. Modern easy divorce and remarriage has opened new avenues of temptation to stepfathers and stepbrothers with girls in their new family from a previous marriage.

Finally, don't think it "can't happen in a religious home." Babylon flourishes in religious homes. Babylon is exceptionally religious. Incest can happen in homes where the dad and mother both know enough about right and wrong to carry a real load of guilt when those standards are violated. A recent study of child prostitutes in San Francisco turned up a horrible fact: a large number of the girls on the street came from religious homes. The majority of them ran away because their dad committed incest with them. Incest is rife in the churches.

RESULTS OF INCEST

(1) *A sharp sense of BETRAYAL of trust* "a kind of trust we can now never have. . . . I will never have a loving, care-taking father." When the incest comes from a father, this leads to all kinds of damage to a girl's image of God.

" 'Pray about it,' I am told. 'What good will it do?' I ask myself. 'If God wasn't around all those times when daddy used me to satisy his sexual urges, why should God care about me now?' 'God is your father,' I hear ministers say. Then who needs God? Fathers cannot be trusted. If God is my father, I can't trust him either" (*Becky: An*

Untold Story op. cit. p. 53).

"Someday, maybe," said Erick Erickson, "there will exist a well-informed, well-considered and yet fervent public conviction that the most deadly of all possible sins is the mutilation of a child's spirit, for such mutilation undercuts the principle of TRUST, without which every human act, may it feel ever so good and seem ever so right, is prone to perversion by destructive forms of conscientiousness" (*Journal American Medical Association*, 1972).

Likewise, when incest comes from a brother or stepbrother, a girl's spiritual image of friendship with boys is made sensual or fearful. Girls I have counselled who have been sexually abused by boys in their family have difficulty in building healthy and honest relationships with other guys even in God's family.

(2) ALIENATION from BOTH parents. "Mother must know. Why doesn't she say something? Why doesn't she help." Often the alienation carries on in life to others; "When I was growing up there was just such a feeling of isolation—like I couldn't tell my mother—but it just carried over into almost everything. Like I couldn't tell anybody. And I was always very much a loner. Never really had any close friends. And I could never deal with my feelings openly" (*Armstrong* op. cit. p. 54).

Every child has strong needs for love, affection and attention from both parents. Little girls have a loyalty and sometimes even an infatuation with their fathers. They sometimes need to be cuddled, carressed and spoken gently to by a dad who genuinely loves them and can be an image of care, protection and love. Any child wants to be safe knowing they can just be a kid with their parents. Incest is the psychic murder of all of these; destroy a normal parent/child affection and you also defile other future friendships. Two-thirds of those who have had incestuous assaults have been found to be emotionally disturbed; 14 percent seriously in the short-term; perhaps only 10-20 percent reach adulthood without apparent long-term negative effects.

"Fury, you know, just fury. On top of everything . . . he was invading the only relationship I had—my relationship with my mother. He was alienating me by saying, 'Don't you ever tell your mother about this or I will kill you.' Not only did he abuse, but he took away the only relationship I really had. Annihilated that completely" (*Armstrong* op. cit. p. 109).

(3) ANGER. Deep, deep anger. Actually rage. Hurt and anger always go together. Dr. Richard Dobbins says, "How can someone hurt you without making you angry? People resist acknowledging this. . . You should know yourself well enough to know that mixed in with the pain and sadness of what you are experiencing is anger" (*Your Anger Is Not Your Enemy, Charisma* July 1984 p. 53). Incest is one of the profoundest possible betrayals of childhood. It can create the greatest hurt, and thus a deep anger and even hatred. "Anger and rage . . . are common emotions for the sexually abused. When a trusted relationship turns into sexual exploitation, bitterness and anger usually follow. Often the victim is left with an urge to kill. This rage and mistrust may be transferred from the father to all men" (*Dr. Alice Murray;* op. cit. p. 52). "I was crying and in hysterics. I ran into the bedroom screaming obscenities. I cried so hard I almost vomited. I wanted to die I was so mad and didn't know if I could take this life I was leading much longer. I contemplated overdosing but was so choked up I couldn't even swallow my own saliva" (*Armstrong,* op. cit. p. 85). The flattery of a prostitute is not love; it is hatred. Incest destroys geniune affection on all levels.

(4) FEAR. Fear when it begins, fear each time it happens, sickening fear as the pieces drop into place and the patterns are learned as to how it is being set up to happen again. Fear of losing a family relationship; fear of losing the family. Fear of being found out, being thrown out, arrested, and put in jail. How alien to the bibilcal pattern: "God has not given us a spirit of fear; but of power, and of love and a sound mind" (2 Tim. 1:7). Incest links sex with force, domination and fear; how directly opposite to God's purposes! "There is no fear in love; but perfect love casts out all fear" (1 Jn. 4:18). Incest is the element of REVERSAL at work in the dad's care and protection of his daughter.

(5) GUILT. Without exception, the victim and the perpetrator know that this relationship is wrong. Even though incest often begins before the child is old enough to know right from wrong, the sense of abuse and violation is quickly understood. "I used to think I brought it on, you know. Just by being female. I knew it was strong. Maybe that came from religion. We had Sunday School stuff. . . . I considered it adultery. Because it was against my mother. My

father's wife. So I felt like a sinner" (*Armstrong* op cit. p. 50). The violator certainly knows it is wrong. He takes elaborate precautions to not be found out, swears his victim to secrecy, threatens them with violence or arrest or divorce if they tell. Incest is sin; against the marriage, against the family and against God.

Betrayal, alienation, hate, hurt, fear and guilt. All manifest signs of the kingdom of darkness. When Babylon rules, the family dies. Of course, even without the healing power of the living Christ, some survive. None are unscarred. Some, like Becky, bury it, and it only comes out in nightmares. Some are like Sandy who says she has "learned to cope with it." Sandy had a whole string of sexual affairs at school that somehow never worked. She says she now "knows why" they never did. Sandy, robbed of all true fatherly affection, has become a lesbian. Some take out their rage and hurt in militant feminist movements. Some are driven back into the embracing arms of the very goddess that spawned this destructive pattern. The closer the relationship of the perpetrator and the victim, the number and duration of times, the degree of force, of fear, shame, guilt—the greater the impact on the child. Sometimes sexually abused children begin to relate sexually to other adults. They offer themselves as a sad and damaged way of getting attention and affection. Some abused children are even made to bear the blame. Strangely enough, when incest is revealed, the child often is made to feel responsible!

Karen Zelas says, "The family suffers terribly from the shattering disclosure of sexual abuse and will try to cope with the guilt and shame by affixing blame—commonly on the child." But all bear the scars, and all are somehow hurt—*suffer, little children.* No wonder Jesus said:

"But whoso shall offend one of these little ones which believe in me, it were better for him that a millstone were hanged about his neck, and that he were drowned in the depth of the sea. Woe unto the world because of offences! for it must needs be that offences come; but woe to that man by whom the offence cometh! (Matt. 18: 6-7).

MOTIVATION FOR INCEST

Why does the father, the brother, the relative do it? The spirit of

Moloch. The exaltation of dead things over life; the glorification of the creation and not the Creator. Using people and loving things.

"It is immoral to use people for any reason," says Neil Gallagher. "People who are used are people who hate. Prostitutes confess they hate men. Less than one percent successfully marry. They've never learned love. They've been used" (*How To Stop The Porno Plague*, p. 46). Louise Armstrong notes: "Weak or authoritarian . . . (the father) must have a perception of his children as POSSESSIONS, as objects. He must see his children as there to meet his needs rather than the other way around" (p. 268). But that perception is the consequence of a spiritual dimension to life. A society that believes man is nothing more than a machine cannot help but see others as objects:

> " 'My love,' she said to me
> 'When you get right down to it
> We are nothing more than machines . . .'
> So I chained her to my bedroom wall for future use
> And she cried" (Steven Turner)

PREVENTION OF INCEST

Prevention must begin early. Children can be taught the difference between *bad* and *good* touching by using something like tickling as an example to teach them it is all right to sometimes say *no* to a relative or an adult if they are threatened by it. "Do you like to be tickled? That's good touching, isn't it? Well what if someone tickles you too hard? That's bad touching. What would you say if you didn't want them to? You could say 'No'. That is all right.

Karen Zelas boils it down to three simples rules you can teach your child:

(1) *Say NO!*

(2) *Get away.*

(3) *Tell someone.*

"Incest can only happen in secret. If parents, preferably BOTH parents, sit down with a child at the age of four or five, or whenever they tell her about not getting into cars with strangers and so forth— and at the same time tell the child that no one has the right to touch her in certain ways—NOT EVEN IF IT'S SOMEONE SHE KNOWS AND LOVES—that child is being given a power she needs. And if parents intrude when anyone—grandfather. . . touches a child, handles a child, in any way that the child objects to, that child is getting another message she needs; her body belongs to her. She's allowed to say no. She's permitted to object" (*Armstrong* op. cit. 276).

LEGAL GUIDELINES ON DEALING WITH CHILD ABUSE

Laurie O'Reilly, legal counsellor for the New Zealand Child Abuse seminar, points out "There is a risk that the damage done by putting a child and family through the legal process may exceed the damage done by the sexual abuse in the first place." The interests of the child here are paramount. New Zealand, like other countries, has both Court and a Family Court with specialist judges, independent counsel for the child, and supportive services available that are distinct from Criminal Court. Yet she says, "Sexual abuse of children is a crime that our society abhors in the abstract but ignores in the reality." Like many nations, there are inadequate laws regarding reporting, inadequate professional investigation, cooperation and processes in this area (Sexual Abuse Of Children; Postgrad. Medical Committee U. Auckland; 11 Sept. 1984). In the United States, as already mentioned, some major improvements in both law and counsel recently have been initiated.

Here are some other guidelines for helping children:

At all stages we must believe the child and protect them.

We must protect the child from the abuser, but we must also protect the child from the legal system.

Hearsay evidence is usually non-admissible in court. However, what the victim (or even the accused) has said to someone else is acceptable. It must be reported promptly to be admissible. It must not arise from leading questions. Accurate recording of these questions and answers will spare the child from having to repeat these statements in court. Courts are reluctant to convict on the evidence of the victim alone. They require corroboration, and distress is one form of this. Record promptly details of what you learn. This can also be used as court evidence.

Try hard to keep the child out of court. For that reason, follow all the rules of evidence as closely as you can in order to prevent a defended hearing. Ideally, use all methods to get a confession. False accusations are rare. False recantations are common.

Karen Zelas says a good response to a properly made case against incest will minimize: (a) Need for the victim to repeat their story; (b) The need to testify in court; (c) The need to be "punished" by separation from family; (d) The likelihood of re-abuse; (e) Adverse emotional sequels; and (f) Maximize opportunity for re-integration of the family (not necessarily including the offender).

So much for the legal. But at heart, incest, as with all sexual abuse, is a spiritual and moral problem. The answer to Babylon and Moloch is not just the scales of justice, but the hand of God. Morally clean parents who love God, each other, and their children do not abuse his laws or each other. We need a revival that shows us the true heart of a loving God.

HELP AND INSTRUCTION

Because these forms of abuse usually come from within the home itself, they are both terribly destructive and difficult to deal with. Law and government often hesitate to step in. There is always the concern that legal or public action will further destroy the home. Society only recently has become aware how large the problem is, and much more needs to be published and made available on dealing with physical and sexual child abuse in a Christian context. There is already much good material in the church on the key problem: strengthening the marriage and the home.

An hour-and-40-minute videotape *"The Exploiters"* (produced by WMAZ-TV in Chicago and geared towards young people or adults) is available. Contact Paul & Lisa, Inc., a national non-profit program for the prevention and rehabilitation of sexually abused youth. It deals with child victims of prostitution, pornography and sexual assault. ($60 and shipping; Box 588, Westbrook, CT 96498)

A state-wide telephone confidential counsel and advice service is available for those parents who have had battles with any form of child abuse and need help. Phone the parents Anonymous Hotline

1-800-421-0353.

The Christian Society For Prevention of Cruelty to Children has developed a family study program kit called "Protecting Your Child From Sexual Assault" with a parent's teaching guide and a child's activity workbook. Order from: Little Ones Books" P.O. Box 725, Young America, Minnesota 55399. ($10 and $1.50 postage).

Youthletter lists some of the better books available:

First-person accounts:

"The Abusers"
Gary Fisher (Mott Media: $4.95 TPB)

Cry Out!
P.E. Quinn (Abingdon: $10.95 HB)

Carole's Story
Chip Ricks (Tyndale House: $4.95 PB)

Academic Studies:

Child Abuse & Neglect: A Guidebook for Educators (1981)
Edsel L. Erikson and others
Learning Publication ($9.95)
3030 S. 9th St.
Kalamazoo, MI 49009

Child Abuse Help Book
Jim Haskins (1981)
Addison-Wesley ($9.95)
One Jacobs Way
Reading, MA. 08167

Coping With Abuse In The Family
Wesley Monfalcone (1980)
Westminster ($5.95)

Family Violence
Richard J. Gelles (1979)
Sage Publications ($24.00)
275 Beverly Drive
Beverly Hills, CA 90212

Sexual Abuse of Children: Resource Guide
Benjamin Schlesinger (1982)
U. Toronto Press (& 10.95)
33 E. Tupper St.
Buffalo, NY 14203

Violence In The Family
Murray Straus & Suzanne Steinmetz (1974)
Harper & Row ($14.50)

Books For Children:

"What If I Say No?"
Jill Haddad & Lloyd Martin
M.H. Capp & Co. ($3.50PB)
Box 3584 Bakersfield, Ca 93385

Private Zone
Frances Dayee
Chas. Franklin Press ($3.00PB)
18409 90th Ave.
W. Edmonds, WA 98020

   For early warning and prevention: See Appendix
"Steps To Take In Protecting Your Child."

WAR ON THE STREET —THROWAWAYS, RUNAWAYS AND CHILD PROSTITUTION

"He shall turn the heart of the fathers to the children and the heart of the children to their fathers lest I come and smite the earth with a curse" (Malachi 4:5-6).

So said the Lord about Elijah the prophet who was to come before "the great and dreadful day of the LORD." The last promise and the last warning in the Old Testament was on the reconciliation of fathers and their children. It was the sign of the last days, the final promise before God's judgment. *And we need an Elijah today.* The attack on the home has resulted in what David Wilkerson called "The Throwaway Generation"—a growing army of hurt, neglected, rejected or just plain abandoned children. We have been warned. Unless something happens to begin to heal the hurt of the home, the judgment of God will come in our time.

LATCHKEY CHILDREN

How does it start? For millions of children the answer is simple; *the parents don't have time to be there or to care.* And why not? Because we have given our culture and our aims over to the spirit of Moloch. Parents have disobeyed God, flaunted his laws and abandoned their responsibilities to each other and their children. Divorce has eaten out the heart of the nation's marriages; the children have been burned. September 10-17, 1984, was made, by an act of Congress, "National Latchkey Children Week." It called attention to "one of the most significant trends in basic family structure and living patterns;" the fact that perhaps five million American children under the age of 10 have no one to look after them when they come home in the afternoon. Some estimate 500,000 preschoolers under the age of six are in a similar predicament.

There are other reasons besides the rising divorce rate. These days most parents of young children work outside the home. Two-job parents have become the RULE rather than the exception and the number of single parents has DOUBLED in the past decade. (Working married women with children under six: 2.5 million in 1960; 3.1 million in 1965; 3.9 million in 1970; 4.4 million in 1975; 5.2 million in 1980; 6.2 million in 1984; working single women with children under six: .42 million in 1960; .57 million in 1965; .64 million in 1970; .96 million in 1975; 1.3 million in 1980; 1.8 million in 1984.) (*"What Price Day Care?" Newsweek* Sept. 10, 1984 p. 14). Why are mothers working? Some no longer have husbands. Some never did. Some have become entranced with an affluent lifestyle. Some have been lured by promises of fulfillment outside the "oppressive" limits of taking care of a husband, a home and their children. But whatever the reason, the result is the same: parents just aren't there when they are needed.

"The typical scene of mom welcoming a child home with a glass of milk and fresh cookies is kaput. Also gone is something more important than milk and cookies; the after school debriefing, the cherished and valuable time for just plain talk about how the world is treating the child, who beat up on who, and the terrible teacher who was unfair" (*Youthletter* Nov. 1983 p. 82).

What do working parents do when they won't or can't stay home to take care of little children? They put them in *day-care centers*. "Guilt is the one reason we've been so successful," says Perry Mendel, the king of day-care-for-profit. "Working parents feel guilty that they have to work, and more guilty having to leave their children in sub-standard facilities. His chain of 900 plus "Kinder-Care Learning Centers" currently handles about 100,000 'units'—Kinder-Care parlance for a child" (*Newsweek* op. cit. p. 14).

How many are we talking about? About *TWO MILLION children* are under formal licensed day-care; more than *FIVE MILLION* other children aged three to five attend nursery schools or kindergartens which, for many parents, serve the same purpose. Additionally, uncounted millions are looked after informally by unlicensed babysitters . . . in a wave of fundamental social change day-care is becoming a basic need of the American family. "Ten years ago when you talked about day-care you were talking about welfare mothers; today you're talking about everybody" (*Patty Siegel*, a California State child-care adviser, p. 14).

There is a dramatic rise in the number of mothers who work outside the home. Despite the fact that it is almost always more expensive for a mother to work an outside job and somehow hire help to take care of her children, two-job families have risen from 18.9 million in 1967, 20.5 million in 1970, 22.3 million in 1975, 25.6 million in 1980 to 26.1 million in 1980 (*Bureau of Labor Statistics and U. S. Census Bureau.*)

How do the children handle all this? Teenagers and children left alone at home go through all kinds of pressures. If the parents care at all, they usually worry enough to lay down the law as to what kids can and cannot do when they are gone. Hedged in by these parents' rules to protect them, many kids feel like prisoners. Some don't want to go home at all, and the local video arcade becomes an attractive alternative.

Leila Moore, Penn State professor says the loneliness is worse than the fear. Girls suffer more than the boys in this because their parents—fearing possible pregnancy—don't allow them to have friends over (*Youthletter* op cit. No. 83 p. 82).

How do those infants and toddlers get on in day care centers compared with those in the consistent care of one person? Because of teacher turnover, a two-year-old in a center for a year with three or four teachers "has it really tough and it happens all the time." Dr. Burton White, director of Boston's Center for Parent Education, doesn't like day care at all. "A child needs large doses of custom-made love," he says. "You can't expect hired help to provide that. I see the trend towards increasing use of the day care as a disaster." He has no patience with the idea that families NEED two paychecks these days. "That's a typical middle-class comment," he says. "Both parents don't HAVE to work—they both WANT to work to maintain a house or a lifestyle. They are putting their desires above the welfare of the baby" (*Newsweek* op. cit. p. 16).

Demand for day care is sure to increase. Many of the post-war "baby boom" generation put off having children until relatively late in life. Now they are making up for lost time and the "resulting baby boomlet in this decade will push the number of children under 10 to 38 million by 1990, an increase of five million" (p. 15).

WHAT HAPPENS TO LATCHKEY CHILDREN?

Latchkey children are not only more prone to emotional problems, more likely to commit crimes and be the victims of crimes; they are left in situations that create loneliness, fear and frustration that open the door to experiments with drinking, drugs and sex. The latchkey child is placed in an unguarded Eden, emotionally starved and left with a whole array of forbidden fruit.

"Young people's sexual awareness runs breathlessly ahead of their emotional development. . . At the same time, a vast increase of working mothers has provided a convenient sexual setting; the empty house after school. . . The prevailing ethos of this new culture has been summed up as 'no waiting,' an ardent belief that any pleasures available to adults should be . . available to the young" (*Newsweek* Sept. 1, 1980. P. 51).

THROWAWAY CHILDREN

Then again some children can't handle their home situations at all. "Running away," says Dotson Rader, "Is one of the ways our children tell us that life at home has become unendurable. About 35 percent of runaways leave home because of incest. Another 53 percent because of physical neglect." "The rest," says Rader, "are throwaways—children kicked out or simply abandoned by parents who move away. Every state has laws against incest, child pornography and the procuring of children but they are rarely enforced."

Linda was 14 when she ran away from home. She had been sexually abused by her father since the age of five and says, "I waited for years for the chance to get out." One month after leaving home she became a prostitute in Denver. "It was easy to say 'Yes' to nice clothes and a nice place to live. I felt miserable at home. Being a prostitute was a lot better than going home to my father." She is one of over a MILLION children who run away from home each year. Most runaways don't live long—150,000 disappear every year. They suffer from starvation, drug-related sicknesses, sexual damage and disease. A major cause of death among runaway boys who get caught up in prostitution is rectal hemorrhage.

The *Runaway Hotline* established in 1973 after the discovery of the mass murder of 27 youths in Houston, fields between 200 and 300 calls every day from teenagers, up nearly 100 calls a day over 1979. . . . Increasingly it is parents who toss the children out . . . "throwaway children" whose parents drop them off at runaway centers saying, "I can't handle you. You're too much." The average age of children coming to one center dropped from 14 to 12. What kind of kids are they? More than 80 percent are white, from middle-class and upper-class families. Rader comments, "Without exception, those I met seemed starved for affection and regard, but fearful, filled with resentment against parents whom they believe never loved them. Oddly enough they blame themselves and wonder what is so bad about them that made their parents love them so little. The majority of runaways are never reported as missing by their parents" (*Who Will Help The Children?* p. 5).

Rader, himself once a runaway, crossed the country from the east coast to the West and back, interviewing hundreds of runaways, public officials, social workers, parents and clergy. His *Parade* cover story on runaways (Feb. 7, 1982) generated thousands of letters and stirred hearings in Congress. Rader returned to his travels and interviews with street runaways in the summer of that same year to see what had happened to them. His article "Who Will

Help The Children?'' (*Parade*, Sept. 5, 1982) is a moving, powerful glimpse into the tragic world of the runaways. Their average age, like Daniel, is 15. Here are some of their stories.

DANIEL

"Huddled in a doorway near Woolworth's was a slight, hungry little girl of 12 who had run away from California months ago. 'Wendy's got no place to live,' Daniel said. 'And she's scared of everybody. She had an abortion two weeks back.' He paused, then added quietly, sadly, 'She's not going to make it when the cold weather comes.'

Late that night we went to the bus depot where Daniel got his small bag of clothes out of a 25-cent locker. I rented him a room at my motel. He had nowhere else to go.

" 'What's going to happen to me?' he asked. 'I can't get a job. There aren't any for runaway kids. How am I going to finish school without money and no place to live? The tricks already want boys younger than me. You tell me what to do.' "

"When I didn't reply, Daniel mumbled something angrily under his breath. I asked what he had said."

"I said 'Nobody gives a damn about kids.' "

GINA

"Gina is 14, a pretty girl, self-assured, almost defiant, like many children too long on the streets. She was born and raised in Seattle. Then her father died, and her mother moved away, leaving Gina and her little brother in care of their stepbrother and his wife. 'Two and a half years ago,' she said, 'me and my little brother ran away together because of what my stepbrother done to us all the time. He beat us up all the time. Then he raped me three times. So we ran downtown. My stepbrother found out where we were. He broke down the door and smacked me with his hand and took us back. When he got us home, he started beating me. I jumped out the back window and went downtown. I was on the streets about four months and then my little brother ran away and found me. He lives with me.

"I asked her how old he is. 'Eleven', she replied smiling. 'He's small for his age. We live in cheap motels. I brought him a TV, a black-and-white. He loves TV. . . he's all I got. I got to take care of him."

Rader asks her how she gets the money to support them both.

"Hustling," she answered. "That's the only way you can survive down there. I first heard about it from a girlfriend. . . . I was 12. There's been a lot of men since. Do you know something? I don't really like sex. And except for my little brother I don't think anybody ever loved me." Gina laughed, embarrassed by what she had admitted.

"I'm a Catholic," she said. "A lot of times I think 'What's going to happen to me when the world comes to an end?' I try to go to church. I get lonely, that's when I go and I think about what God's going to do to me. But hustling's the only way I can support my little brother. I would have done ANYTHING else, but I couldn't get a job. There aren't any for street kids."

LOUIS

"My first night in Albuquerque, I met Louis, 14. Two years ago his mother threw him out of the house, saying she couldn't take it anymore. She never told him what 'it' was.

" 'I heard about runaways staying up in the heights,' Louis said. 'So I camped here with these three kids who were dealing dope. It was the first dope I ever smoked. After a few days I heard about an abandoned motel, and I split, walking all the way down.' He paused, shaking his head at the length of the trek. 'I stayed nights at the motel. There was no lights. The toilet didn't work. I ripped off food from a market. That's how I eat . . .' "

Radar asks if he's ever gotten caught." 'Yeah. A couple weeks later. There was a security guard, but I didn't care because I was so hungry. I was busted and sent to D home (juvenile detention center) for a night. The next day a friend got me out. He was a Christian so I became a Christian. I stayed the rest of the summer with him. That was a year ago. Then he said I had to get out because he didn't have money to take care of me. A lady at his church said they'd find a Christian family to take me in. They never did.'

"I just hang out. I stay in parks when I can't crash somewhere.

Sometimes the park or the graveyard toward the airport. It scares me though. I think someone might kill me when I sleep. I ain't too big a kid, you know. There's nothing to do. I keep thinking the church will get me adopted. But it's been a while now, so I guess it won't be happening like they promised" (p. 6).

RICHARD

His last afternoon in San Diego, Rader visited for several hours with a group of runaways living together in a small house. As he was leaving he saw a small boy outside. He was blonde, light-eyed, slight—vulnerable in appearance, lost and unhappy.

"I sat beside him on the grass," says Rader. "He wore cut-off blue jeans and a torn plaid cowboy shirt. He was 11 years old.

" 'Why don't you go home?' I asked. 'It's getting late.'

"He stared at the grass."

" 'I'm sure your parents miss you. You should go home.'

"He glanced up, raising his left arm for me so see. Like his entire body, his arms were thin, like sticks. Across his left forearm between wrist and elbow was a deep red gash.

" 'My mom did that,' he said without emotion. 'My mom did that,' he repeated, as if I didn't believe him.

" 'Why?'

" 'I don't know,' Richard said. 'She just doesn't like me.'

"I asked how it happened.

" 'She got mad because my room was messy, and she started screaming at me and whipping me like crazy. She's always screaming about something.'

" 'And that's how your arm got hurt?'

"He dropped his arm and looked down, watching his fingers braid blades of grass like strands of hair. He didn't like talking about his mother.

"I asked him again to tell me.

" 'Mom held my arm against the door (frame) and slammed the door shut.'

"Richard stood up; he was about four feet tall. Facing me, he carefully removed his shirt, then turned around to show me his back. There were bruises on his body, and on his left shoulder was an ugly burn larger than a man's hand covered with a scab just beginning to heal.

"Richard pulled his shirt back on, wincing. 'It don't hurt much,' he said.

I wanted to know how he got such a wound. He said he had a fight with his mother when she was cooking dinner. He didn't know what started it. It was one of those things that happened all the time for no good reason. She had gone into a rage, grabbed him, lifted him and shoved his bare back against the hot oven.

" 'She doesn't want me anymore,' he said ruefully.

" 'Where will you go if you can't go home anymore?' I asked him.

"He sat down again on the grass but didn't answer for a while. He was thinking hard. At 11, it's the kind of question that scares a kid.

" 'I'll run away,'' he finally said. 'I'll run away for good.'

"And then what? I wanted to know.

" 'I'll just run away.' "

A BROKEN-HEARTED FATHER

"He was a Christian so I became a Christian," said Louis. "I stayed the rest of the summer with him. A lady at his church said they'd find a Christian family to take me in. *They never did.*"

Hungry, lonely, abandoned. "They *said . . . they never did.*" When did you last hear that phrase? Was it the words of those before the awful Throne?

"Then shall they answer Him saying, 'Lord when did we see You hungry, or thirsty, or a stranger, or naked or sick or in prison and did not minister to You?' Then shall He answer them saying, 'Verily I say to you, inasmuch as you did it not to one of the least of these, you did it not to Me ' " (Matt. 25:45)

And how do you think *God* feels about runaways? How do you think his father's heart is affected? And what do you think the one who gave us the unforgettable story of the Prodigal has in mind for them?

Long before our time, perhaps the Father looked down the corridor of history and saw the age in which you and I would be born.

He saw the hurt, the rejection, and the pain of hundreds of thousands of children. He saw a generation of selfish, Moloch-worshipping parents who either would or could not care for their own children. And what did he do? He gave us a promise: "In the last days I will pour out of my spirit upon all flesh" (Joel 2:28). *That spirit is the spirit of Adoption.* The Father said: "If their own parents will not take care of them, then I will. I will pour out of My spirit of adoption, and they will be MY sons and MY daughters. If no one else will take care of them, then I will. I will raise up an army from the abandoned. I will call together a family from the shattered and disinherited. The prodigal sons and daughters will come home, and I will be there with open arms to welcome them. Then they and I together will show the world what a real Father is like."

A young man called *David* said it centuries ago: "When my mother and father forsake me—the LORD will take me up" (Ps. 27:10). He who first came to earth as a baby will not allow the abandonment of children to continue without intervention. "Your sons and your daughters shall prophesy . . . your young man shall see visions." Perhaps the greatest spiritual awakening among the young of all time is still to come. Someone is going to reach the street children. Someone is going to mobilize that unharnessed potential for good or evil. Someone will see them touched amd molded into power to affect the world. And God helping you and me, it must be the Church.

WHAT YOU CAN DO TO HELP?

All the runaway shelters in the United States combined can only help around 44,000 runaways a night. Much work is needed to be done by both government and public organizations; but the one group that could really help, the church, is often largely unaware of the scope or the urgency of the problem.

The federal government only allotted $10.4 million in 1981 to help runaways. Rader says, "that's about the cost of lunch in the Senates's subsidized dining room." Some Christian and other public agencies have begun to build *shelter, half-way houses* and *adoption placement services.* What is desperately needed are *street ministries* modeled after the work of George Mueller and the Booths that can reach these children who are "14 going on 40," love them to Christ, help them relearn what it is to be children again, and put them into a caring and loving Christian family. Another avenue to explore is to bring together *grandparents* whose own children have grown up and left home with these converted street children; to bring the old and the young together in the service of Christ and the future of redeemed man seems to be the heart of the fulfillment of Joel's prophecy of the "last days."

Counsel and Help: See Covenant House, Centrum addresses, or check your own local situation:

For local runaway shelters call toll-free:

The *National Runaway Switchboard* 800-621-4000 (In Illinois 800-972-6004) or Hotline 800-231-6946 (Texas 800-392-3352)

Support and information contact:

The National Fund For Runaway Children
1511 K. St. Suite 805
Dept. P
Washington, D.C. 20005

The war on the streets puts a large majority of the abandoned, rejected and throwaway children into the ultimate destruction of innocence: child prostitution.

CHILD PROSTITUTION

Ken Herrmann, a U.S. board member of Defense For Children International testified before a Senate subcommittee of a worldwide market for children in sex. Those who enter this market he said, "usually unwittingly or unwillingly are most commonly street children. Of the *170 MILLION such children worldwide,* only about 500,000 receive support or services from professional agencies." Investigations revealed examples of international child exploitation like:

People posing as foster parents to recruit children for pornography and prostitution. A sex syndicate in Melbourne (the *Australian Pedophile Support Group)* was involved in a "systematic program of child pornography with Filipino boys taking some to Australia for illicit sexual purposes under the banner of foreign foster parent support groups."

Children bought and sold at auctions in Amsterdam, reportedly not an isolated event. It was "the buying and selling of children by photograph for the purposes of pornography production and child trafficking for such purposes," he said. (Dutch authorities denied the allegation). International traffic in children was conservatively estimated as a $5 billion business.

"Child sex tours" offered in West Germany, the Netherlands, Japan and the U.S., taking participants to Sri Lanka, Thailand, the Philippines and elsewhere (*Auckland Star New Zealand* Dec. 3, 1984).

Two years ago, a 12-year-old calling herself Linda, was sold knowingly by her mother as a prostitute for $50. She has since serviced as many as 4,000 men. "I was terrified," she explained. "I said to the Madam, 'I don't want to be that kind of girl.' She said, 'Once you become that kind of girl you can't go back.' The first time it was $250; the second, $180. Then my price dropped, until I couldn't charge a special price." Now she can be bought for $9, of which she gets $3.45. Two so-called Chinese Teahouses in the Prakanong District of Bangkok bought more than 100 girls under the age of 18 who were offered to patrons as prostitutes.

Tim Bond, who works for the London-based *Anti-Slavery Society* presented a report "The Price of A Child" to the United Nations Commission on slavery. He actually bought two tiny children in Bangkok for $20 each and returned them to their parents. The face of a little girl he could not save still haunts him. "It is like a cattle market" (*TV & Radio Times* Aug. 13, 1983 p. 3).

One police investigator who heads a special unit in Los Angeles dealing with child abuse estimates there are some 30,000 sexually exploited children in that city alone. "Nationwide estimates on the number of boys and girls under 16 who are engaged in prostitution range from the tens of thousands to MORE THAN A MILLION. The figures DOUBLE when 16- and 17-year-olds are added."

When the question is asked, "What can be done to help these kids?" one name stands out: *Father Bruce Ritter.* Here is a man who let his compassion become a consuming conviction, and with faith and guts, is doing something about it. Founder-operator of New York City's Covenant House and the "Under 21" sanctuaries for homeless kids, he tells a Congressional Committee what happens too often to youngsters who try to survive on the streets. In one three-week period, he says three girls under 17 were found murdered within five blocks of their homes; two boys, 14 and 15, were picked up by homosexuals, raped and slashed badly; a pimp entered "Under 21" to offer $500 for a 13-year-old girl; a 14-year-old boy held captive for six weeks in a nearby hotel escaped and reached "Under 21" just a step ahead of his captor" (*Child Prostitution: How It Can Be Stopped* John G. Hubbell, *Reader's Digest* June 1984 p. 202).

"Without dealing in myth or exaggeration, there are 500,000 kids younger than 17 involved in prostitution," says Ritter. "Nobody will dispute that. They have nothing to sell but themselves." Father Ritter's Covenant House programs have become the yardstick by which others are measured. His aim is simple: to provide as many beds as possible each night to give kids an alternative to selling themselves. His is tough love. Any staff member who refuses a child is instantly fired. In New York he takes in 12,000 a year; the Toronto Center handles 3,000 more. The Houston shelter expects 5,000 this year. . . "Honest to God, in all my life I've never met one boy or girl prostitute who didn't start out as a runaway. And how can we prevent runaways? The key is the home. Kids ordinarily don't run away from warm loving families. And those who do, invariably return home" (*Streets Of The Lost, LIFE* July 1983 pp. 35, 42).

Bruce Ritter is a 1980's John the Baptist, a thorn in the side of an often callous and immoral Herodian society. *Covenant Houses'* address is 460 West 41 Street, New York, N.Y. 10036; Ph. (212-613-0300).

In the late 1970s, John Rabun, a Kentucky Baptist minister and senior social worker who managed half a dozen Jefferson County shelters for runaway and throwaway kids, found as many as 12,000 kids a year were deserting their homes and on the streets working for pimps. At first ignored by police, Rabun spent most of a year writing down license plates and building a mapped profile of the principals in Louisville's sex industry. Judge/Executive Mitch McConnel organized a task force to study the situation, and in July 1980, created an Exploited and Missing Child Unit(EMCU). Rabun was put in charge with the help of four social workers, half a dozen policemen and the Police Department's Intelligence Commander, Major Wesley Cruse.

Their effective tactics were three-fold:

(1) A massive countrywide *INFORMATION CAMPAIGN* with warning brochures and posters requesting child pornography informants to call in. "Parents were encouraged to educate— but not frighten—their children . . . to keep close track of them, form neighborhood watch-groups and ask school principals to immediately notify parents whose children failed to reach school.

(2) *A STAKEOUT* at a Louisville park that attracted large numbers of youngsters. As cars stopped, picked up kids, and drove off, plain-clothes men and roof spotters radioed parked police cars who trailed the cars out of the neighborhood and then pulled them over. They asked both driver and passenger for names, addresses and occupations; why they had been in park and if they knew each other; where they were going; what they were going to do. "We were pleasant and respectful" says Cruse, "No one had to answer our questions but they all did. We wanted these people to know that we were there watching and knew who they were."

(3) Soon police made ARRESTS, and while officers interrogated adults, Rabun interviewed the kids, spending as long as necessary to gain their trust. By the spring of 1983 they had successfully completed 28 major prosecutions.

"It became apparent that this was a statewide problem . . . state law now provides for a child victim's trust fund to finance 'body safety' education programs; a statewide clearing house for information about missing children; authority to permit out-of-court pretrial video-taped testimony of children under the age of 12 to be used as evidence of sexual-abuse cases; no probation for certain sexual offenses against children."

A PRESIDENT'S CONTRIBUTIONS

President Reagan (well-known for his opposition of abortion and determination to influence legislation in favor of these baby victims) took a further step in 1984 to help endangered children. He signed into U.S. legislation, new and tougher laws against child pornography and prostitution. The Reagans have both shown a commendable commitment to the care and protection of children. Nancy Reagan has been active in opposing drug abuse, promoting child adoption and bringing together unwanted children and caring, lonely grandparents. Reagan is the only president in contemporary history to release a book on a politically sensitive yet significant moral issue during an election year, *Abortion and the Conscience of a Nation (Thomas Nelson)*. He has continued this commitment by also establishing, in April 1984, the *National Center For Missing and Exploited Children*. Its directors include *Jay Howell*, former Senate investigator who conducted nationwide hearings on the problem; *John Walsh* whose own young son was abducted and murdered, and *John Rabun*. This center can help parents find children, assist and train law-enforcement agencies, and help mobilize public opinion to press for strong legislative action.

CENTRUM

Founded in the late '70s as a consequence of the Jesus Movement outreaches of that decade, CENTRUM is one of the many new organizations whose concern is with the street child prostitutes. *John Dawson,* a young expatriate New Zealander working with the Centrum leadership, and with the help of some Hollywood people, developed a powerful film, "Hollywood's Delusion," documenting the tragedy and terror of the street child prostitute. John and the Centrum staff drew on a noble tradition; their dreams for the film were to awaken and shock the conscience of a people who seemed careless or unaware of what was going on all around them in California's media-influencing society. Over a century before, *Bramwell and Florence Booth* of the early Salvation Army had discovered the same awful trade of child entrapment and prostitution in London. One of the most radical challenges ever made to sin in society came by their controversial media exposure that rocked a nation.

Managing the "Refuge," a temporary haven for runaway girls, streetwalkers and hookers, Florence was prepared for evidence of London's widespread prostitution, but not for what she discovered: a terrible network entrapping young girls—innocent children often younger than thirteen or fourteen—fraudulent employment agencies, hideous initiations, and then shipping them as human sexual slave traffic to rich debauchers through England and sometimes (drugged and nailed alive into coffins) to the Continent. The "age of consent" in "moral" Britain was then only *thirteen* to the Continent's twenty-one; yet *three times* legal efforts to raise this age in England were met with defeat, one member of Parliament wanting it lowered to 10."

"London was steeped in prostitution; *one in every fifty English women was a hooker,* with 80,000 prostitutes in the city and 2,000 pimps working Charing Cross alone. Their clients were 'men in high places'; not only members of Parliament, but Queen Victoria's cousin, the King of the Belgians who spent 1,800 pounds a year debauching English girls" (Richard Collier, *The General Next.To God,* Fontana, 1965 p. 111). Another lecher proudly boasted he had "ruined 2,000 women." One home near Farnham for "fallen children" housed *40 girls under 12;* one at Newport, another *50 under 10.* "In only four instances had any of the perpetrators been punished. Two London men had outraged, respectively . . . a dozen children; only one was convicted. The plea—the children over thirteen had consented; and those under thirteen 'could not know the nature of the oath'! In eight weeks no fewer than thirty cases involving injury to forty-three girls between three and thirteen years old were brought before the courts" (*Maiden Tribute,* Madge Unsworth, *S.A. Publishing,* 1949 pp. 17-18).

"With her own baby daughter beside her, thinking of other little girls' anguish and degradation, Florence cried herself to sleep night after night. Bramwell, her tenderhearted husband was shocked, but secretly doubted it could be so bad. Determined to check it out, he shortly after met a 17-year-old girl, Annie Swan, who had escaped during the entrapment process. Further questioning to other rescued street girls confirmed the horrible truth; a slave-traffic that 'could not be matched by any trade in human beings known to history.' The 26-year-old Salvation Army Chief of Staff then wrote, 'I resolved—and *recorded the resolve on paper*—that no matter what the consequences might be, I would do all I could to stop these abominations, to rouse public opinion, to agitate for the improvement of the law, to bring to justice the adulterers and murders of innocence, and to make a way of escape for the victims!" (*Echoes & Memories;*

Bramwell Booth p. 120).

THE GREAT EXPOSURE

"Working with a new convert, Rebecca Jarrett (a thirty-six-year old ex-drunkard and brothel-keeper for twenty years), and the famous London editor William T. Stead, the Salvation Army launched a fantastic plot to confirm and expose the children's slave traffic. It was one that was eventually to embroil the Army in bitter controversy, and result not in the arrest and conviction of the child traders, but of Jarrett and Stead! Jarrett posed as a procurer and Stead as 'one of the wealthy debauchers to whom so many hundreds of the children of the poor were annually sacrificed.' Obtaining a pretty child called Eliza Armstrong for two pounds from her own mother, they played out and documented the entire process, releasing it in the July 6, 1885, issue of the *Pall Mall Gazette*.

"It took the British public by storm, in a way that can be hardly paralleled in newspaper history. Where it was opposed, young Bernard Shaw himself offered to go out and sell the paper; where it was in demand, enterprising newsboys sold the last copies at exorbitant prices. The 'dead' Criminal Law Amendment Bill was suddenly resurrected before a packed and excited House of Parliament; within seventeen days over *343,000 signatures* filled the Salvation Army's 'monster petition' to the House of Commons, *two miles in length*, carried by eight Salvationists onto the floor of the House. In a month the Bill was law, the age of consent raised to sixteen. But the underworld, outraged at their exposure, counterattacked. They took Stead and Jarrett to court indicting them under an 1861 abduction act! This 'most sensational trial of the 19th century' ended in Bramwell's aquittal, but Stead and Jarret respectively received three and six month sentences. They had succeeded; it cost them all dearly, but they broke the back of one of the most vile and vicious practices in England's history" (*"Revival; Principles To Change The World"* Pratney, pp. 296-299).

CENTRUM'S 20th century film and video version of this early Salvation Army expose' of child prostitution and slavery, "Hollywood's Delusion," is one of the new media tools being made available to alert and awaken people to the need. As with most of these ministries, usually understaffed, desperately short on refuge space, and too minimally-supported financially, CENTRUM nevertheless provides a powerful and effective center of care and compassion. Contact them at *CENTRUM of Hollywood, P. O. Box 29069, Hollywood, CA 90029. They staff a 24-hour Lifeline (213) 463-5433 (or GOD-LIFE for crisis intervention).*

How can the ordinary person help? It is obvious that every state agency in a nation, combined with every established organization and ministry dedicated to finding, sheltering and rehabilitating these kids, still cannot meet the awful need. The real heart of the problem is that society has lost its moral moorings, and is becoming a worshipper at the shrine of the spirit of Moloch. Only a massive spiritual awakening can reverse this tide, save the marriages and families of a nation, and stem the exodus of children to the streets. But something can be done in the meantime. Something *must* be done. A good part of the answer lies in the willingness of people who care about God and others to add their individual weight to help tip the balance.

Because child prostitution is fed from the breakdown in the *family, support all pro-family movements,* organizations and legislation. Mark those with a record of support to Moloch and help vote them out of office. If child prostitution and pornography makes you angry, DO something about it; "Be ye angry and sin not." Cultivate a sensitivity to every issue where the family, marriage, or the genuine care of children is being laid on an altar of sacrifice and speak out wherever you can. Don't let Moloch get away with murder. Put on the robes of an Elijah and go to war against every ideology and popular imagination that allows this kind of evil to entrench itself. Create a moral atmosphere of anger against this wrong and give decent men and women in line for leadership a chance to win.

OPEN UP YOUR OWN HOME. All relief agencies together cannot possibly meet the need for shelter. But there are easily enough people who profess Christianity in a fraction of the churches in America alone who could conceivably adopt a needy street child. The widows, orphans, and the poor were never to be the prime responsibility of government. They were to be the responsibility of the CHURCH. We are faced with a whole generation of orphans; an entire generation whose needs must be met by someone. The pimps and chickenhawks will take them if you won't. Children don't just need an institution; they need a home. They cannot survive on *legislation;* they must be *loved.* And government organizations cannot provide for that with a budget. It must come from people who genuinely and really care about these kids. Do *you* have a home? Do you have room in it for a lost and lonely abandoned kid? You see pictures of the starving children in OTHER lands; are you aware of the ones outside your door?

CHILDREN MEETINGS. Out of an initial attempt to reach small children without church or Christian influence, the street ministry of *Agape Force* began a Saturday or Sunday afternoon children's gathering they called a "Jamboree." Clowns went door to door and through the streets to invite local children to a borrowed church building for an afternoon hour of fun, games and Bible stories. Kids came at first by the score, then by the hundreds. The need for material that would cross religious and anti-religious barriers became apparent; out of this need they created plays and parables, songs and stories that could speak to children about God's love and care for them.

The result? *"Agapeland,"* eventually a full dramatic and multimedia production with a cast of eighty that pulled crowds of excited children (and often even, at first-reluctant parents) of up to 2,000 at a time, playing finally at such key family entertainment places as the *Goodtime Theatre* at *Knotts Berry Farm.* A further result; *"The Music Machine,"* the best-selling Christian album of all time, one of the few Christian gold albums and the first Christian album with the potential to go platinum (over a million copies sold). With its companion, *"Bullfrogs And Butterflies,"* also recently certified gold, *The Music Machine* fronts the list of an impressive and powerful array of character-training and evangelistic albums.

With its creative and capable Executive Director *Tony Salerno* at the helm of its productive arm, the *Agape Force* has continually expanded and intensified this ministry of concern for children. His wife, Kathy, has been especially concerned recently over the plight of runaways and street children and has contributed her own musical gifts to the various projects. Other dramatic productions and accompanying curricula developed are now used in many nations and even in other languages as outreach and training materials. Tony also founded *Gingerbrooke Fare,* a national touring dramatic clown troupe that presents biblical principles to families through both live shows and film. Another venture is the pilot of a fully animated *children's cartoon series* for prime-time children's television in conjunction with one of the best and most respected of the ex-Disney animators; and even a full *Christian production studio* to aid in the development of films, video, plays, books, comics and records that can influence and minister to children; street or otherwise, who have never known "Majesty" or become a citizen of "The Land Called Love." Similar concerns, even on much smaller scales, need to be multiplied in every nation to help turn the tide. (*A/F Productions:* P.O. Box 9000, Tacoma, Washington 98424 Ph. 206-922-2028).

Here are some legal steps that must be taken:

(1) *State and local governments* should re-examine laws and where necessary make even a first offense punishable with a heavy fine and a mandatory long-term prison sentence without probation. In 1982, the Federal Court and 47 states had statutes specifically directed against child pornography; the Federal Protection of Children Against Exploitation Act of 1977 (P.L. 95-225, 92 Stat. 7) makes it a Federal crime to either "transport minors across state lines for immoral purposes, or to contribute in any way to the production of transportation of visual or print media showing minors engaged in sexually explicit conduct." The basic penalty for any violation is a fine not exceeding $10,000 and/or imprisonment not exceeding 10 years. Second-time convictions draw a fine of up to $15,000 and prison for at least two and up to 15 years. Four new bills in the Senate and six in the House expound and strengthen present legislation; the most comprehensive proposals H.R. 322 (Rep. Marriot June 15, 1983) and S. 1469 (Senate July 16, 1983) toughen the fines, increase the age of "Minor" from 16 to 18, and delete any "obscenity" and "commercial purpose" requirements to enforce existing laws. (*Child Pornography: Legal Considerations.* Issue Brief 1883148 Updated 02/21/84; *Congressional Research Service)*

(2) Recognize that the customer, the "john" is a partner in crime with the pimp and should be punished for making the trade profitable.

(3) Provide care for runaway and throwaway children. Warns

one Jefferson County EMCU member, "Society had better look after these kids, or society is going to become their victim." Industries must become concerned and involved. Business and industry should be urged to provide expanded shelters and professional care for such kids. . . " The only way you can fail to find child exploitation in our major cities," says Wesley Cruse, "is not to look for it" (*Child Prostitution: How It Can Be Stopped*, op. cit. p. 202).

THE WAR ON INNOCENCE:
CHILD PORNOGRAPHY

"In Manhattan Beach, California, they already PREY in school."
(*L.A. Herald Examiner* cartoon)

SICKNESS TO DEATH:
THE EVOLUTION OF PORN

Few ordinary people realize just how bad pornography has recently become, Paul C. McCommon writes:

"There was a time when pornography bookstores and movie theatres were confined to the decaying inner areas of large cities. There was a time when most of us were untouched by pornography and its effects. There was even a time when pornography consisted of pictures of partially nude women posing alone. *Those days ended at least ten years ago.*"

John Quinlan, in a "blockbuster" Grand Jury report, said:

"We believe pornography is one the the most evil, immoral and degrading social problems of our times. . . . (It) develops perverted attitudes among young and old, toward love, marriage and morals. It corrupts the young and sickens the old. . . . Adult films . . . now show all varieties of anal and oral sodomy, male adults sexually abusing young children, intercourse and oral sodomy with animals, homosexuality in unbelievable manners, sadism, masochism, adults urinating on each other and including every form of moral depravity the human mind is capable of except cannibalism" (Quoted by Neil Gallagher, *How To Stop The Porno Plague,* p. 29).

Dirty bookstores and theatres infect urban areas and most small towns and cities in every major Western nation. Approximately 90 percent of the pornography in the U.S. seems under the control of three groups with the "blessing and cooperation" of national crime syndicates. The porn industry has gained in *physical* and *political* power, even interviewing a former president (Jimmy Carter), a former U.N. ambassador and Atlanta mayor (Andrew Young), and a presidential candidate and minister, (Rev. Jesse Jackson). American society has been pervaded by filth, *and people whose idea of pornography is an early '70s "Playboy" magazine have no idea of what is being sold in the 1980s.*

"Material now," McConnell says, "explicitly depicts both heterosexual and homosexual intercourse; explicit group sex, oral sex, and sex between people and various types of animals including dogs, pigs and horses. "There is sado-machismoistic sex depicting bondage, torture, rape and even murder." Films of real rape/murder—(girls' throats slashed with razors)—were recently seized in one of our large Mid-Western cities. In Garden Grove, California, authorities searched for two men charged with the murders of two teenage girls believed killed during the filming of porno movie scenes. (Paul McCommon; *"Pornography 1984; Its Pervasive Presence In American Society"* pp. 1-2; C.D.L. Inc. 2331 West Royal Palm Rd. Suite 105, Phoenix, AZ 85021 (602) 995-2600).

Evidence now clearly links pornography and violence. A New Hampshire University for the American Society of Criminology shows American states with the biggest readership of "men's magazines" also have the most reported rapes. Alaska (with no laws over distributing obscene material) led with 72 rapes per 100,000 people and the highest percent of male magazine readers— about a fifth of the state's adult population. Nevada was number two both in reported rapes and in sales of porno magazines. Lowest was North Dakota, where men's magazines ranked 31st. Low also in both sales and reported rapes were Iowa, Maine, Rhode Island and West Virginia (U.P.I. *Arizona Republic* Dec. 9, 1983).

Yet around 80 percent of American college men read magazines like *Playboy.* While researchers emphasize you cannot "prove" one causes the other, the study shows a "strong association" between sex magazine readership and rape. Yet in the past, people even said the very OPPOSITE was true; that legalizing pornography would REDUCE national sexual offenses! But does it? When Denmark did this, it first decriminalized pornographic fiction in 1967 and then pornographic photos in 1969.

WHAT REALLY HAPPENED
IN DENMARK

A Christian Danish study team writes: "Many Danes do not like pornography. It was inflicted on them by a minority who, before anybody could realize what was going on, flooded Denmark with a tidal wave of filth. . . In those critical days the supreme court could really decide what was 'art' and what was 'pornography'— so pornography in *print* was let loose. It was claimed that when the forbidden fruit was no longer forbidden it would die. And that philosophy was right—to a certain extent. Some reduction in sales of porn books was noted. But pornography itself did not die. On the contrary, a chain reaction started. Lust turned to stronger stuff. People could no longer be satisfied by reading mere words . . . they wanted to see *pictures.* Again there was heavy pressure on the law, and the government decided to allow pictures uncensored. But pornography still did not die. . . the decision was made to remove all censorship on films. This has influenced the whole Danish film industry—and this, in its turn, had a certain influence in television."

It didn't stop there. "Then it was no longer satisfying to see porn on films (which were now unrestricted)—people wanted to see the *real thing* done in front of them by living human beings on a stage. So we got the so-called 'lives shows' which, of course, are really a new name for centers of prostitution. These have developed into disgusting places of cruelty and bestiality and performances which we will not mention . . . But lust knows no bounds until it reaches the final destruction of human dignity. And when it's impossible to think of more methods of defiling MAN—these forces will throw off their mask. Their ultimate effect is to defile the holy things of GOD. Pornographic films about the Lord Jesus Christ are being made. And now heavy pressure on the law has begun to claim the freedom to blaspheme God publically" (*Den Lille Hvide.* Facius, Noer & Stage: pp. 42-26: Forlaget Perspektiv, Copenhagen 1971).

The sociologist *Kutchinsky* studied the effect of Denmark's increasingly legalized pornography on sex crimes. His initial findings DID show a drop in certain areas like exhibitionism, peeping, statuatory rape, and verbal indecency. He theorized legalization was the "direct cause" of the drop in sexual offenses: that it acted as a "safety valve" for offenders.

But do these claims "prove" sex crimes in Denmark "decreased"? "If we . . . cut down every parking meter, there would of course be tomorrow a decrease in the number of parking offenses. . . . Something on these lines has happened in Denmark. Certain former sex crimes have been made exempt from punishment and are therefore no longer reported. Homosexual prostitution, for example, has become exempt from punishment and the laws against incest have been weakened. Such activities continue but they don't get reported as they are not classed as crimes" (*Facius, Noer & Stage,* op. cit. 48).

Later research shows *almost no actual evidence* supports Kutchinsky's "venting" idea at all (Berkowitz 1971: Straus 1974). Although the total number of sexual offenses decreased, reported rapes in his data either continued as before or actually *INCREASED!* (Kutchinsky 1973: 166). "The change in the composite number of sex offenses hides an INCREASE in the number of rapes. The fact that rape, one of the most serious sex crimes, did not decrease after porn was legalized led Court (1976: 144) to contend that this outcome represents a 'Pyrrhic victory' (*Family Violence Research Program;* 18 Nov. 1983: Dept. of Sociology U. New Hampshire

Durham N.H. 03824). Today as much as 90 percent of child pornography entering the United States comes from Denmark and the Netherlands.

"Pornographers say that pornography does no harm because (a) books have 'no effect' on anyone and (b) books about sex or violence 'purge away sex and violence in all of us harmlessly.' These arguments cannot both be true. Actually, they are both false. Books like the *Bible, Das Kapital* and *Mein Kampf* have had tremendous influence on people. Good or bad." (*The Black & White Book:* Cook & Lean, Blandford Press p. 72).

PORN & VIOLENCE

The fantasies of porno violence can blunt your ability to care in real life. A 21-year-old mother of two children goes into a New Bedford bar to buy cigarettes. Inside, she is grabbed by four male customers and while screaming and pleading for help, is gang-raped for two hours on a pool table. Not only does no one call the police or step in to stop it; but some even clap and cheer, as at least 15 other customers and the bartender look on! "Pornography does hurt. Pornography hurts women by portraying them as only sexual objects. And it hurts men and boys, especially those exposed to it at an early age, by giving them a limited, leering view of women" (*Readers Digest* June 1982 Canada "What You Should Know About Pornography").

Trading on the new technology, porn has gone video and cable in the last decade. We are only beginning to understand the impact of this media on the consciousness of the nation. Approximately 90 percent of all research on TV's influence on behavior has only been done in the last decade—(some 2,500 titles!) But what has already been found underlines the expected. Films and television that portray violent sexuality DO increase male acceptance of violence against women. (*Malamuth & Check* University of Manitoba; American Psychological Association Montreal, Canada Sept. 4, 1980). Excessive sexual arousal and aggression ARE at higher levels, encouraging attacks against others; and the more a man sees sexually violent films, the less sensitive he is to violence against women (*Robert A. Baron*, Purdue University; *Donnerstein*

& Linz "Sexual Violence In The Media": *Psychology Today,* Jan.
1984 pp. 14-15).

SMUT & CRIME

Smut is the moral smog of a city. There are over 15,000 so-called
"adult" bookshops in North America. ("Three times more than
MacDonald's restaurants," boasts *The Adult Business Report,*
porn industry trade newsletter). It sells well too; the 10 leading sex
magazines reportedly generated nearly $475 million in 1977; the
nation's 800 X-rated theatres grossed over $360 million. In the
capitol of the nation (all within view of the Justice Department) are
37 dirty bookstores, eight movie theatres specializing in X-rated
shows and 15 topless or totally nude bars. Despite its own exaggerated popularity, Porn IS big money. In 1981 alone, this "industry" took in an *estimated six BILLION dollars* (almost as much
money as conventional movie and record sales combined) from
more than 400 pornographic magazines on the market, of which
over 260 are child-pornography magazines. A single *Playboy* article
pays $3,500. Organized crime like the Mafia now heavily infiltrates
money-making porn films like "Deep Throat" ($25 million), *"The
Devil in Miss Jones"* and *"Wet Rainbow."* Where they do not have
a direct financial share in the film, they have made further millions
from pirated and illegally distributed copies. Porn money has given
several porno movie-makers with Mafia connections money to
produce and distribute legitimate films. New York Capt. Lawrence
Hepburn is concerned that 'If the trend continues, these people are
going to become a major force in the movie industry within a few
years' (*Gallagher,* op. cit. p. 26).

If pornography affects adults, can pornography affect children?
Katherine Brady, sexually abused by her father from age eight to 18
said: "Pornography trained me to respond to my father's sexual
demands. (It) frightened me; it confused me; and yet it excited me,
and I felt trapped." Brady is now an activist in child-abuse prevention. (Los Angeles Times 8/9/84) "Can pornography affect
children?" Yes, sometimes in even more awful ways:

ST. PETERSBURG, FLORIDA: A seven-year-old boy and his
nine-year-old brother sexually assault (with a pencil and a coat-

hanger) *an eight-month-old baby girl.* She dies in the attack. The seven-year-old testifies that he and his brother were just "imitating actions they had seen in their mother's sex magazines." Their 24-year-old mother "baby sitting" the infant at the time, admits keeping pornographic magazines her boys "could have had access to" (*Arizona Republic* UPI April 21, 1984).

PORN & CHILD MOLESTATION

Shirley O'Brien (*Child Pornography;* Kendall/Hunt Publishing Co. 1983) says police report they almost never arrest suspects in child molestation cases without finding child pornography. Child molesters use it to both justify their own evil actions and condition children to accept abuse. FBI agent Kenneth Lanning, exhibiting to a Senate subcommittee a pedophile's sick pamphlet *"How To Have Sex With Kids"* testified that the "hundreds of thousands" of pedophiles in the United States "almost always" are collectors of child pornography and erotica (Los Angeles Times *"Pornography Called Trigger for Child Molesting";* Joan Radovitch 8/9/84).

A Michigan State Police study by Detective Lt. Darrell Pope showed that of 38,000 sexual assault cases on file, 41 percent involved pornography "just prior to or during the act" (*West Michigan News Review* 7 May 1979).

John C. Quinn in his *U.S.A. Today* editorial said:

"Child pornographers are exploiting and terrorizing America's children. There are as many as 1.2 million victims— as young as six months old and as old as 16. Sexual abuse of children is a major problem in society, and many fear that kiddy porn can entice a sick mind to prey on a child. . . . Two years ago the Supreme Court ruled that child pornography isn't protected by the First Amendment. In November, the House passed a Bill to make the use of children in pornography a crime. But still the crime continues."

Films with sick titles like "Kindergarten Orgy" and magazines like "Sex Babies" are just more blatant in a society where children are even exploited by more respected media advertising in fashion magazines and TV ads. "But," says Quinn, "Children have the right to be children. They need the rich, happy, innocent experiences of childhood to become well-adjusted adults. Child pornography robs its victims of their innocence and subjects them to physical and emotional abuse. That's why police and prosecutors should throw the book at child pornographers" (John C. Quinn *USA Today* Opinion Editor, Wed. Jan. 25, 1984).

Just how bad is pornography? Charles Nelson, Asst. Chief Postal Inspector is interviewed by Senator Arlen Specter, Chairman, Subcommittee on Juvenile Justice. He asks for an example of child porn intercepted through the mail inspections:

Specter: "What kind of photographs were present there?"

Nelson: "It involved homosexual photographs of anal and oral intercourse, young ladies in lesbian-type affairs. There was one instance where there was a child approximately 10 months old . . ."

Specter: "And what was the 10-month-old child doing?"

Nelson: *"As I recall, it was an effort by an adult to make penetration"* (*Hearing, Subcommittee on Juvenile Justice* Wash. D.C. Nov. 5, 1981; Serial J-97-78).

Summing up the destructive effects of pornography, Neil Gallagher shows it is a *spiritual, civil* and *legal* problem. It affects the moral fiber of a nation replacing self-discipline with self-indulgence. It infects the local community, and feeds billions into the pockets of syndicated crime. *Pornography cannot be tolerated on ANY level. It always gets worse; and it always eventually kills children.*

AN INTERNATIONAL NETWORK

The reports come in from everywhere. A vast worldwide underground network exists in pornography of the particularly vicious kind, the war on small innocence.

In just four years (1978-1982) U.S. Customs agents seized more than 247,000 pieces of pornography; between 60-70 percent of it child porn.

In May 1982, agents in Los Angeles arrested a Rolls-Royce-driving mother of five who may have operated the "largest single distribution center for child porn in the nation." Seized were over 200 originals of films which "included sexual acts between children, children and adults, adults and animals, and acts of excretion, mutilation and forced sex." And she had a huge clientele. In her four-year-old daughter's crib, they found a list of some 30,000 buyers!

" As many as one million children a year, aged from under a year to 16, are estimated to be sexually molested and then filmed or photographed either for the abuser's pleasure or profit" (*Rita Rooney "Innocence For Sale" Ladies Home Journal* April 1983, p. 127).

The record makes sickening, shocking reading. Although the "typical" child pornographer is a white male between the ages of 25-50, "don't look for him in a seedy trench coat and slouch hat, a crazed look in his eye and flecks of sweat glistening on his lips . . . More likely, he's well-known to his victims as the parks and recreation worker, the neighbor down the street or as a friendly adult" (*Jayne Clarke: Phoenix Gazette* June 27, 1983). You can find them in almost every state and major city, even in small towns. Here is a welder, a beauty pageant photographer, an ex-Mormon missionary, a Marine and a Navy engineer. Some are deacons, DJs, day care centers owners, computer analysts, retired old couples, lawyers, doctors and executives of major corporations. These "quiet, hard-working, unassuming community figures" traffic in the death and destruction of unprotected little lives. By their exaltation of money, pleasure and power, they worship at the altar of the spirit of Moloch.

LOS ANGELES, California: Carleton "Corky" Mayberry, all-night disc jockey for country music radio station KLAC is charged with trying to recruit a 26-year-old listener AND her seven-year-old daughter as prostitutes. When they call to request a song, he asks about her daughter. Described as "pretty and bubbly," he then asks if her little girl would "dress up in high heels, panty hose and a bathing suit to make perhaps $60,000 a week." Convinced he was "up to no good," the woman tells police, who tape-record a conversation in which she is asked to bring her daughter to the station so he can teach her about "sexual response."

Describing himself as "the middleman" for film-makers, he asks the mother if she would engage in a variety of sexual acts for money, reportedly telling her that "if the seven-year-old saw her doing them she would want to imitate her" (Ted Rohrlich, *Times* Staff Writer, *Los Angeles Times* Sept. 8, 1983).

ALBUQUERQUE, New Mexico: Police raid the Northeast

Heights home of a computer systems analyst. They seize about 2,000 video-cassette tapes; a link in a multi-state pornography ring. (The tapes sold for $80-$500 each). Still photos of children in sexually explicit poses and similar slides were confiscated from rooms also filled with video equipment, children's toys and posters. He was "very cooperative," police said.

MIAMI, Florida: Michael Jamison, 39, accused child pornographer, kills himself, apparently when police tried to arrest him for the second time in a week, based on new evidence from developed rolls of his impounded film. "I feel the game is totally over. My reputation is totally ruined. My parents are totally embarrassed in this community" (R.A. Zaldivar, *Miami Herald* Sunday Aug. 19, 1984).

ALEXANDRIA, Washington: San Diego police arrest a Navy engineer from Alexandria on three counts of child molesting in connection with an investigation of child pornography in four states. Acting on a tip from Los Angeles police, Alexandria agents search the Old Town apartment of Ron Woodward. They find boxes of photographs of nude children, 14 reels of film, five rolls of undeveloped film, a 35 millimeter camera and two movie projectors. Woodward, while in Los Angeles for a two-week stay, supposedly engaged in sexual activity with children and traded photographs of children with others (*Washington Post*, Aug. 4, 1983).

BUZZARDS BAY, Massachusetts: U.S. Postal and Customs agents raid the Main Street office of Richard L. Sanford, 42, manager of Sanford Studio of Photography, member of the Greater Bourne-Sandwich Chamber of Commerce and photographer for past years of the Miss Cape Cod beauty pageant in Hyannis. They impound some 200 obscene video-cassette tapes, many involving child pornography.

"Many of the tapes show lurid sex scenes of pre-teen boys and girls having sex with each other and various animals. Officials say they seized at least one so-called 'snuff' video-cassette, an hour-long film showing torture and murder scenes for the purpose of sexual stimulation," reports said. Sanford charged customers $100 for each child pornography tape. Adult pornography tapes were "negotiable" but he was "firm" on the $100 for each pre-teen and child pornography cassette. The raid was the second involving child pornography there in three years. In March 1980, Robert Mohr-nann was convicted of child pornography charges. Police confis-cated an array of bondage devices and some 20,000 slides and photographs from his home (Daniel Ring; Staff Writer: *Cape Cod News* Hyannis Mass., Nov. 29, 1983).

SALT LAKE CITY, Utah: Arthur Gary Bishop, 30, is charged with killing five young Salt Lake County boys. One, four-year-old, Alonzo Daniels, disappears while playing in front of his apartment. Danny, another four-year-old, from a supermarket. Troy, six, from a street corner; Kim, 11, after leaving home to sell his roller skates to an unidentified man; and Graeme, 13, right out of his home.

Bishop, a former Eagle Scout, honor student and ex-Mormon missionary, is described by almost everyone who knew him as "quiet, unobtrusive, clean-cut, hard-working and kind" who, after capture, expressed "concern about those families involved."

His lawyer said, "He also knows the grief the families have felt through this."

The mother of a 13-year-old boy who lived with Bishop over the last two years said he was a "kind man, a perfect role model for her son."

A police search of his house results in the "recovery of a sig-nificant number of pornographic photographs, exposed film and videotape all depicting nude children, some engaged in sex acts," according to reports. Investigators said there was no photographic evidence recovered to support the claims that Bishop may have been involved with necrophilia—perversion involving sex with the dead. He would not comment further on the topic.

Three of the boys apparently had been beaten to death with a hammer-like instrument. One had been shot and another strangled.

"I didn't have any idea," said one shocked woman. "I've never even seen him with even a cruel expression on his face. He was always cute with kids. It was almost like he was one of them. I'm so scared. It's like he was two different people" (Jerry Spangler and Kris Radish; *Deseret News* July 29, 1983).

CARSON CITY, NEVADA: A stunned Senate Judiciary Com-mittee listens to James Reyman, 27, (part of a former child prosti-tute ring using children and young adults, ages 12-18) describe how he was seduced by a church deacon and used as a sexual tool for six years. The man used child pornography to convince him the things he was asked to do were "right." Since his experiences, he has tried to commit suicide three times and is still undergoing psychiatric treatment. "I'm doing great now," he told lawmakers, but added somberly; "I lost out on a lot of my life and teen years."

The man operating the "kiddie porn" ring also used his own children and grandchildren, but was never arrested or charged. "The man was never brought to trial because I was afraid to say anything. I felt guilty and dirty about what was happening to me and didn't know how to stop it," said one who had personal knowledge of the situation.

Las Vegas FBI agent Roger Young says child porn exists for three reasons; (1) sexual gratification; (2) as a tool to seduce children; and (3) for its "tremendous" money-making potential. At least three national organizations exist to promote pedophilia. One, the 5,000 member *Rene Guyon Society,* actually campaigns for the "RIGHT" to have sex with children. Their motto is "Sex before eight or it's too late!"

Leola Armstrong of Carson City calls child porn the worst crime committed against children "because it isn't done because of anger, sexual gratification or even perversion. People involved in child pornography are in it for the money; greed, pure and simple, devoid of any human emotion" (Dale Pugh: *Las Vegas Review-Journal* March 31, 1983).

REDWOOD CITY, CALIFORNIA: A San Carlos construction worker and his wife (Raymond, 53, and Gillian Mary Thomas, 60) stand trial on felony charges for possession, duplication and using children for pornographic purposes. Evidence suggests they operated a mail-order service in California, Nevada and Arizona for child pornography. The couple sold pictures of children engaging in sex acts as young as six years old. Detectives seized about 20 albums containing 10,000 photographs from the couple's home. One picture shows Thomas engaged in intercourse with a young girl, while another shows Mrs. Thomas lying nude in bed with a different girl. The mother of a 15-year-old identified her daughter in two of the seized photographs. Neighbors of the Thomases describe them as a "quiet, unassuming couple" whose arrest this summer shocked the neighborhood (*San Carlos Times* Jan 14,

1983).

SAN JOSE, CALIFORNIA: Walter Holbrook, 58, retired Marine, and Earl Magoun, 60, welder, are charged with a total of 16 counts of sexually molesting children and procuring children for prostitution. Deputy Chief Larry Stuefloten says Magoun operated a pornography business catering to so many customers in the U.S., Europe and Asia they used two computers to keep track. The business ran for more than a decade, involving hundreds of children, teenagers and women in various poses and sexual acts. Its extent was "mind-boggling."

Stuefloten said: "We found file cabinets filled with envelopes containing thousands of photographs, all coded. He dealt in every sort of pornography, every perversion that I think we know of." Teenage girls were recruited from supermarket bulletin board ads offering housework, then seduced. The girls then got paid extra money for posing, usually $20-$50. "They were attractive young ladies, middle-class from good homes. They could be anyone's daughter . . . " he said.

"Something's going on in our society," he warned. "Whether we're just becoming more aware of it now, I don't know."

It is probably impossible to measure the impact of violent pornography on society, but noting recent serial murder cases and the reports of molestations at child-care centers, he added: "I think all of this should be telling us something." (Robert Lindsay *How Pornographers Prey on Children For Commercial Gain: Inquiry Reveals World-wide Operation, N.Y. Times* News Service).

TRADING KIDS LIKE BASEBALL CARDS

Shirley O'Brien warns: "The problems of child pornography have not gone away. The effects of the July Supreme Court ruling which came down hard on producers and distributors simply pushed kiddie porn further underground . . . Networks of child porn buffs criss-cross America. They trade stills, films and slides like baseball cards. It is estimated that the child pornography market accounts for seven to 10 percent of the sex-selling industry—up to 1 billion a year. Police estimate that up to a million boys and girls have some filmed sexual involvement with an adult. Products range from black and white 8mm film to full-color 64mm movies; tape recordings of voiced sexual abuse to videotaped child sex orgies. The camera focuses on genitals, not facial expressions. But it is obvious that the children are not willing participants as the perpetrators testify. Though they may be following orders physically, they are not participating emotionally.

"What kind of children are they? Though child abuse may cross color, religion and national origin, child pornography focuses on children as young as three, light-skinned, light-eyed, blond, beautiful, innocent and naive. Where do they come from? Some are on their own on the streets willing to try anything once for a few bucks. Others are children of porn stars, pretending sexual arousal, dutifully taking direction from the moviemakers. But most are the Jimmys and Susies who live at home with busy and preoccupied parents. They seek out adults who take them places and give them attention" (Shirley O'Brien Guest Columnist, *USA Today* Wed. Jan. 25, 1984).

"KIDDIE PORN CHIC IS DANGEROUS, DESTRUCTIVE"

Another guest columnist for *U. S. A. Today,* Florence Rush, adds: "With sexual abuse of children reaching epidemic proportions such erotic message are downright dangerous. It gives pedophiles . . . permission to act out their lasciviousness."

Devasting statistics arise from a society where children are offered up as alluring femme fatales. Twenty-five percent of all females experience some form of sexual abuse (from fondling to rape) before they reach 13. Half of the reported rape victims are under 18; 25 percent of that number UNDER 12.

One and two-tenths million children are annually exploited in prostitution and pornography.

One hospital found more children admitted for sexual abuse than broken bones and tonsillectomies. They required medical attention for genital infections, abdominal pains, lacerated vaginal and anal walls, foreign bodies in the rectum and vagina, and throat infections from oral sex.

"Few victims escape emotional trauma. Most develop eating, sleeping and school disturbances, chronic fatigue and withdrawal from friends and play. In later life, the repressed experience can explode in severe neuroses, depression, psychoses and even suicide... But the child molester whose warped perceptions are nurtured by such images insists, when caught, that 'little girls are sexy' and 'they really ask for it.'" The lucrative but destructive combination of 'sex and innocence' widely used to sell blue jeans, cosmetics and magazines, makes a mockery of childhood suffering and undermines the efforts of adults who struggle to protect our young" (Florence Rush: Opinion Guest Columnist, *U.S.A. Today,* Jan. 25, 1984).

Sickening as it is, the war on innocence is only a part of the war.

WAR ON THE MIND—MEDIA EXPLOITATION OF CHILDREN

One of the most memorable summaries I ever heard of the works of darkness was from my friend Ken Talbot. He said, "The devil has one purpose: to *take out all the life he can from anything* and *inject into it all the death he can.*" Ken picked up an orange. "If Satan got hold of his, he would suck out all the natural goodness, the vitamins and nutrition. Then he would inject it with artificial flavor, preservatives and carcinogenic dyes and repackage it labeled as 'New, Improved and Extra Healthy.'"

Something like that is happening in the media to children. Not only are they presented with attractively packaged death in what they are exposed to, but that same culture is also marketing their innocence.

John Quinn took a swing at this dangerous trend in a 1984 *U.S.A. Today* editorial:

"We live in a society where there is growing exploitation of children. Advertisers use children to sell products. One respected magazine, *Harpers Bazaar,* used a young child in seductive poses in a December issue photo feature called "Tiny Treasures." The child, heavily made up and bare-chested was shown in a feature pushing perfume. The magazine made her look sexually attractive and showed her holding a bottle of perfume beneath copy that said, "For seduction with just a hint of innocence." That feature was in exceptionally bad taste. It tried to make a child look like a sexually provocative adult for commercial purpose. Some called it 'kiddie porn chic'. . . . Children have the right to be children. They need the rich, happy, innocent experiences of childhood to become well-adjusted adults" (John C. Quinn *USA Today,* Opinion Editor, Jan. 25, 1984).

In reply, Anthony T. Mazzola, Editor-In-Chief of *Harpers Bazaar,* apologized for the layout, pointing out that as the magazine was a woman's magazine for women readers, the suggestiveness was "unfortunate, and certainly unintended." He promised to try "in the future to be more sensitive to the unusual ability of photographs to convey unintended messages."

Perhaps true. But pick up a magazine and chances are good you will see children posed in adult fashion to sell something.

CLOTHING DESIGN AND FILMS

Some clothing manufacturers lead the bandwagon by setting up children in adult or sexual situations in efforts to develop new lines in children's wear. "The Jordache Jean company hypes its contour-explicit pants by picturing scantily-clad teenagers astride each other in such proper media as the *New York Times Magazine,*" says a *Newsweek* article. Madison Avenue regards 10-year-olds as among the best models for makeup.

There are *child sexploitation films* for the regular movie-goer. "Provocative films like *'Foxes'* (four Los Angeles teenagers blundering through sexual initiation), and *'Little Darlings'* about two 15-year-olds competing to lose their virginity at summer camp, pack movie theaters with agog adults and kids" (*Newsweek* Sept. 1, 1980, p. 49). Films like *"Blue Lagoon"* further established Brooke

Shields as a child sex symbol. She first posed nude at 10 years old.

Taboo themes are proliferating both on TV and films. A film historian notes only six movies about incest during the whole of the 1920s, 1930s and 1940s, but 79 in the 1960s.

Child prostitution in a feature movie involving an abused *girl* might make many people angry and upset. But films with actresses like Jacqueline Bisset have helped overcome this resistance by focusing the prostitution instead on a immature but willing *boy*. In Bisset's roles in movies like *The First Time, Secret Worlds* and *Class* she plays an older woman seducing or sexually involving a young boy (Franky Schaeffer, *Bad News For Modern Man*, p. 36).

Not every young actor (even in Hollywood) supports the move to emphasize sex at high school or junior high levels. *Matthew Broderick*, the 21-year-old star of *Wargames* strongly disagrees with the teenage sex movies trend.

"High school is not a big fun party where you're trying to see a naked girl all the time. High school is going on your first date and you're terrified and you kiss her and everytime you see her again at school you're embarrassed." So what of the image of all those high schoolers into little else but parties, music and sex? "Maybe," says Matthew, "if you're just an insensitive piece of blubber you can spend your high school days just staring at girls. But mostly it's painful." And the movies? "I think what those movies are offering is some kid of adult fantasy of what adults wish high schools were like" (*Youthletter* August 1983 p. 58).

DIVISION BETWEEN ADULT AND CHILD DESTROYED

What are the social factors of the war on the mind? Some commentators believe one of the most significant factors of our time eliminating the idea of childhood is the advent of television. Neil Postman *(The Disappearance Of Childhood)* actually believes that TV is the chief culprit. As the printing press helped create childhood (by facilitating democracy and empowering Reformation ideas to affect the culture), television will end it. Not only has TV affected

WHAT we know, it has changed even the WAY we know.

Since 1945, 99 percent of U.S. homes have had a TV set. On an average evening 80 million people watch TV; 30 million will be watching the same program. The average household set is on more than six hours a day; with a child, more than eight hours. That is roughly HALF of the non-sleeping part of the day. And what kid of perception does it encourage?

Jerry Mander notes that "In one generation . . . America has become the first culture to have substituted secondary, mediated versions of experience for direct experience of the world. Interpretations and representations of the world were being accepted as experience and the difference between the two was obscure . . . A new muddiness of mind was developing. People's patterns of discernment, discrimination and understanding were taking a dive (*"Four Arguments For The Elimination of Television"* p. 24-25).

TV not only muddies ADULT minds by substituting an electronic image for reality, it translates that substitution down to the lowest common denominator. What did the switch from print to TV do to *children* in the communications revolution?

Like Postman, Joshua Meyrowitz thinks it helps "eliminate childhood as a distinct special stage of life." A New Hampshire University communications professor who has studied this effect for more than five years, Meyrowitz says TV often reverses child and adult roles: "Children now speak more like adults and adults more like children. Children wear designer clothing and adults wear jeans and sneakers. Children commit armed robbery and murder; adults play video games." TV bypasses the protection children had from some of the hard realities of the adult world. With print, children have the natural barrier of language to adult ideas. Words too hard or complex for them shield them from adult themes like sex or incest, suicide or murder. But TV puts "all the cookies on the bottom shelf." It gears most of its daily programming to an eight-year-old level and thus tends to eliminate the child/adult distinction. If books expose children to the adult world only slowly, TV gives it to them all at once with no protection—what Ken Talbot calls *splat media.*

Meyrowitz calls the change in children a "social earthquake that

has shaken many old assumptions and disrupted many institutions"
—like schools, churches, courts and families (*Youthletter* Sept.
1983 p. 67). And we will not mention here latchkey children feeding
on porn cable channels.

BOOKS

While we are speaking about print, what happened to all the good
children's books? Best-selling children's writers like Judy Blume
make their living selling so-called "realistic" novels that explore
involvement of children in situations like rape, prostitution, divorce,
voyeurism and homosexuality. Blume, who gets over 1,000 letters a
month from her young readers, despises "the idea that you should
always protect children. They live in the same world we do. They
see things and hear things" (Rodney Clapp "Vanishing Childhood"
Christianity Today May 18, 1984 p. 14). Judy's work, which sells
in the millions, has no specific moral tone, and she is criticized for
writing books some call "pandering, salacious and trashy," dwel-
ling too much on the physical and sexual side of growing up. But
perhaps part of her popularity is not only her easy-to-read first-
person narrative style. Her books appeal to children who have no
one to talk to about their feelings and problems. She says she "writes
the way she wishes someone had written for her when she was
growing up" (*Youthletter* Oct. 1983, p. 75).

In a 1983 *Seventeen* poll, 40 percent of the children read five or
more books a month, another 29 percent, three or four, and only 4
percent didn't read any. In a study of 3,400 Connecticut children,
grades four-12, sports led the list for boys (41 percent), then sci-fi
(29 percent), horror/supernatural (27 percent), adventure/survival
(26 percent) and mystery/suspense (26 percent). Girls preferred
love and romance (57 percent), mystery/suspense (33 percent), and
problems of growing up (32 percent).

Students in all grades reported the most fear-filled topic was
homosexuality. One-fourth said they would stop reading a book if
they discovered it was about this subject. The percentage was even
higher (33 percent) among high school boys. Newspapers are not so
popular, only 29 percent read one every day and then mostly for
comics, entertainment, advice columns and front-page news.

(*Youthletter* op. cit. p. 75).

C. S. Lewis and George MacDonald would not have agreed at all that children always want realism. There is still a place in a child's heart for the tender and mysterious. We need a great rebirth of good and lovely stories that are not on sex, drugs and horror.

In a 1983 *Radix* article (July-August) Jane Stephens calls for support of more books like *Jack and the Beanstalk, The Wind In the Willows* and the *Narnia* series. They teach without the pain of too much adult reality. "Allow them the full bracing pain of stories like 'The Ugly Duckling' (in which they can learn the hope of heaven—transformation) where they can face the whole measure of emotion 'undiminished by the constraints of realism.' "

CHILDREN'S CARTOONS

Parents who are concerned about their children's futures should take a good look sometime at Saturday morning cartoons. Although Mighty or Mickey Mouse still put in appearances for "old times sake," there is a whole new ballgame on the tube today. A great deal of today's children's cartoons have occult themes or heroes. Magic, spells and witchcraft are the order of the morning.

Take, for example, the children's cartoon of *Wonder Woman*. Here is Semiramis, the goddess, repackaged for the 1980s; "Tamus" (Tammuz) her "little boy" assistant was "born of a sunbeam." *Wonder Woman*, in regular life, goes under the name of *"Diana"* (one of the other names of the goddess)—Diana Prince. She has abilities and powers that can only be described as supernatural. Take a whole morning and just make a note of these cartoon super-heroes. What they can supposedly do, how they get the power to do it and what a child might do to be like them.

Besides the spiritual potential for familiarizing a child with oc-cult imagery, cartoons are also blatantly ruled by another char-acteristic of the spirit of Moloch—they are *prime tools for market-ing*. Some were deliberately designed to do just that—a multi-mil-lion dollar series of commercials. Others are quickly picked up by toy or other children's manufacturers once the series prove popular enough for "commercial potential." Friends of mine developing a new Christian character-based cartoon series for secular TV ran into this problem: "But what does it SELL?" Their excellent pilot is of the highest standard, it has good storylines, animation under the supervision of some of the best in the business and the music is of award-winning standards. But it doesn't "sell" anything. And in a Moloch society, why should a cartoon be *on* unless it sells something?

HOW CAN YOU WATCH TV?

If Christian parents are going to let their younger children watch television at all, they ought to at least sit down with them and watch a sampling of the cartoons that come on every Saturday. *Ask questions* as you watch together. Help your child to make some value judgments based on a biblical base. Point out what is unacceptable and what must not be watched.

There may be some surprises. Some of the programs usually allowed as "innocent" would get a big black mark in a biblical framework. Shows that show a weak, vacillating or unwise father like *I Love Lucy* would be discouraged. *Sesame Street,* that hallowed teacher of numbers and letters, might also pull a surprising number of negatives; no real parents on the show, bad manners and eating habits taught by furry little green guys who live in garbage cans. Sometimes even the *Muppets* promote occult ideas or Eastern thought in their guest shows. And not all the shows that have bad or violent things happen may be outlawed.

As Bill Gothard (who is certainly no supporter of TV watching) points out, the real harm of TV violence is not in the FACT of that violence. Violence is in the Bible. The real danger lies in the fact that TV rarely offers any clear distinction between right and wrong. Kids have to choose between people who are bad and people who are worse. Wickedness presented as ending in judgment (the bad guys get punished) is the biblical way of relating violence and wrong.

"BACK OFF MAN:
I'M A DEMON-BUSTER"

Sometimes a parent can use the wrong in media against itself. The devil is a copycat. In order to do anything effective he has to borrow from the good. Much of the power of the media works on this principle. When an occult "super-hero" borrows from biblical qualities or characteristics, the parent can, with the child, sometimes point out those originals and relate them back to God's Kingdom.

For instance, the hugely popular *He-Man* cartoon series contains obvious elements of the occult. *He-Man* lives in "Castle Greyskull." All dangerous. Yet the popularity of *He-Man* can be traced not only to its excellent animation and stories; as myth it also draws on biblical elements. *He-Man* is the "Mightiest man in the Universe." He wears a chest harness in the shape of a cross. He fights with a sword of light. He never lies, cheats, steals or betrays a friendship. He is in ordinary life, "Prince Adam," a royal inhabitant of "Eternia." *He-Man* and his friends are in constant conflict with the patently nasty Skeletor and his henchmen who at least have the virtue of being consistently evil and consistently foiled and beaten. Young Prince Adam comes from a royal family who loves him, and has a commitment to truth and justice, if not the American way. And each *He-Man* episode teaches some sort of character principle by a reprise at the end that speaks directly to watching children about the lesson they can learn from that story. *He-Man*, for all its weaknesses, is an example of powerful and effective children's cartoon programming that ought to be done from a biblical base.

THEY STILL CALL THEM "COMICS"

Go down to the local book or speciality store and take a look at the current crop of children's comics. A "comic" was originally supposed to be *funny* or *humorous*. So what can you find to laugh about in most of these? Then ask youself this question: from where in the world (or under it) do the adults get their images who "cartoon" much of this recent stuff supposedly for children? If there was an enforced rating system for modern comics, a large percentage would be R-rated, and many of them even X-rated. Horror, explicit violence, immorality and the demonic are the order of the day.

TOYS

Visit your local toystore today if you want a real example of the occult attack on children. If there is one thing kids do more than anything else in the world, it is *play*. Their imaginations are continually on high. They spend hours every day acting out "scenarios." And play is without doubt one of the finest and best ways to learn. In the last decade, toys have become the target for an occult attack on children unlike any other in history. From the *Ouija* board made available as a parlor game in the '60s, to the *Dungeons and Dragons* roleplaying games and figurines of the 1980s, the young are being educated in the world of supernatural evil long before they are able to understand its spiritual implications. A retail manager, when asked what kind of toys sold best, replied, "Any toy which deals with fantasy or the supernatural. We can't even keep them in stock."

Dungeons and Dragons is perhaps the best-known of a whole series of fantasy roleplaying games that emphasize the imagination. Played by around four million people in the nation, many of them children and teenagers, *D&D* and other related "modules" that involve supernatural warfare is a classic example of marketed occultism. Its dangerous power consists precisely in the fact that it demands immersion in highly detailed and complex role-playing made as "authentic" as possible by often using the characteristics of *actual demonic deities* of past cultures as models. The power of imagination is that it is essentially a *function of the human spirit.* It is the way by which we "image out" into the real world that which is the focus of our hearts. *Whatever captures our imagination ultimately gets our commitment: whatever gets our commitment gets our worship.* The devotion of some *D&D* players is legendary. Some children become so entranced with the game they lose touch with reality.

"This game lets all your fantasies come true. This is a world where monsters, dragons, good and evil, high priests, fierce demons and even the gods themselves may ENTER YOUR LIFE," (*D&D Rulebook*, p. 7).

Pick up a *D&D* manual yourself sometime if you have never done so and browse through it. You will see multiple examples of genuine occult lore all set to an entrapping simplicity.

Dr. Gary North says:

"After years of the study of the history of occultism, after having researched a book on the subject, and after having consulted with scholars in the field of historical research, I can say with confidence that these games are the most effectively, most magnificently packaged, most profitably marketed, most thoroughly researched introduction to the occult in man's recorded history." (*"None Dare Call It Witchcraft"* Quoted by Linsted "Entertaining Demons Unaware" South West Radio Church P. O. Box 1144, Oklahoma City, OK. 73101 p. 25).

"The Magic user must memorize and prepare the use of each spell. Its casting makes it necessary to reabsorb the incantation consulting the proper book of spells before it can be cast again. As with all other types of spells these of the Magic users must be spoken and read aloud" (op. cit. p. 25). These spells have often been pulled out of actual magic books.

MUSIC—THE CENTRAL DOOR

Perhaps the most direct and powerful path to a child's mind is through their music. If I had to name the single most powerful influence on a 1980's child during the critical years of their life, the answer would be easy: music. Know what kids like listening to and you will know what they are really like. Professor Allen Bloom (University of Chicago) writing in the *Wall Street Journal* says rock music's great success among the young is an "amazing cooperation between lust, art and commercial shrewdness." He claims rock and all that goes with it is a more powerful formative influence on children between 12 and 18 than anything else, including church, school or the home.

"Hey teachers/Leave those kids alone" are popular lyrics by (*PINK FLOYD—The Wall*) sings: *Alice Cooper* in his *School's Out for Summer* says:

"School's out for summer
School's out forever!
School's been blown to pieces
No more spelling, no more books
No more teacher's dirty looks."

MUSIC today, not mothers, "rocks the cradle" that rules the world.

Frank Zappa, the "godfather" of explicit sex in rock, noticed it as far back as the '60s when he said.

"The only real loyalty that exists for the American teenager today is his music. He doesn't give an actual damn about his country, his mother, his government or his religion. He has more actual patriotism in terms of how he feels about his music than anything else. And this just has never happened before."

There are notable exceptions, of course. But for millions of kids, Zappa's evaluation is practically pretty "right on." If you don't believe me, criticize anything you want to in front of a teenager, and *then* criticize his music. See which gets the biggest reaction. Again, even a cursory glance through the array of albums in your friendly local record store may give even a liberal parent reason to wonder. Check out the jackets and the lyrics.

Modern rock groups, in an effort to make an impact on a (in more than one sense) "decaying" market, have pushed any sense of propriety or decency to the absolute limits and then beyond. Rock idols today have gone far beyond the "naughty sixties" where the newspapers headlines the occasional drug bust or sexual orgy. Today in both lyrics and stage performances almost literally anything goes. If you can think up something horrible, bestial or perverted enough, you will probably find a group who (at least in their act) did it. Groups now strip, masturbate and act out sexual intercourse; in their stage acts decapitate babies, worship the devil, spit, vomit or urinate on their audiences; cut themselves, throw equipment, bottles, cans and sometimes themselves at their fans. The barbed wire, spikes and leather of sado-masochism is the dominant dress of heavy metal performances. Rock concerts today sometimes look like church services from hell.

But rock is the *single most powerful unifier* of the youth culture. Now we have walkmans, boom-boxes, C.D. and music videos to go with Victory tours, chartbusters and mega-concerts. New forms of the constantly driven music scene surface to vie for kid's affection, adoration—and especially money; names that reflect an ugly and painful worldview like *Twisted Sister, Iron Maiden, Quiet Riot,* the *Scorpions, Rock Goddess* and *Judas Priest.* Many flaunt their disgust or opposition to society, school, the church and Christian values, and go out of their way to incite this in their audiences:

"Rebellion is the basis of our group. Some of the kids who listen to us are real deranged, but they look up to us as heroes because their parents hate us too much" (*Alice Cooper: Time* March 28, 1973, p. 83).

Some performers make a living acting outright satanic or the occult like *Black Sabbath, Blue Oyster Cult* and *Motley Crue.* Violence, rebellion and the overtly demonic characterizes recent brands of demented rock like that known as "Black Metal." Groups like *Venom (At War With Satan),* whose members assume demonic names like Cronos, Mantas, Abbadon, are affectionately known as *"Satan rockers."* Although many of the grossest and most occult-based appeal to older teenage and college audience, younger and younger children are pulled by peer pressure from the more "innocent" groups they listen to in grade school.

"It wasn't like we sat down before our first gig and said, 'I'm going to drink blood from a skull and throw raw meat into the crowd.' Those are things that just developed as we played more and more shows. We decided to be as outrageous as possible. We don't mind being a little controversial. We've been getting letters from feminist groups complaining we actually kill young girls on stage. They get caught up in the illusion we create . . . Hopefully they won't get so involved with the visuals that they fail to listen to the music. That's where we'll really hook them. . . I imagine most of them have heard the stories about the blood, the women and the chainsaws. It's all part of our plan to take over the world" (Blackie Lawless, *W.A.S.P. Hit Parader* Oct. 1984 p. 28).

Some concerned people have even pushed for legislation to put warning labels similar to those on cigarette packets on albums that contain dangerous, perverted or subliminal messages. Both music and cover-art parallels what has happened in pornography. Wendy Williams of the *Plasmatics* (the ultimate sex and violence act to date) calls her act "pornography rock."

The jacket art of some albums alone in some cases should be brown-wrapped. Groups have done everything possible to market perverted visuals to match their lyrics without them being outrightly banned, and losing sales. *Blind Faith* won a "literary art" cover award using a 13-year-old girl to pose nude for their album. *Fleet-wood Mac,* the *Stones, Led Zepplin* and other more recent groups have all used children in some way exploitatively or pornographically on album covers. One of *Van Halen's* record jackets shows a small, old-young winged cherub smoking; an album cover statement of the war on the heart.

MTV & MUSIC VIDEO

MTV—music television and music video—is the most recent marketing and access tool to the head, heart and pockets of kids. It is another example of the loss of child/adult distinction. Although the majority of kids who buy records are between 12 and 19, music video consistently screens products that are adult in theme and content. One of the major networks said to a friend they only accept music videos if they are either *sensual or bizarre.* War, sex, death, the occult and other perversions of adult mentality are regularly broken down to images eight-year-olds can absorb. Even the "safe" groups preferred by the younger kids are infected: *Michael Jackson's* best-selling *Thriller* celebrates in fun the occult and the horrifying; *Duran Duran,* in their desire to remain one of the best masters of music video, explore more deeply occult imagery; and gentle *Boy George* feels compelled to flaunt his drag queen image to the limit. Part of their popularity is, of course, because they shock, and both children and teenagers love to be shocked and shock others; "shock sells."

A CHRISTIAN RESPONSE
TO THE WORLD

All Christians, and especially Christian parents concerned about children exposed to media, need to think of the dual role each individual Christian is called on to play in our kind of world. We are faced with *two problems:* how to live in *this world without becoming worldly,* and *how to be holy without living in a hole.* Our desire to know and do God's will sometimes seems in direct conflict with the need to know and understand our culture in order to minister to it. We are somehow to identify without being identical. Those who especially work with children and teenagers, whose entire world-view and beliefs are largely shaped and molded by the media, face this dilemma every day.

Worldliness, we understand from the Bible, is not a thing—it is a HEART-ATTITUDE. It is to take goals and beliefs and values as your own from a society that violates God's principles and commandments. Worldliness is a commitment to the patterns and principalities that rule a secular culture. Those principalities and powers and spiritual wickednesses in high places are not only demonic personalities, but *structures and images that embody their values.* But it is not the fact of that secular culture around us that ultimately has power to change us. It is what we think of its values and how much we allow ourselves to be influenced or molded by them. Although Jesus was talking about physical food in Mark 7:18-22, his words apply equally to *mental* food also:

"Whatsoever thing from without enters a man it cannot defile him . . . That which comes out of a man, that defiles the man. For from within, out of the heart of men, proceed evil thoughts, adulteries, fornications, murders: thefts, covetousness, wickedness, deceit, lasciviousness, an evil eye, blasphemy, pride, foolishness; all these evil things come from within, and defile the man."

No one *deliberately* feeds on poison if they want to stay alive. But sometimes in the busines of living we eat things that will not feed us properly, or that are not as traditionally and properly washed as we might wish. When we walk through our dirty world to serve it, sometimes we too will get dusty. But Jesus has come to wash both our hearts and our feet.

TWO SETS OF EYES

I believe we need to look at the media which is today's major source of "truth" for children with *two sets of eyes:* the eyes of a *prophet* and the eyes of *an evangelist.* As a prophet, we are called to speak out against sin and deviation from biblical norms; as evangelists we are to see those elements of hunger in people's lives that correspond to biblical reality. As prophets, we denounce sin; as evangelists, we love sinners.

To *church kids,* who ought to know better, participation in ideas or thought-forms that can harm or damage our spiritual lives and grieve the Holy Spirit must be exposed and forsaken. God has given us a sacred responsibility to lovingly and clearly steer children clear of unhealthy and dangerous mind and heart traps. But like the apostle Paul who was familiar enough with what he called "certain of your own poets," we can sometimes use the things a child already knows as illustrations of the beauty or truth they do not yet understand.

I remember the boy that went back to the theater again and again (over *200 times)* to watch the first *Star Wars."* Occult as it is, *Star Wars, E. T.* and other offerings from the Lucas-Spielberg stable, nevertheless embody elements drawn from something unable to be really captured in two-dimensional fantasy. They were widely successful with children as well as adults because they tried to meet a great and worldwide hunger in the heart.

To street children who have never known the real "Prince of Eternia," we must point them with compassion beyond the shells and substitutes to the eternal reality from which all good myths, including the modern ones, draw their example. And if enough Christians can affect the media politically, economically and creatively enough to begin again to create new and fresh images of the "old, old story" we can win the war of the mind. Like salt is supposed to, we can bring back some *taste* into the culture of our children.

CHARACTERISTICS OF CHILDREN

Here are just a few off the top of my audiences' heads. You can probably come up with many others with a little thought:

(1) *Children have a simple FAITH*—they implicitly believe what is told them by a reliable authority without argument or debate.

(2) They are *full of TRUST* and bring out whatever real care or compassion is in an adult's heart (Prov. 3:5-7).

(3) They have a *FRESHNESS* and brand-new approach to looking at life; the one essential ingredient it seems (besides a high IQ) for what we call in adults, "genius" ("Except a man be born again, he cannot see the kingdom of God" (John 3:3).

(4) They *ask QUESTIONS* all the time; they are perpetually

curious, constant learners (Luke 10:21).

(5) Little children *FORGIVE quickly* and do not hold grudges easily. "And be ye kind one to another, tenderhearted, forgiving one another, even as God for Christ's sake has forgiven you" (Eph. 4:32).

(6) They are *HERO-WORSHIPPERS:* it is the easiest thing in the world for them to look up to someone and try to be like them. "Be ye therefore followers of God as dear children" (Eph. 5:1).

(7) Children *Seem to be always HUNGRY* "As newborn babes desire the ... Word" (I Pet. 2:2).

(8) The *HUMILITY* of little children Jesus referred to is the un-self-conscious knowledge that they are only little and have much to learn from someone bigger, wiser and stronger than them (Matt. 18:4).

(9) Unspoiled little children are *INGENIOUS* (or uncool); they have not yet learned to be sophisticated, jaded and cynical. (Can you imagine how uncool it was for Joseph to tell his brothers about his dream? Gen. 37:5-11). And yes, despite the Fall, there is,

(9) An *INNOCENCE:* the "eternity in every baby's eyes" ("I was alive without the law once," said Paul, "but when the commandment came, sin revived and I died" (Rom. 7:9).

(10) Unhurt children are *JOYFUL*—they enjoy little things hugely, and laugh a lot.

(11) *LOVING:* they find it natural to hug and cuddle and throw themselves into their parent's arms. "For you have not received the spirit of bondage again to fear; but you have received the Spirit of adoption whereby we cry, Abba, Father (Dearest Daddy)" (Rom. 8:15a).

(12) *PLAYFUL:* children spend a large amount of time just playing. It is the primary way they develop and learn. And that, says some of the best motivation teachers in industry and business, is one of the all-time finest ways to develop creatively and solve problems.

(13) *SIMPLICITY*—children live in an uncomplicated direct-approach world. They live, love, laugh and play without complexity (Luke 18:17).

(14) *TACTLESS*—Children say what they see, and cannot see any reason to make things any different from what they really are.

Bill Gothard calls them "God's little spies;" "Speaking the truth in love" (Eph. 4:15).

(15) *Wholly relaxed*—when they sleep, they really pass out.

(16) *ZEALOUS:* whatever they do, they "do it with all their might" (Col. 3:23).

(17) They live in a world of *ABSOLUTES;* things are either right or wrong, bad or good. They have not learned the meaning of the word "compromise" (I Jn. 3:7-10).

Take a good look at this list again. This is not only a description of childhood; this is also a description of WHAT THE FATHER THINKS A CHRISTIAN LOOKS LIKE. All that makes a little child loveable are the marks of the kingdom in the life and heart of a true lover of Jesus.

> *Let the little children alone and do not hinder them from coming to me, for the kingdom of heaven belongs to such as these." (Matt. 19:14).*

What then is God's purpose in childhood? *Childhood is a perpetual reminder to all alike of true Christianity,* an unspoken sermon to every decent parent in the world of that which makes the world worth living in. Children are little time capsules, "living messages sent into a future we may never see."

> *"And whoso shall receive one such little child in my name receiveth me" (Matt. 18:5).*

And adults? *Children* adults? What are THEY to look like? What does God want CHRISTIANS to look like in the world? Forgiving. Trusting. Knowing how much we need to learn. Living in a world of clear right and wrong. Full of joy, faith and love. Fresh every morning; getting into everything with our whole heart; looking at everything like it has never been looked at before; playful, simple and direct; and at the end of the day totally relaxed in rest. *Is that what adults—even Christian adults look like today?* Would you think that is a fair description of most Christians you know? What, on the other hand, would you say is the very OPPOSITE of child-likeness? The skeptic? The cynic? The sophisticate? The proud, the arrogant, the bitter? The worldly wise? The weighed-down, burdened, mechanical approach, half-hearted "I've seen-and-tried-it-all-before" man or woman who carries the burdens of the day and then spends half the night worrying and looking at the ceiling?

No wonder God hallowed childhood. It is a constant rebuke to our failure to be like God. It is a universal witness to the heart of Christ in the world. Little children are God's ongoing witness of his kingdom; a continual illustration of the Divine ideal; a perpetual reminder of what it means to belong to the Father. Children are a God-designed sermon in every home for simplicity, joy and humility. They remind us what it means to be a real Christian.

So what will happen to the world if it loses its childhood?

VANISHING CHILDHOOD

"There are children who are not childlike. One of the saddest and not least-common sights in the world is the face of a child whose mind is so brimful of worldly wisdom that the human childishness has vanished from it as well as the divine childlikeness. For the CHILDLIKE is the divine" (George MacDonald *Creation In Christ* p.30).

In *Vanishing Childhood (Christianity Today:* May 18 and June 15, 1984) Rodney Clapp gives an excellent two-part overview of some of the social pressures modern children face that we have dealt with in some length in this book. He says "Childhood— a span of 12 to 17 years in which a child is protected and prepared for life— may appear to be a biological fact. Parental protection of children may appear to be as natural as breathing . . . But whatever is assumed, none of these is the case. There are many signs that children are increasingly less appreciated in our society, and that childhood as we know it is threatened with change to the point of extinction. The boundary protecting children is no concrete, biological wall as unchallengeable as the law of gravity. It is a thin, cultural veil, gradually raised in the past for good reason. It tears easily. And anyone who listens can hear it "ripping" (op. cit. May 18 p. 12).

Clapp points out that children have in the past been treated more as miniature adults. In Agricultural-Age medieval days, children did work as young as two or three; but they were at home shooting crows away as their parents sowed seed or herded cattle. Though they were at seven considered adult and apprenticed to craftsmen, this early work was humane. Apprentices were protected by guild rules, and taught a trade useful to them as adults. But when the Industrial Revolution came, children again began to suffer. Chil-

dren. especially poor children in both America and England, were
exploited by industry. working in coal mines and cotton mills. as
chimney sweeps and carriers. again sacrificed to a Moloch mentality of wealth and power.

Clapp says that in America many children over seven worked
"from dawn to dark six days a week with two and a half days off
every year. (Some industrialists incredibly claimed that *23-hour
workdays* would not be too long for children). Those between six
and 16 earned over half a woman's wage and one-fourth a man's.
Child workers in some mills were fed so poorly they raided pigsties"
(op. cit. p. 17). It was the Christian gospel, flowing from Jesus' care
and special honor to the children of the world, that eventually gave
them a special place in society. Christians fought abortion and
infanticide, gave them training and loving discipline in place of
abuse and abandonment and took costly steps to see they were
sheltered and protected by society as well as their homes. One of
those men was *Anthony Ashley-Cooper.* (Lord Shaftesbury) the
Christian politician and statesman of England; and his biography
makes eye-opening reading.

SHAFTESBURY'S DAY

In August, 1840, Lord Ashley asked a Commission to enquire
into the working conditions of poor children in the mines. In May,
1842, they issued their first report. Few studies of this kind were
ever so widely read. Continental, as well as English reformers and
philanthropists, "studied its fearful disclosures with intense interest." It unveiled "a mass of misery and depravity about which
even the warmest friends of the laboring classes had only a faint
conception." The testimony was overwhelming yet it was "utterly
incredible that in the most Christian and civilized country of the
world such enormities could be permitted . . . and if we dwell
briefly upon a few of the details it is only that this generation may be
better enabled to realize what was the actual state of things in the
'old time' before them and how great a deliverance Lord Ashley was
instrumental in effecting" (pp. 220-221).

MINE CHILDREN—A NIGHTMARE

"A very large population of the workers underground were less than 13 years of age; some of them began to toil in the pits when only four or five; many when between six and seven and the majority when not over eight or nine, females as well as males. "A man must have strong nerves who, for the first time, descends a deep shaft without some uncomfortable sensations. In a young timid child, the descent was a cruel terror; nor was the first impression of the mine less horrible. It was deep, dark and close, with water trickling down its sides, the floor ankle-deep in black mud and around a labyrinth of dark, gruesome passages.

"Young children were often made 'trappers,' opening and shutting the complex of doors that guarded a mine from chain reactions of an accidental explosion. From the time the first coal was brought in the morning until the last 'whirley' had passed—that is to say for 12 to 14 hours a day—the trapper was at his monotonous, deadening work. He had to sit alone in the pitchy darkness and the horrible silence, exposed to damp and unable to stir for more than a dozen paces with safety lest he be found neglecting his duty and suffer accordingly. He dared not go to sleep—the punishment was 'the strap' applied with brutal severity. Many of the mines were infested with rats, mice and beetles and other vermin, and stories are told of rats so bold they would eat the horse's hoof in the presence of the miners and had been known to run off with the lighted candles in their mouths and explode the gas. All the circumstances of a little 'trapper's' life were full of horror and upon nervous, sensitive children, the effect was terrible, producing a state of imbecility approaching almost to idiocy. Except on Sunday, they never saw the sun; they had no hours of relaxation, their meals were mostly eaten in the dark and their 'homes' were with parents who devoted them to this kind of life" (p. 221).

Clapp says of this time, "We can only too accurately imagine that for these children reality was more hellish than most contemporary children's nightmares."

Both women and children had to crawl on their hands and knees to draw enormous weights along shafts choked with coal dust or as narrow and wet as common sewers; women remained in this work until the last hour of pregnancy. . . . Coal-bearing—carrying on their backs on unrailed roads, burdens varying from a half a hundredweight to a hundredweight and a half—was almost always performed by girls and women. It was common for little children of the age of six or seven to carry burdens of coal of half a hundredweight, that in the aggregate equaled an ascent 14 times a day to the summit of St. Paul's Cathedral (365 feet high).

"Sometimes children in the mines were required to work 'double shifts,' that is to say, 36 hours continously! This cruelly protracted work was not tending self-actuated machinery but the heaviest kind of bodily fatigue; pushing loaded wagons, lifting heavy weights, or driving and constantly righting trains of loaded "corves."

"In addition . . . children, especially the apprentices, suffered terribly from the cruelty of the overlookers who bargained for them, dismissed them and used them as they pleased. Brutal punishments too sickening to dwell on were inflicted for the most trifling offenses, and their food (eaten irregularly) was not only invariably insufficient, but of the coarsest kind.

"Education was totally neglected, and the morals of the people were in the lowest possible state. Nor can this be wondered at when it is remembered that in a great number of the pits men worked in perfect nakedness, and were in this state assisted in their labors by females of all ages, from girls of six years old to women of twenty-one, these women being quite naked to the waist, their only garment being trousers" (p. 223).

Why did society permit it? Revolting cruelty was practiced upon these children of the poor employed in mines and collieries. They suffered dreadfully in their premature and destructive labor. Horrible indecencies daily passed before their eyes, inviting their imitation; and for all ignorance, licentious habits and social disorganization springing out of this state of things, what was the main excuse given? That *"without the employment of child-labor the pits could not possibly be worked with a profit;"* that "after a certain age, the vertebrae of the back do not conform to the required positions and that therefore the child must begin early. *Unless early inured to the work and its terrors, no child would ever make a good collier."*

For eleven years, Shaftesbury prepared and fought for reform.

When he was finally able to present his case to Parliament, he showed that women and children had to travel between 17-30 miles a day and had to lean over a machine and return to an erect position, while doing this not less than 4-5,000 times a day! He showed the disastrous effect by the death rate, poverty and disease among the poor; and the breakdown of the home. "He demonstrated by incontrovertible facts and arguments that this unnatural toil engendered every possible form of moral evil. Intemperance, impurity and demoralization were the inevitable consequences. All the arrangements and provisions of domestic economy were annihilated. Dirt, discomfort, ignorance and recklessness were the portion of almost every household when the time of the wife and mother were monopolized by factory labor" (p. 292).

Sir James Graham, his opponent (reacting to public pressure), introduced his own "Factory Labor Regulation" to the House of Parliament. All he wanted was time for children to be educated (without a proviso for that education) and that the definition of "children" be extended to mean those between nine and 13; that their working hours be reduced to eight and those above, or "young persons" (13-18) to 12 hours a day! Also that no "young person" would have to work earlier than 5:30 a.m. to 7:00 p.m. in summer or 6:30 to 8 p.m. in the winter.

Shaftesbury didn't agree. He wanted it further reduced to only 10. After that long battle, Shaftesbury finally prevailed on July 26, 1850. His Bill reduced the legal working day for all young persons and women to the time between 6 a.m. and 6 p.m. with one and a half hours for meals, which has been ever since (British law. P. 374). It had taken 17 years.

He said to Parliament, "We fear not the increase of your political power or envy your stupendous riches; 'Peace your walls, and plenteousness within your palaces!' We ask but a slight relaxation of toil and a 'time to live and a time to die;' a time for those comforts that sweeten life and a time for those duties that adorn it. And therefore with a fervent prayer to Almighty God that it may please Him to turn the hearts of all who hear me to thoughts of justice and mercy, I now finally commit the issue to the judgment and humanity of Parliament" (p. 293, March 15, 1844).

Shaftesbury's love and compassion for people flowed out of his love for God and his lifelong dedication to care for the poor—and the children. He wrote near the end of his life: "when I feel age creeping on me and know I must soon die—I hope it is not wrong to say it—but I cannot bear to leave the world with all the misery in it." (p. 771, July 1883).

What Shaftesbury did was but one result of the long stream of Christian men and women over the centuries who, in the light of Jesus' words, constantly and consciously protested against the mistreatment of children. Finally, others began to take up the refrain. Even non-Christians joined in; *Jean-Jacques Rousseau* published *Emile* in 1762, a romantic view of childhood that deeply affected the whole of Europe.

In England alone, says Clapp, "the book triggered more than 200 tracts on benevolent child-raising. Mothers, who only a year before would have sent their children to nurses, now suckled them. Schoolmasters eased discipline and enlivened their lessons. A new spirit swept the world, and after the turn of the century Victor Hugo staked a claim, "Christopher Columbus discovered America; I have discovered the child."

But now here in the 1980s we are in danger of seeing it all thrown away. Clapp warns us how historians agree that childhood as we know it took form only beginning in the 17th century.

"This childhood, waning perhaps since 1950, will not be naturally sustained but must be *consciously maintained* by individuals and society" (op. cit. p. 19).

Christian reform must not only attempt to influence government and the media to be more hospitable to children, but keep its own house clean. In our haste to protect society we must be careful not to play into the hands of those who would manipulate legitimate concern for their own humanistic purposes. Our own speaking, writing and preaching must be searched for loaded words that are placed in our minds by a secular society whose media is often the mouthpiece of Moloch.

David, one of Clapp's friends and a father of four mentioned in his article, calls children "exciting and intoxicating, extremely creative and innovative and unpredictable." He enjoys most their *freshness;* "a purity and innocence that you cannot duplicate once lost." "Children," he says, "are really children for parents. Their lives are a gift for parents . . . They keep me in tune with the very important issues of life—the real values—not just making more money or whatever. They teach the value of the individual for the individual's sake. Children aren't impressed with whether or not their daddy is famous. Children love people for who they are. I wake up in the morning with a fishbowl mouth but my daughter kisses me. She appreciates who I am without dressing up."

To marry, to have children, Michael Novak writes, "is to make a political statement. It is a statement of flesh, intelligence and courage."

Clapp concludes: "Childbearing and protective child-raising verge in our culture on being subversive activities. To stop the erosion of childhood, to preserve it, will require energy and sacrifice. It will require energy of all Christians—not simply parents—who use the public media, determine government and live and work and play affecting the thoughts and actions of neighbors in a hundred small ways. . . It is a testament to the triumph of Christ's attitude that even now, with childhood corroding, it stretches the imagination to think of children as an oppressed group. . . . In this world, Christ's kingdom is only realized partially in fits and starts, in glimpses and glimmers. . . But in a child—there Christ is embraced and wept over and kissed a trillion times daily" (Clapp, op. cit. June p. 24).

God help us give of ourselves to win the war on the heart.

BOOKS ON VANISHING CHILDHOOD

Christianity Today lists some important books in this area:
   Childhood Without Childhood
   Marie Winn (Pantheon 1983)
   Best sociological survey of culture's threat on children.

   The Disappearance of Childhood
   Neil Postman (Delacorte, 1982)
   Communication specialist emphasizes TV's role.

   Our Endangered Children
   Vance Packard (Little, Brown 1983)

Statistical verification of trends unfriendly to childhood:

In Defense Of The Family
Rita Kramer (Basic Books 1983)
Brilliant apologetic for the traditional family.

HISTORY OF CHILDHOOD:
Children Through The Ages
Barbara Kaye Greenlead (McGraw-Hill 1978)
Simply written survey.

Images Of Childhod
Anita Schorsch (Mayflower Books 1979)
Excellent illustrations of children in the past.

Centuries of Childhood
Philipps Aries (English transl. Knopf 1962)
Standard scholarly history of childhood.

CHILD RIGHTS & EDUCATION

If there is one thing calculated to make parents mad, *pick on their children.* Perhaps the war on childhood has made you angry enough to want to do something. You will, of course, want to support any legislation that protects children from abuse. You may be able to throw considerable weight to get such laws passed in your area. But before you sign on the dotted line, *read the fine print carefully.* The enemy never agreed to fight fair. Under the guise of compassion and concern, Moloch has taken up another collection for his altar and with the support of those who didn't recognize his horns under the halo. Beware. Not all the laws to save the children are made to save them at all.

Do you believe children should:

Have the right to divorce their parents and receive "alimony?"

Be *eligible for minimum wages* if they do household chores?

Be able to *charge their parents with child abuse* if they use biblical disciplinary measures?

Have the right to *sue their parents* for being "forced" to attend church or to avoid going places with them?

Decide whether to have an *abortion, quit school* or *hire their own attorney?*

Ridiculous, you say. Absurd. But all the above are either in effect or under serious consideration for adoption.

"As radical as these ideas may sound most have already been upheld by court decisions or are being proposed for enactment into state or Federal law. The "liberation" of children has been underway for nearly two decades. So gradually that most parents are unaware of it" (*Presidential Biblical Scoreboard:* Ed. David M. Balsieger and Colonal Donor, *Biblical News Service* P.O. Box 10428 Costa Mesa CA 92627. 714-850-0349).

Emphasize *responsibility* with children, says Bill Bothard, and you promote revival in the nation; but emphasize *rights* "and you promote rebellion."

The Bible is not romantic in its loving treatment of children. It requires both parents and children to bear responsibilities that recognize a higher authority than either the family or the state. Today, some under the guise of care for the children, are promoting amoral or anti-family legislation that on inspection shows up just as rotten as the crime it is suppose to guard children from.

Richard Farson outlined a *"Child's Bill of Rights"* in Gloria Steinam's *Ms. Magazine,* March 1974, (thus endorsed by the feminist movement) specific reforms he considers "essential to the true liberation of all children, including his own."

They include the right to:

(1) *SELF-DETERMINATION:* to decide matters which affect them most directly.

(2) *ALTERNATIVE HOME* Environment: Choice from among a "variety of arrangements: residences operated by children, child exchange programs, 24-hour child-care centers and various kinds of schools and employment opportunities."

(4) *INFORMATION:* All information available to adults—"including and perhaps especially, information that makes adults uncomfortable."

(4) *EDUCATE ONESELF:* Children should be "free to design their own education, choosing from among many options the kinds of learning . . . they want, including the option of not to attend any kind of school."

(5) *Freedom from PHYSICAL PUNISHMENT:* Children should "live free of physical threat from those who are larger and more powerful than they. Corporal punishment is used impulsively and cruelly in the home, arbitrarily in the school and sadistically in penal institutions. It does not belong in our repertoire of response to children."

(6) *SEXUAL FREEDOM:* "To conduct their sexual lives with no more restriction than adults . . . the right to information about sex, non-sexist education, and the right to all sexual activities that are legal among consenting adults." He reasons, "They are denied any information about their own sexuality or that of others. We keep them innocent and ignorant, then worry they will not be able to resist sexual approaches." In his book, *Birthrights: A Child's Bill Of Rights* (MacMillan 1974), his call for sexual freedom includes the "right" to incest.

(7) *ECONOMIC POWER:* "To work . . . receive equal pay for equal work . . . own property, develop a credit record, enter into binding contracts . . . obtain guaranteed support apart from the family, to achieve financial independence."

(8) *POLITICAL POWER:* To vote and be included in the decision-making process. "Eighty million children in the U.S. need the right to vote because adults do not vote on their behalf."

(9) *JUSTICE:* "The guarantee of a fair trial . . . an advocate to parents as well as the system and a uniform standard of detention."

Pending in Congress now is HCR 109 (sponsored by Beard of Rhode Island, et. al) "to express the sense of Congress that children possess both fundamental human rights and rights attributable to their status as children . . . and to grant children ADDITIONAL rights equivalent to the rights now possessed ONLY BY ADULTS."

But as the *Pro-Family Forum* points out, with "every right is a responsibility. To give children all adult rights is to burden their immature and inexperienced minds with responsibility of forming judgments and making life-determining and far-reaching decisions which are difficult for even the most mature adults. THIS IS CHILD ABUSE IN ONE OF ITS CRUELLEST FORMS! One of children's most basic needs is loving and concerned adults capable of giving mature guidance and support. One of the cruel injustices of the so-called 'Childrens Rights' movement is that children are being stripped of this fundamental support because parental rights are being systematically destroyed and parental values are being systematically undermined and ridiculed. THE BASIC QUESTION NOW UNDER DEBATE IS: Who has the *primary right* in childbearing: the parent? the child? or the State?" (*Pro-Family Forum* P.O. Box 8907, Fort Worth, Texas 76112 Monthly Newsletter $19).

Dr. Mary Jo Bane, associate director of Wellesley College's Center for Research on Women said, "The fact that children are raised in families means there's no equality . . . In order to raise children with equality we must take them away from families and raise them." And who is "we"? The State, of course. Swedish authorities in 1982, under the "Youth Care" act, removed 12,000 children from their parent's homes for state-sponsored "protective upbringing."

All this points up, of course, the encroaching power the State has over the family when the spirit of Moloch rules in a nation. John Conlan points out biblically based Bills of Rights For Children have been drawn up free from the "hidden agenda" implicit in the others. One such Bill includes: (1) The right to the affection and intelligent guidance of understanding parents; (2) the right to be raised in a decent home and be adequately fed, clothed and sheltered; (3) the right to the benefits of religious guidance and training; (4) the right to a school program which offers sound academic training plus maximum opportunity for individual development and preparation for living; (5) the right to receive constructive discipline for the proper development of character, conduct and habits; (6) the right to be secure in his or her community against all influences detrimental to proper and wholesome development; (7) the right to individual selection of free and wholesome recreation; (8) the right to live in a community where adults recognize that the welfare of their children is of primary importance; (9) the right to receive a good adult example; and (10) the right to a job commensurate with his or her ability, training and experience, and protection against physical or moral employment hazards which adversely affect wholesome development" (*Children's Ideals* Vol. 27 #4 Ideals Publishing Milwaukee 1970; *Beyond 1984* pp.42-43).

Altered to the humanistic intent of the United Nation's promotion of "The Year Of The Child," defenders of the traditional family like Tim and Beverly La Haye helped block the hidden agendas from being pushed through; but as Conlan pointed out, the "battle against families will continue to be waged disguised as compassion for children" until the humanists either establish their agenda or the traditional family makes a permanent comeback. Legally for the moment, the children are safe; but the other problem is a ticking time bomb.

ILLITERACY AND DECAY IN THOUGHT

There are two more obvious areas in which young people face a real war on their futures. One of the dramatic collapses among children today is their inability to read deeply and think clearly. Both are necessary for children to handle the future in an Information Age where they will be bombarded in every direction with ideas clamoring for a hearing.

Dorothy Sayers, that friend of C. S. Lewis and fellow-Inkling, whose sharp wit and penetrating insight said, "We let our young men and women go out unarmed in a day when armor was never so necessary. By teaching them all to read, we have left them at the mercy of the printed word. By the invention of film and the radio (to which we can add now TV) we have made certain that no aversion to reading shall secure them from the incessant battering of words, words, words. They do not know what the words mean; they do not know how to ward them off or blunt their edge or fling them back; they are a prey to words in their emotions, instead of being masters of them in their intellects. We who were scandalized when young men were sent to fight armored tanks with rifles are not scandalized when young men and women are sent into the world to fight massed propaganda with a smattering of 'subjects'; and when whole classes and whole nations become hypnotized by the arts of the spellbinder, we have the inpudence to be astonished" ("The Lost Tools

Of Learning"; from selections of Dorothy Sayers, *A Matter Of Eternity,* p. 119).

Savers suggested a return to the medieval practice of teaching *Grammar, Dialectics* and *Rhetoric* through the use of a language. A method of teaching that suits the three stages of a child's growth she characterized as the Parrot (absorbs and memorizes everything), the Pert (delights in riddles and in tricking adults), and the Poet (goes into room not feeling like lunch because she is going to write a song or a poem). Teachers who use this same approach to each subject will develop in a child the ability to take an unknown subject, understand, analyze and present it. *Grammar* is the collection of words, ideas or facts. *Dialectic* involves clear and accurate distinction, definition and arrangement of these. *Rhetoric* is the art of clear and moving presentation in written or spoken word. Those families that train their children to learn by collection, categorization and communication will produce leaders in an age when leadership belongs to those who master precisely these skills.

IS TV TO BLAME?

Again, TV has been blamed for the sharp decline in children's scores on the Scholastic Aptitude Test. After all, by the age of 16 most children have spent 10-15,000 hours watching TV. Much more time than they spend in any school. As some of these TV children graduated in the '60s and '70s, an Adult Performance Test found that "20 percent of the American population was functionally incompetent." That is, they could not perform basic tasks of reading, writing or computing: like counting their change, addressing an envelope, reading a want ad or filling out a job application. "The result," says Paul Copperman, president of the Institute of Reading Development in San Francisco, "is that society may be compelled to support an increasing percentage of dysfunctional or only marginal functional citizens" (*U.S. News & World Report* Aug. 2, 1982).

Nearly 40 percent of today's 17-year-olds tested cannot draw inferences from written material; only one-fifth can write a persuasive essay; and only one-third can solve a math problem requiring several steps. Some 23 million adults, 13 percent of 17-year-olds and up to 40 percent of minority young people, are functionally illiterate; they cannot read a bus schedule, a want ad or a label on a medicine bottle. Another 34 million are just barely capable of simple reading tasks. The National Commission On Excellence in Education said bluntly in May, 1983, "If an unfriendly foreign power had attempted to impose on America the mediocre educational performance that exists today, we might well have viewed it as an act of war" (*Presidential Biblical Scoreboard* op. cit. p.18). And an act of war it probably was.

A TURNING POINT IN HISTORY

But TV is certainly not entirely to blame. Language, like all of the rest of creation, suffers from anthropy, a tendency to become more and more simple, with less and less available energy unless that system is open to a higher order of intelligence and energy that can organize it. More deeply at fault are modern liberal experiments in education that have contemptuously rejected the discipline and structure of older methods of teaching in favor of progressive approaches. Examples are the "New Math" which has helped students not to be able to count, and the rejection of phonics which has also helped students not to be able to read. Harry Blamires recalls a young woman graduate who spoke to him as a fellow-educator and made a comment that stuck in his mind pointing to a watershed point in educational history, perhaps in cultural history.

"I was lucky," she said. "I was educated under a backward county authority and came too soon for all the change."

Blamires thinks it deeply significant that "Educated people can and do say now what would have been unthinkable 20, 30, 40, 50 years ago; that they are glad to have escaped what the young are now getting . . . Surely if there has been one constant over the past hundred years and more of public education—until the last decade—it has been the genuine envy of each generation of the educational provisions made for the next . . .

"It begins to look like a turning point in history" (Harry Blamires; *Where Do We Stand?* (Servant Books, Ann Arbor MI 48107, 1980; p.13).

ILLITERACY AS A
WORK OF DARKNESS

Bob and Rose Weiner of *Maranatha Ministries* believe that this growing illiteracy among children is directly related to the works of darkness. Language is so important to mankind it was given to him as a gift of God, and even Christ himself, the express image of the invisible God is called "the Word." God spoke the creation into existence by his Word (Gen. 1:3: Ps. 33:6,9); C. S. Lewis used the lovely image of Aslan singing the stars into existence.

The Weiners note, "The highest purpose of language is to fit man to commune with God . . . Although we can feel the power of love it is through words that the full meaning of that love can be comprehended. In the biblical accounts of God's revelation to man . . . God always spoke to man through words. Words are God's principle form of communication with men . . . The larger and more vast your vocabulary, the greater your comprehension. This explains why Satan, the enemy of our souls, works towards the degeneration of language" (*Whatever Happened To The English Language? The Forerunner,* July 1983 Vol. IV #3 pp. 13-14).

So what happens to a culture when its children grow up no longer knowing many of its words? When we are poor in language we never gain an ability to understand or an ability to share. *Noah Webster,* who ultimately mastered 26 languages in order to complete the first American dictionary, was not only a Christian; he was an educator par excellence and took up his massive task because he felt that the future spiritual and moral health of the nation rested on its ability or failure to keep its language clear, pure and strong. He wrote:

"The English language is to be the instrument of propagating sciences, arts and the Christian religion to an extent probably exceeding that of any other language. It is therefore important that its principles should be adjusted and uniformity of spelling and pronunciation established and preserved" (*Webster's 1828 Dictionary.*" Introduction p. 23. Facsimile First Edition: *Foundation For American Christian Education,* P.O. Box 27035, San Francisco CA 94127).

Illiteracy can be viewed as an attack on the ability of a culture to understand itself and others, but even more deeply, an attack on its ability to express itself to others. It is significant that on the Day of Pentecost, the first major public witness of the resurrection of Christ to the world by the outpouring of the Holy Spirit, was marked by communication in many languages, the "wonderful works of God." Without a grasp of words, we will always find it difficult to deepen our praise to God or widen our ability to speak of him adequately to others. Christian parents who intend to live by God's Word and to instill its stories, principles and precepts in their children's hearts have a unique opportunity now: bring up a generation that will have the power and the authority by their mastery of the Word and words to take back the land.

THE SECRET OF GREAT LANGUAGE

I will never forget a particular Shakespeare-loving English teacher I had in high school. He was memorable for two things. First, he wore his hair parted dramatically in the middle, and let it fall down both sides of his face like the pallid and fashionable poet he was at heart. Secondly, on one rare day we made him really angry. That day we had been goofing off in his momentary absence and contrary to his explicit instructions. He burst in the door, paused only a moment to take in the sight of us still snickering in the back. Then, white with rage, he gave the entire class an absolutely incredible three-minute tongue-lashing. It was awesome. He unleashed such a string of words that we were all utterly cowered. I mean, scarcely daring to breathe. And yet, I did not recall that he ever once swore in that astonishing tirade that reduced all of us to shocked silence. And so perhaps the best single advice I ever got about the use of words was later from him who had proven himself such a master. He said:

"There are *three stages* of great thinking and great writing. The first is when you have *small ideas and small words*. The second is when you have *big ideas and big words*. But you never reach greatness until you can put those *big ideas* in *small words*. Big words are not the secret of good thinking, speaking and writing, but the right short word only comes when we know enough to make the exact choice. Study the words of Jesus. Here you have the greatest mind in the Universe, with the most profound thoughts ever uttered.

And yet there is scarcely a word he uses that has more than two syllables.

ALTERNATIVE EDUCATION

Children in Colonial days were taught the basics by their parents. After the need for national unity following the Revolutionary War created a demand for standardized texts, Noah Webster's *Blue Backed Elementary Speller* and the *McGuffey Readers* were developed. These books were character-connected, and stressed patriotism, belief in God, honesty, thrift and courage. More than 100,000 reprints of these 1896 Readers were sold in 1982 (Mott Media, 1000 E. Huron St., Milford MI 48042).

The Foundation for American Christian Education, under the capable leadership of professional historians and librarians Hall and Slater, has accomplished the mammoth task of collecting and reprinting original key documents from America's true "hidden history" — the influence of real Christians in its political, legal and educational genesis. Included in these quality collections is a one-volume issue of the original two volumes of *Webster's 1898 Dictionary*, key documents on the origin of the Constitution and the Revolutionary War, and a teaching manual with accompanying curriculum for what they call the *"Principle Approach"* to learning.

Christian and private schools have moved into the gap created by the failure of much public education. Many are also beginning to explore home education—the original way many of the nation's best thinkers and writers learned in the past before the Industrial Era began to regiment and separate families to fit into factory shifts. A new Christian school opens somewhere every day; and many of these students in grades one to eight score in Stanford Achievement Tests from 16 to 19 months ahead of the national average.

Many such parents who are *not* Christian have opted to send their children to such schools. Not only does the education level tend to be higher, but the crime rate is certainly lower! Schools without biblical elements of discipline and love, of unified understanding built around moral principle and percept, have become "Blackboard Jungles." Today it is downright dangerous to go. Secular humanism values clarification, situation ethics, sensitivity training and amoral if not immoral sex education courses, psychodrama and evolutionary concepts have ruled the classroom long enough for people to appreciate the difference such "higher education" can bring.

IT'S DANGEROUS IN THERE

"Animals" is another poem by Christian Steve Turner who writes for *Rolling Stone Magazine.* He talks in it of some horror a gang of kids in Britain were caught doing. It was such a brutal murder that the local paper called them "Animals."

"Animals," muses Turner. *"That's what my biology teacher told us."*

Each month *three million* secondary school students are victims of in-school crime. *Two and a half million* of these are robbed or stolen from. More than 250,000 suffer physical attacks. In large cities, eight percent of the juniors and seniors missed at least one day at school a month because they were afraid for their lives. The average attendance in some violence-prone schools is only 53 percent.

If it's tough to be a student, it's worse to be a teacher. Each month 6,000 are robbed, 125,000 threatened with physical harm and at least 1,000 a month so violently assaulted they need medical care. "As far back as 1976 we were paying over $200 million each year to repair the results of school vandalism" (John Conlan *"Beyond 1984"* p. 56)

In 1940 the top offenses in public schools were, in order: (1) *Talking;* (2) *Chewing gum;* and *(3) Making noise,* followed by running in halls, getting out of turn in line, wearing improper clothes and not putting paper in the wastebasket.

In 1982 the top three school offenses were: (1) *Rape,* (2) *Robbery;* and (3) *Assault,* followed by burglary, arson, bombings, murder, suicide, absenteeism, vandalism, extortion, drug taking or pushing, drinking, gang warfare, getting pregnant, having an abortion and contracting venereal disease (Mel Gabler, *Educational Research Newsletter,* Nov. 1982).

We've come a long way, baby.

Phyllis Schlafly (president of *Eagle Forum,* a national pro-family organization, records the "remarkable real-life drama" of hundreds of parents, teachers and concerned citizens traveling to one of seven city locations where their testimony was heard before the U.S. Dept. of Education on proposed regulations for the Protection of Pupil Rights Amendment. They recorded more than 1,300 pages of testimony summarized in Schlafly's book, *Child Abuse In The Classroom.*

They were people who loved kids and were mad at what was being done in the name of education. They explain, says Schlafly:

". . . WHY we have 23 million adult illiterates who have graduated from high school, and WHY young people are experiencing high rates of teenage suicide, loneliness, premarital sex and pregnancy. . . HOW schools have alienated children from their parents, from traditional morality such as the Ten Commandments and from our American heritage . . . WHAT children have been doing in those classrooms instead of learning to read, write, spell, and subtract and the essentials of history, geography and civics. These Hearings explain HOW children learn in school to be 'sexually active,' take illegal drugs, repudiate their parents and rationalize immoral and anti-social conduct when it 'feels' good in a particular 'situation.' These Hearings speak with a thunderous voice of hundreds of parents who are angry at how their children have been emotionally, morally and intellectually abused by psychological and behavioral experiments during classroom hours when the parents THOUGHT their children were being taught basic knowledge and skills. . . indignant at the way educators' change agents,' spending federal tax dollars, have used children as guinea pigs for fads and experiments that have been substituted for real learning."

Phyllis Schlafly is real mad. And with good reason, it turns out. Even the court-appointed stenographers who are considered the most accurate and experienced of recorders generated a whole page of misspelled words in transcribing the verbal testimony. The United States is in a bad way, and the burden is falling on the children.

Child Abuse In The Classroom has two valuable appendices for parents that help them to evaluate any school's curriculum and/or sex education course. Order from: Pere Marquette Press, P.O. Box 495, Alton, Illinois, 62002 $4.95 each, discounts on bulk orders).

HOPEFUL SIGNS

Much has been done recently among Christians to correct these conditions by the infusion of biblical principles and concepts as well as believers into these teaching systems, and curricula are constantly and carefully revised in the light of new scriptural insights. New kinds of higher education have been launched like *Youth With A Mission,* Pacific and Asian University (PACU) where each subject is assigned an entire living complex, and students are immersed wholly and totally in that subject until it becomes a part of their lifestyle. Much time and thought has been invested in developing each distinct discipline in the total light of God's Word, and relating each system to his centrality and kingdom.

Bill Gothard has made some quality contributions towards a character-based curriculum, and his educational efforts, like his *Character Sketches,* have won national book awards for their sheer clarity, quality and beauty.

Others like *Tony Campola* of Eastern College in Pennsylvania aim to infuse their own special brand of scholarship, compassion and enthusiasm into the liberal arts colleges, while creationist researchers and scientists continue to publish and willingly debate secular evolutionists on their own turf and in their own disciplines. The trickle-down effect of the '60s and mid-'70s Jesus movement is releasing a whole crop of new Christians into fields that are hungry for some creative and determined leaders. But there is still a long way to go. And in the meantime, the battle for the future rages on.

BOOKS ON CHILD RIGHTS AND EDUCATION

The Battle For The Public Schools: Humanism's Threat To Our Children, Tim LaHaye, (Fleming Revell, Old Tappan, NJ)

Child Abuse In The Classroom
Edited Phyllis Schlafly (Pere Marquette Press, P.O. Box 495, Alton, IL 62002)

Communicating A Christian World-View In The Classroom
Robert L. Simonds (NACE: Box 3200, Costa Mesa, CA 92628)

A Guide To The Christian School
Robert Billings (New Century Foundation, Washington, D.C.)

Homegrown Kids: Homespun Schools
Raymond and Dorothy Moore (Word Books, Waco, TX)

The Siecus Circle: A Humanist Revolution (Sex Ed.)
Claire Chambers (Western Islands Publ., Belmont, Mass.)

LEGAL RIGHTS

Home Education and Constitutional Liberties
John W. Whitehead and Wendell R. Bird (Crossway Books, Westchester, IL)

Freedom Of Religious Expression In Public High Schools
John W. Whitehead (Crossway Books, Westchester, IL)

ORGANIZATIONS

Citizens For Excellence In Education (CEE)
Box 3200, Costa Mesa, CA 92628

Eagle Forum
Alton, IL 62002

Family Life Action Coalition
217 E. Main, Genoa, IL 60135

The Foreunner
P.O. Box 1799, Gainesville, FL 32602

Foundation For American Christian Education
P.O. Box 27035, San Francisco, CA 94127

Institute In Basic Youth Conflicts (Bill Gothard)
Oak Brook, IL

The Mel Gablers
P.O. Box 7518, Longview, TX 75607

National Association of Christian Educators (NACE)
Box 3200, Costa Mesa, CA 92628

Pro-Family Forum
P.O. Box 8907, Fort Worth, TX 76122

WAR TO THE DEATH—CHILD
& TEENAGE SUICIDE

Every now and then you hear a particularly horrible story. Some-where, someone just seems to totally flip out and goes on an insane and murderous rampage. Innocent people passing some multiple-story bell tower or sitting down at a local family restaurant look up to see someone who is trying to kill everyone in sight in all direc-tions—men, women, children and even babies, until the police or local SWAT team charges in to finally "take them out."

The papers, radio and TV are full of the incident for a couple of days. Reporters take pictures, magazines run cover stories on "What Really Happened," and the world shakes its head until the next week when everything is mercifully forgotten.

The ones that stick most are the sad stories of the dad who careful-ly gathers all his children and his wife together, then uses a gun on everyone in his family just before he turns it on himself. But a lot more people, hurt and angry with a world where they do not feel they fit in, or where it will not behave the way they wish, do not kill OTHERS. The ultimate trophy of Satan's war on children is not murder of or by another. It is when a child, a teenager or a college student who cannot handle things any longer, makes the fatal choice deliberately. *They kill themselves.*

One of the best recent books on child suicide is *A Cry For Help* by Dr. Mary Giffin and writer Carol Felsenthal (Doubleday & Company 1983). Giffin and Felsenthal's book is an excellent resource and MUST reading for practical help on recognizing and dealing with would-be young suicides. It forms much of the basis of this chapter. Two others by Christians are *Suicide* by Dave Wilkerson (Wilkerson Books, 1978; excellent for young people as well as parents) and *What You Should Know About Suicide* by Dr. Bill Blackburn (Word 1982).

"Suicide rates are increasing among youngsters of all ages. The youngest person we describe is two and a half years old. The oldest is twenty-four; (*A Cry For Help:* from the Introduction). Among 15 to 24-year-olds, suicide is the THIRD leading cause of death after homicides and accidents. Around 2,000 kill themselves every year. Researchers at the National Institute of Mental Health report that suicide ATTEMPTS outnumber actual suicides 50 to one. About 250,000 teenagers will try it this year.

EVERYDAY an average of 18 young Americans "twixt twelve and twenty" kill themselves—between 6,500 to 8,000 a year. Every HOUR, 57 children and adolescents attempt to take their own lives—well over 1,000 attempts a day.

At a Chicago-area suicide hotline, the phone rings every 20 seconds. Dr. Michael Peck, one of the country's leading suicidologists estimates that each year in the U.S. "somewhere in the neighborhood of a million or more children move in and out of suicidal crises . . . Many more young people die of suicide than cancer. Each year the death rate for childhood cancer falls (43 percent since 1950) but the suicide rate rises (a shocking 300 percent since 1950).

DISGUISED AS "ACCIDENTS"

Giffin thinks that a great many of the deaths that go down in the records AS accidents or homicides are really suicides and that the number of suicides, is AT THE VERY LEAST, twice what is reported. Not only family shame keeps the real numbers so low. National Center for Health Statistics officials don't record a death AS suicide unless there is proof that it was intentional; a suicide note is normally required. But only 15 percent of suicides leave notes.

She says, "Many of us believe that suicide is really the number one killer; that many of the accident or homicide victims are really suicides in disguise. A recent Philadelphia survey revealed that more than 25 percent of murder victims caused their own deaths by picking a fight with someone who had a weapon. In one case, a teenager who knew his gun was unloaded brandished it at police officers inciting them to shoot him in self-defense . . . We call these 'chronic' suicides—the daredevil who shouts 'Looks, no hands' as he rides his bicycle on a two-lane highway, the 12-year-old wearing his Superman cape who jumps from the roof, the hundreds of thousands of adolescents slowly destroying themselves with drugs and alcohol."

Then there are those kids with cars who sometimes find a quick way to exit life without looking like they tried. Car deaths, 37 percent of all fatalities among 15-to-24-year-olds) probably represent the biggest block of suicides disguised as accidents . . . Forensic experts think perhaps one quarter of these 'accidents' are deliberate; adding these 'autocides' to suicides they argue easily makes suicide the number one killer." Then there are the "accidental" poisonings; each year among children aged five-14 there are 100,000 cases of intentional self-poisoning (op. cit. p.79).

Official statistics, while "only the shadow of reality," are disturbing enough. Between 1955 and 1975, the rate of teen suicides almost TRIPLED from 4.1 per 100,000 in 1955 to 11.8 per 100,000 in 1975. Between 1974 and 1975 (the latest statistics available) the rate rose by a walloping 10 PERCENT! While more older people commit suicide than young, the rate of INCREASE of young suicides far exceeds that of older groups.

EVEN THE VERY YOUNG

An eight-year-old makes a will. It reads:
"*I want to not
live no more.
Mickey gest my
bank and Mommey my stamp book.*"

Even the *very young* are now trying to kill themselves in record numbers. At the 1982 convention of The American Psychiatric Association, psychiatrist Perihan Rosenthal described her encounters with six suicidal children who had at least one thing in common—*they were all under five years old.* Four-year-old David wrapped himself in a blanket and set it on fire. When asked why, he answered, "Because David is a bad boy, there will be no more David."

Following his parents' divorce, Benji (two and a half) stopped eating for two weeks, threatened to throw himself in front of cars, and bit himself until he bled. In therapy, he made a doll plunge from a dollhouse roof and the top of a toy truck.

"Why is the little boy hurting himself?" Rosenthal asked. "He is a bad boy. Nobody loves him," Benji explained.

The National Center for Health Statistics does not even compute figures for children under 10. People erroneously believe that suicide in children that age is so rare as to be unmeasurable. Yet when Pittsburgh psychologists surveyed 127 elementary school children, 41 percent admitted having thought about it!

Michael Peck indicates that "up to 10 percent of youngsters in any public school classroom may be considered at some risk for suicide." There ARE figures for 10 to 14-year-olds. They have risen nearly as fast as the rate for 15 to 24-year-olds. In the decade between 1968 and 1978 the rate increased by 32 percent (*A Cry For Help* op cit. p. 101).

COLLEGE STUDENTS—AN EPIDEMIC

For college age, it is officially the SECOND leading cause of death having risen from fifth place in the early 1970s. Between 1968 and 1975, suicides among the 20 to 24-year-olds MORE THAN

DOUBLED. In 1976 HALF the deaths on a large midwestern campus were due to suicide—a figure that remains constant nationally, especially among freshmen. One Columbia University study of college freshmen revealed that 70 percent had thought of suicide in one given year" (Giffin op. cit. p.12).

YET MOST DON'T WANT TO DIE

As high as the suicide DEATH rate is, it seems moderate when compared to the ATTEMPT rate. For every young person who completes suicide there may be 50 to 100 others who attempt it and "fail." Yet most young people who attempt suicide don't want to die. Suicide is the nation's number one PREVENTABLE health problem... They die because they believe they are not loved... "Until the very last moment that the bullet or barbiturate finally snuffs out life's last breath, the suicidal person wants desperately to live. He is begging to be saved," one expert noted.

Dr. Bill Blackburn, a Christian authority on suicide, notes that the desire to live and the desire to die "exist side by side... engaged in a powerful struggle. At one stage... these conflicting wishes are expressed in a resigned attitude of indifference: 'I don't care whether I live or die.'"

A suicide loses this tug of war between life and death. *Marilyn Monroe dies clutching a telephone; the poet Sylvia Plath* has a note asking that her medical doctor be called; and people often drive up to the emergency room of a hospital and shoot themselves!

"In what are strangely humorous instances, why would a potential suicide obey when a policeman rushes into the room with pistol drawn and orders him to drop his gun? In one instance, a man jumped off the Brooklyn Bridge in New York City and refused to grab a life preserver thrown to him. A policeman from the bridge shouted, 'Grab that life preserver or I'll shoot!' The man grabbed the life preserver and was pulled to shore. Ambivalence reigns" (*"What You Should Know About Suicide,* Bill Blackburn, p.19).

Nobody commits suicide out of the blue. Studies show that approximately 80 percent of the people who committed suicide gave repeated warnings. Some seem to court death like a lover. Janis Joplin, who reportedly died after having shot liquid cement in one arm and LSD in the other, was remembered by friends as "playing delightedly with death even as far back as high school days" (*Blackburn* op. cit. p. 29).

Barbara, a three-time attempter who called in to a Chicago radio station's program on teen suicide said, "I don't want to commit suicide. I want my parents to recognize that I feel so terribly bad and I want them to help me; to make me feel that I'm cared for. . . I was hoping to be saved by them, that it would shake them up to realize that they should, you know, share their love while they had the chance."

Nine out of 10 teenage suicide attempts take place in the home. Seventy percent of teens who attempt suicide do so when their parents are home. And they do só between the hours of three in the afternoon and midnight when they can be seen, stopped and saved. If they REALLY wanted to die they would not take the chance of being discovered. (Adults choose the hours between midnight and dawn to kill themselves). In the few months before committing suicide, 75 percent of the victims visited their family doctor and many also were seeing a psychiatrist (Giffin, op. cit. p.16).

CONSEQUENCE OF DIVORCE

Failure in school, a problem that frequently plagues suicidal children, is more common among children whose parents are divorced. Children from one-parent families are more likely to be discipline problems; three times more likely to be suspended from school; and twice as likely to drop out (Giffin op. cit. p.152).

Psychologist Carl Tishler found that kids who attempted suicide from 1978 to 1980 had parents who were more depressed than normal, drank more and had lower self-images. Mothers of suicide-prone teenagers often considered suicide themselves, more so than either their husbands or parents.

Calvin Frederick, Chief of Disaster Asssistance and Emergency Mental Health at N.I.M.H., found that 93 percent of suicidal teen-agers he examined reported a lack of communication between them and their parents.

"A fairly typical suicidal male," he said, "has either lost his father between age 16 or has one with whom his relations are strained. This leads to depression, smoking, drinking, drugs, falling grades and poor behavior—and ultimately perhaps a suicide attempt."

The heart of the problem," he says, "is the breakdown of the nuclear family" (*Youthletter,* Feb. 1982, p.12).

David Wilkerson said in his 1978 book *Suicide:*

"Last year there were more than one million new divorces with 10 million kids victimized by these and previous divorces. On the Judgment Day I see a generation of lonely, mixed-up kids rising to witness against parents whom they believe let them down. The prophet Isaiah must have been thinking of our broken homes when he said:

"Prepare slaughter for this children for the inquity of their fathers" (Is. 14:21).

CAUSES FOR SUICIDE

Why do kids try to kill themselves? There are many reasons, but some of the most recurring pressures given are these:

(1) *Desire to MAKE THE OTHER PERSON SORRY they didn't love them.*

"Suicide," says Blackburn, "is almost always a hostile act . . . Often directed toward the survivors. A child threatens: 'I'll die and then you'll be sorry.' In fact, one school of psychotherapy maintains that a person who takes his life is fulfilling a childhood vow 'If it ever gets bad enough, I can kill myself.' The threat of suicide can be a tool to manipulate others: ('If you marry him, I'll kill myself')—the 'trump card' played after all other cards have been played . . . used by children against parents, husbands against wives, girlfriends against boyfriends, workers against co-workers" (Blackburn, op. cit. pp.21, 23).

(2) *Abnormal Social Development.* The end of a life of bitterness (hurt that has never been forgiven) is often a desire to end it all. Suicide is a self-inflicted punishment, although not always the chief motivation. A deep sense of personal guilt is a key factor in many suicides.

Judas said, "I have sinned . . ." and the chief priests and elders said, "What is that to us . . . ?" And he cast down the pieces of silver in the temple and went and hanged himself (Matt. 27:4-5). Some who misguidedly feel they have committed the "unpardonable sin" take it on themselves to pass sentence on their failure, when the effects of that sin are the exact opposite of the moods that lead to suicide. The unpardonable sin is a final rejection of the convincing and convicting power of the Holy Spirit who calls us to salvation. The chief sign of such a rejection is a careless, hardhearted attitude about personal guilt, and a complete loss of feelings of guilt over known wrong.

(3) *Romeo and Juliet ROMANTICISM*—a "creativity, love or genius too pure for this world." Young Romeo, discovering the apparent body of his Juliet, says, as he drinks poison to join her in death:

> *"Eyes look your last/Arms, take your last embrace*
> *And lips, O you the doors of death/Seal with a righteous*
> *kiss*
> *A dateless bargain to engrossing death."*

A *West Side Story* suicide has sometimes become a glamour exit to the romantic young who have not seen the gassed, blasted, or purple-faced corpses of kids who dated death thinking it would be like the comics. To live in a real world where one may have to grow sick, frail, or old has been sold as a fate to be at all costs avoided. "Die young," sang Debbie Harry, formerly of Blondie, "Stay pretty."

A teenager from a home without strong family support falls desperately in love with someone. That person becomes their entire world. Then the whole thing is threatened. The person loses interest, finds someone else, or parents or relatives step in to break it up. A situation like this triggered an entire wave of high school teenage suicides in Arlington, Texas, in 1983.

"Following the breakup of a romance or marriage a suicide may also be a distorted and tragic way of letting the other person know just how much he or she was loved . . . The same phenomena is present in some murder/suicides or joint suicides. The thought of living without each other is so strong that both partners decide to walk the path together to death, reenacting the sad story of Romeo and Juliet" (Blackburn, op. cit. p.30).

(4) *CELEBRITY SUICIDE:* We have so deified power, money

and knowledge in our time that when some celebrity who "seems to have it all"—fame, money, enormous success in the "real" (versus the school world)—commits suicide many young people agonize, "If he who had everything to live for killed himself, what possible hope is there for me?"

The month following Marilyn Monroe's overdose on sleeping pills the national suicide rate rose 12 percent. When 23-year-old Freddie Prinze of *Chico and the Man* fame shot himself to death, the youth suicide rate jumped. John Lennon's death was like losing a member of the family to many kids. After his murder the teen suicide rate again increased (Giffin, op. cit. p. 179).

(5) *A SIGNIFICANT "CAUSE"*—A desire to impress others with significance. Another consequence of the exaltation of Moloch's brand of "success" is the loss of personal value. Kids feel they can't do anything important, and if you don't, you don't count.

Some, like John Hinckley, feeding on fantasy and determined to impress someone, try to kill someone famous. Many, without the imagination or ability to try that, simply decide to kill themselves, and be "famous for five minutes."

Elton John sang on the album *Honky Chateau:*
"*I'm getting bored being part of mankind*
There's not a lot to do no more/this race is a waste of time
People rushing everywhere swarmin' round like flies
Think I'll buy a forty-five/give them all a surprise
Yes, I'm gonna kill myself/get a little headline news
I'd like to see what the papers say/on the state of teenage blues."
"A suicide attempt grabs attention like few other things. People are startled, guilty, concerned, puzzled. Where people previously ignored a person, now they lavish attention on them." (*Blackburn*, op. cit. p. 22).

When this interest wanes, they may make another attempt. It may set up a vicious cycle that escalates until the person (perhaps not really meaning to) actually does kill himself.

(6) *FAILURE to REALLY UNDERSTAND MORTALITY*—Few kids really know of death other than fantasy where an Indiana Jones or James Bond faces death 30 times in a two-hour movie.

survives each effortlessly, or is killed only to be "reborn" in the next TV series (right after the Coke commercial that "adds life").

"Life-like" special effect recreations of death and dismemberment in film, TV, and video create a make-believe world where death only happens on the screen, and at half-time after the smoke has cleared, you can go out again for popcorn. Youth is a time of adventure and exploration, fascinated with the untried and unfamiliar.

"Death seems so remote and young people feel so invulnerable to it, they are drawn to experiment with it, often through drugs, guns or automobiles. Sometimes the experiments are fatal. Included . . . would be drug overdoses, games like Russian roulette and forms of 'chicken' " (Blackburn, p. 28).

Some rock lyrics even advocate teenage suicide like *Blue Oyster Cult's "Don't Fear The Reaper"*:

"Come on baby, do it with me
Take the leap, it's easy you'll see
40,000 men and women do it every day
40,000 men and women are strictly on their way.
Don't fear the Reaper—don't fear the Reaper
Come on baby, let's play."

A depressed girl in Sacramento went out to a tree by their barbecue grill and hung herself. A note on the last few pages in her diary read: "I will not fear the reaper." Her favorite group? *Blue Oyster Cult.*

(7) An increase in BELIEF IN REINCARNATION. Dr. William Worden (Harvard Medical School) speculates that this may be partly responsible for the jump in suicide rates. One college freshman who attempted suicide twice told him, "I'm kind of looking forward to death, just to try something new. It's another place to go. I'm really curious to find out what's on the other side" (p. 86).

Some believe they will go to a better world like 16-year-old Jason Perrine and 15-year-old Dawn Swisher who were "obsessed with the possibility of reincarnation." Friends reported that after the pair read Richard Bach's book *Illusions* (a book with the theme of reincarnation) they began leading lunchtime discussions on suicide and rebirth. They planned their suicide—steal a sports car, die in a famous crash in their old junior high school after which they would move on to a "higher plane of existence." A year later to the day, they crashed into the North Mercer (Washington) Junior High at five a.m. Jason was killed instantly. Dawn, apparently with some last-minute doubts on reincarnation, just barely survived by diving under the dashboard (p. 86-87).

(8) *INABILITY TO HANDLE DELAY:* June 26, 1982. Two teenagers, Ellen Chow, 15, and Edmund DeBock, 16, climb onto the roof of a YMCA building in Chicago. Holding hands they leap to their deaths. They told friends with whom they shared a six-pack of beer they were "looking for a better world."

Eddie asked: "What's it like up in heaven? Let's try it." They wanted to marry so they could be together all the time. They couldn't because they were too young. Waiting until their eighteenth birthday was apparently more than they could bear (p. 88).

(9) *LOSS OF FUTURE.* In *Too Young To Die* Francine Klagsbrun postulated that one reason for a dramatic increase in teen suicide is "life in the shadow of nuclear war." There are at least 50,000 bombs in the world; each 400 times more powerful than the Hiroshima bomb; each can kill 8.1 million in one hit."

Children do grow up with the ominous knowledge that our world can be annihilated in seconds.

Dr. Norman Bernstein, a professor in child psychology at the University of Illinois, attributed the rising teen suicide rate in part to "a loss of belief in the future, not just because of the bomb, but because of the economy" (*A Cry For Help*, p. 91).

But Mary Giffin counters: "the real causes are *internal*, not external. Young people can handle social problems. What they can't handle are their personal problems, feeling hopeless, neglected, utterly alone. MOST OF ALL they can't handle feeling that their parents' love is CONDITIONAL— and that they must perform, beat out the competition if they hope to win that love."

PARENTS ARE THE KEY

"Parents remain far and away the most important people in a child's life. They also remain the most important factors in a young person's decision to commit suicide," Giffin said.

Dr. Eliot Sorel, Professor of Psychiatry at George Washington University Medical School, says the breakdown begins in the first few months of the child's life when wealthy, ambitious and busy parents do not take time to establish a presence for their child that is "consistent, continuous, caring." The failure to establish that bond in infancy colors the trust that children have for their parents through adolescence. Blackburn notes that some kill themselves because they feel they are a burden to others (through sickness, public embarrassment, scandal, etc.). What about kids who feel in some way that their parents do not like or really want them? Instead of being angry or anti-social, apparently compliant and obedient kids may kill themselves to punish their parents' neglect or rejection.

Giffin cites the case of Roberta, a sophomore, whose parents were two successful lawyers. At the end of her freshman year, Roberta wrote in the little box on the inside of her textbook cover: "Condition issued: New. Condition returned: Dead." Just after the start of her sophomore year, Roberta began to vomit in one her classes and, later in the morning, in two other classes ... "She stayed home for the next three days. Early in the morning on the fourth day she killed herself. She had used up her welcome."

Emile Durkeim ("Le Suicide" 1897) argued that suicide came from an individual's sense of isolation from the community. He identified three kinds of suicide: (1) *EGOISTIC* where a person has few ties to his community that impact a sense of belonging. (2) *ANOMIC* where individual adjustment to society is suddenly disrupted. A sudden, shocking "effective-immediately" loss of a job, divorce, loss of a wife, a close friend or fortune are all possible causes. When someone loses a position or responsibility central to their sense of self, they are left with no anchor or purpose in life. (3) *ALTRUISTIC:* someone is overly integrated into society. The group's authority over the individual is so overwhelming, so compelling, he loses personal identity and sacrifices his life for the community like a soldier on the battlefield. (Like Japanese *hara-kiri*, Hindu *suttee* or at Jonestown in Guyana).

In a "Future Shock" society, job transfers, faraway friends, only rare visits to grandparents, and the collapse of the two-or-three generation-extended family all combine to break down community life. Kids are hurting. Parents that focus more on developing themselves than their community, pass on these values to their children who then prefer solitary passive TV watching to community projects, volunteerism or even sports.

"The need to have 'adult children' is not confined to teenagers. Many parents reject out of hand a nursery school that doesn't offer reading training. 'Just playing,' they say, 'is a waste of time.' Even kids' sports teams have turned into serious business; play well 'and eight years down the road an athletic scholarship may be waiting.' Teenagers dress like miniature adults in the latest designer fashions to compete at age 14 for dates, sex, grades and status. But physically and emotionally they are still children. Many pay a terrible price for the rush. When they stumble, as they will, too many have neither values nor understanding parents to cushion the fall" (Giffin op. cit. p.128).

With the extended family out of fashion, no alternative institution has filled the gap. The church—the obvious substitute for, or complement to, the family—has actually declined in influence. The neighborhood can no longer fill in as well as it did once where the family left off.

MATERIALISM AND SUICIDE

April Olzak writing on *Teen Suicide* for Chicago's *Tribune Magazine* opened with this question:

"What can you do to prevent your child from becoming suicidally depressed and committing suicide? Don't make too much money, and don't live in certain high-status suburbs. It could kill your child." This obvious exaggeration still contains an element of truth. With success and sophistication comes higher expectations and invariably disappointments (Giffin op. cit. p.131).

How can children survive in a Moloch culture that replaces love with things? Charles, a five-year-old who was psychiatrically treated for sudden and severe depression after a major house move, said he felt he had "lost all his best friends" when he moved. Especially sad was just what relationships little Charles had. Asked to describe those "friends" he described a bench in the neighbor's yard, the tree outside his window and the steps leading up to his family's front door.

THE ROLE OF DRUGS

In 1979, doctors wrote 81.5-million prescriptions for Valium, the most-prescribed tranquilizer. These sedatives and barbiturates are very often a suicide vehicle. "In 1978 more than 1,500 people died in hospital emergency rooms from misuse of tranquilizers. Valium alone was responsible for an estimated 50,000 emergency room visits that year. In England and Wales alone in 1968, overdoses of barbiturates accounted for 30 percent of all suicide verdicts and 65 percent of all suicide deaths due to drugs" (*Cry For Help* op. cit. footnote). Many world-famous artists, musicians and stage personalities have killed themselves by drug overdoses: *Keith Moon, Janis Joplin, Jim Morrison, Bonn Scott, Sid Vicious, Elvis Presley, John Bonham, John Belushi.* For some of them, drugs were the daily gamble of a self-destructive deathstyle. Power, wealth and success—the spirit of Moloch kills again.

And what is the greatest obstacle to stopping this slaughter? The opposite of love—indifference. We must prove we care. *The cardinal rule of suicide prevention is DO SOMETHING—and NOW.* A suicide attempt is a cry for help.

David Wilkerson says:

"I have a theory that suicide is a result of *misdirected hunger pangs.* Mankind was created with an innate hunger for God that must be satisfied. God so longed for the companionship of the man and woman He created He caused the inner man to experience loneliness as a kind of magnet to draw them back into His presence. . . . God put within man and woman an instinct. It is a very powerful instinct that yearns to return to the Heavenly Father at all times. And loneliness is the force that is designed to make that instinct work.

"Loneliness has nothing at all to do with isolation from people. . . Loneliness is caused by separation from the presence of God. That empty, lonely, depressed feeling is God's way of calling you back to Himself. When you grow cold towards God, when your faith weakens, when you quit feeding your soul with His holy Word, when you no longer pray, when you neglect the things of the Spirit you will become lonely. It is inevitable. Loneliness is God on the line, calling you to come quickly into His presence.

"His presence is the law against loneliness. This fullness of joy (Ps. 16:11) expels all loneliness . . . Unless those misdirected hunger pangs are satisfied and dispelled they can lead to death. Only people who are dead spiritually can commit suicide. That is why it is so extremely important to understand what causes loneliness" (*Suicide:* pp. 10-13).

For signs of would-be suicide, see Appendix 2

A Cry For Help
Dr. Mary Giffin & Carol Felsenthal (1983 Doubleday & Company Inc. Garden City N.Y.)

Suicide
Dave Wilkerson (1978: Route 1, Box 80, Lindale, TX 75771)

"What You Should Know About Suicide"
Dr. Bill Blackburn, (1982 Word Inc. Waco TX 76796)

POSTSCRIPT

The mass murder of children is not new. Babies were slaughtered in the time of Moses; babies were slaughtered in Jesus' day. Satan has put out his demonic contract in times past. *But why? In the records of the Bible each time a mass destruction of children fell on the world, a KEY LEADER was about to be born. Moses, Jesus,* a deliverer was coming, and hell was afraid.

The contract is out again. It has come in our time, and it has come for our children. What does that say to us? What can we learn from this awful slaughter? We must ask ourselves: What is there about *this* generation that makes Satan so afraid? What does he see or sense coming that has triggered such an awful holocaust?

In the times of Moses and the Lord Jesus, that rage missed its mark. The target of that destruction each time escaped. And the ONE THAT GOT AWAY did untold damage to hell's kingdom. There is something precious and important about this generation.

so deeply under attack. It may well be the last generation before Jesus returns. It may have among its ranks of the survivors the makings of a major spiritual miracle. There may be leaders-to-be rescued from the sword and the burning altars of Moloch that will lead an entire generation of the abandoned, loveless and lonely into the promises of God.

We all can do something; we all must do something. But we are not alone. For now, we must be found faithful. Like Miriam or Mary, we must do what we can, and listen to the voice of God. The future of the church, the future of the world is in his hands.

APPENDIX A

STEPS TO GUARD YOUR CHILD FROM DANGER

These steps are general guidelines to teach your child carefulness in a Moloch society. Children are being molested, kidnapped, raped, abused and murdered from all kinds of backgrounds. These rules may help save their lives.

(1) *Lead them early to Christ.* Teach them what it means to love God and trust him. The Holy Spirit is able to warn any believer with a clean conscience of the presence of evil. Scripture has much to say about discerning the intent and motives of others. Even children can often discern evil in a person when they are approached. "Take heed that you despise not one of these little ones; for I say unto you, that in heaven their angels do always behold the face of my Father which is in heaven" (Matt. 18:10).

(2) *PRAY for your children daily.* "The angel of the Lord encamps round about those that fear him" (Ps. 34:7). As we have often stressed here, much of the war on childhood is genuinely demonic in origin. Some tragedies may even be prevented by earnest, specific prayer where children in care of Christian parents can hold them before God for his protection and guardianship.

(3) *Be OBSERVANT.* Teach them to note suspicious, unusual or strange behavior in others. Bill Gothard advocates the teaching of character-quality-discernment based on topics from the book of Proverbs. Tell them how lost people look and behave. Here, the normalcy of a genuinely loving family will be a standard from which they can evaluate any deviations.

San Francisco Detective Dick Vance gives some basic rules for parents to teach their kids to help guard against sexual abuse or kidnap:

Rule 1: *"Get permission* from mommy and daddy whenever any grownup wants to take your picture—even if it's fun-loving Uncle Bob."

Rule 2: "When any adult wants you to keep a secret from your mommy or daddy be sure to *tell us about it."*

Rule 3: "*Never go along with any adult* to help them find a lost dog or cat."

Rule 4: "*Never go near a car with someone* in it even if the person in the car asks for help or directions." Teach them never to accept gifts, candy, toys, money or rides from strangers. They should know beyond a shadow of a doubt that *a stranger will NEVER be sent to pick them up from school,* a store or a movie. They should be told that if someone calls to them from a car they should never get close enough to be snatched or pulled into the car.

Rule 5: "Whenever an adult *gives* you something, be sure *to tell mom and dad about* it."

Rule 6: *"Never enter someone's home without our permission."*

Rule 7: "*Never go with a man who shows you a badge* and tells you he is a policeman unless he is wearing a uniform and is driving a marked police car." (A particularly cruel trap that molesters lay is to tell the children there is an emergency such as mommy was rushed to a hospital and the child must go there immediately" (Comment: *Arizona Republic* 5/19/84).

(4) *Resolve to NEVER hitchhike;* a firm, unbreakable rule with NO exceptions.

(5) *Tape money into a shoe for an emergency* phone call. Teach children to *memorize their name, home address and phone number,* how to use a dial and pushbutton phone.

(6) Teach them not to boast about money, and that personal belongings are never worth risking physical harm. Small treasures are precious to young children. One of the best tactics a child can learn to escape an attack is yelling loudly to attract attention. But fighting back, running or talking their way out of difficult situations are also useful tactics.

(7) *A child can be taught to cry out to the Lord* in life-threatening situations. There have been instances where this has actually resulted in the offender stopping or fleeing. Although God has not promised that Christians will be immune to harm or danger, when that threat is demonic in origin "the name of the Lord is a strong tower: the righteous runneth into it, and is safe" (Prov. 18:10).

APPENDIX B

How To Recognize Danger Signs
Of Child Suicide

SUICIDE DISTRESS SIGNALS

Mary Giffin lists three major stages of a suicide:

1. *GENERAL DISTRESS:* behavior that becomes a fixture or backdrop in the child's personality. Sets the stage for trouble.

(1) Gloom, withdrawal, noncommunication or acting out aggressive, hostile behavior, hyperactivity, manic, frantic behavior and extreme risk taking.

(2) Alcohol and drug abuse. Substance abuse is a key warning sign second only to depression as a spur to suicide. Nearly half the adolescents who commit suicide are drunk or "high" shortly before their death.

(3) Passive behavior. Numbness often hiding enormous rage.

(4) Changes in eating habits. Under- or over-eating. Both anorexia and bulimia are attempts at self-destruction. Anorexia nervosa affects mostly teenage girls (500,000 in the U.S. alone). Anoretics suffer from a profound sense of inadequacy or self-hatred. Bulimia (gorging high-calorie snacks, as many as 16 pounds of food in one sitting, and then purging by inducing vomiting or gobbling as many as 300 laxatives a week) is very serious. The practice is epidemic on some campuses with as many as 25 percent of college-age women involved. They gorge and purge in secret, like addiction to drugs or alcohol.

(5) Changes in sleeping habits. Trouble falling asleep or staying awake. Sleeping around the clock, or staying up around the clock.

(6) Fear of separation. Morbid unnatural fear of losing close friend or relative. Fakes illness to stay home.

2. *SPECIFIC BEHAVIOR CHANGES;* sudden and abnormal wild mood swings, impulsiveness, failure in school, feelings of haplessness. Loss of control or balance.

(7) Abrupt changes in personality. Becomes class clown, or withdrawn and sullen. Overly solicitous or ingratiating towards teachers and classmates. The normally shy and quiet becomes loud

and obnoxious.

(8) Sudden-growing extreme mood swings. Roller coaster persistent ups and downs.

(9) Impulsiveness. On-the-spot decisions.

(10) Slackening interest in schoolwork. Decline in grades.

(11) Inability to concentrate. Cannot focus on anything.

(12) Loss or lack of friends. Tendency to become a loner. Not involved in any extra-curricular activities, no close friends.

3. *FINAL PRECIPITANTS TO SUICIDE* (Events that push the child over the brink): The danger signals of impending doom.

(13) Loss of an important person or thing in the child's life. Parental death or divorce; irretrievable loss of position or place.

(14) Hopelessness. The three H's of suicide are:

(a) Haplessness: one thing after another goes wrong.

(b) Helplessness: person overreacts, and cannot see how he will ever get the energy or initiative to get back on the track.

(c) Hopelessness: the risk of suicide becomes very high when helplessness turns into hopelessness. It means the person has stopped seeking solutions to the problem and sees death as the only way out. "When a kid is going through a bad time I ask him how he feels about the future. If he says . . . 'things will get better,' I relax a little. If he tells me he's without hope I'm always on the lookout for suicide" (p.69).

(15) Obsession with death. A death wish. A "romance with death." May take big risks, have repeated "accidents."

(16) Evidence the child is making a will. Gives away precious possessions.

Here is a brief outline of the biblical versus the Babylonian pattern of the home and family. First we have the scriptural model of a happy home; that of Christ and His church.

The PATTERN OF FAITH (Eph. 5:25)

"Husbands, love your wives, even as Christ also loved the church and gave himself for it; That he might sanctify and cleanse it with the washing of water by the word, That he might present it to himself . . . glorious . . . So ought men to love their wives as their own bodies . . ." (Eph. 5:25-28).

"Wives, submit yourselves unto your own husbands, as unto the Lord. For the husband is the head of the wife, even as Christ is the head of the church: and he is the saviour of the body. Therefore as the church is subject unto Christ, so let the wives be to their own husbands in every thing." (Eph. 5: 22-24).

THE INNER SOUL OF A MARRIAGE

The key reason why so many couples have lost the power to stay in love lies here. Unless husband and wife both belong to Christ AND have learned from him what love is really like, both their marriage and their lives will suffer. Every marriage has a soul—an inner life which is lived out by both partners when they are alone together. This is shared by special tones of voice used in private that reveal what the other person is REALLY like when none is listening who needs to be impressed; by certain "looks" and little actions that form a whole language known only to the husband and wife. Is the soul of your or your parent's marriage Christian? Is your home a practical demonstration of two people following Jesus Christ and wanting to do as he asks for each other's happiness?

The following sets out the biblical pattern, or reality-structure around which a happy home life can be built. Much has been written in recent years concerning home and family responsibilities. We will not attempt to deal with these in any detail here (see Bibliography of Recommended Reading). Our concern here is basically over the spiritual forces that shape family destruction. The biblical answers to this are both widely known, much discussed, and readily available to the Christian public. Consider this as a suggested outline and take the time to study it in your own experience and Bible Study. But you, personally, are involved in one of these two patterns. Each person plays a part in imaging out the purposes of God or the Babylonian pattern. The home is the crucible of history.

HUSBAND—AUTHORITY

"Husbands LOVE your wives (the one under your leadership)
JUST AS (Equivalence—the same way as)
Christ LOVED the Church (Motivation of leadership)

and GAVE HIMSELF up (Sacrifice of independent goals) FOR HER" (Commitment to remain regardless of circumstance).

How is a husband to love his wife? Like Jesus loved the world; unconditionally. Without criticism or complaint; to allow a wife freedom to make her mistakes. Jesus loves us as we are. Dorothy Sayers, the great Christian author of the classic *Lord Peter Whimsey* detective series wrote a fictional dialogue with a fan who was "sure" her storybook hero would end up a Christian.

"From what I know of him," said Miss Sayers, "nothing is more unlikely." "But as a Christian yourself," the fan insists, "you must WANT him to be one."

"He would be horribly embarrassed by any such suggestion," replies Sayers (*Mind of The Maker,* p. 131).

Even God respects his creatures' autonomy. He gives us freedom to fail. To be like God, no good author shall impose his will or God's upon his creature. To be like Christ, no husband shall impose his will—or God's—upon his wife.

The husband is to demonstrate to his wife the same character-qualities Christ shows to his church. Study the relationship of Christ to his church and you discover the perfect marriage pattern.

The faithful husband loves, cherishes, and honors his wife. He gives of his time, his labor and his talents to promote the interest of his wife. And the faithful husband is jealous for his wife's good name. He feels deeply when her feelings or reputation are injured. Christ is the perfect picture of the faithful husband.

NEED: HONOR—(ADMIRATION, RESPECT)
PRINCIPLES: Equivalence of love and patient leadership that can be appealed to: Sacrifice (servant heart) to see corporate fulfillment. Commitment to remain, stand on godly and wise absolutes (security).
RESPONSIBILITY: LEAD Man finds fulfillment in DOING —his WORK (Christ the Creator)

WIVES—INSPIRATION

"Wives SUBMIT yourselves (Voluntary dependence)
to YOUR OWN husbands (making him special focus)

AS UNTO the LORD (as Christians trust Christ)
For the husband is the head of the wife
As Christ is the head of the Church.
Now as the Church submits to Christ
SO ALSO wives should submit to their husbands in everything."
(Eph. 5:22-24 NIV)

The wife is to demonstrate to her husband the same character-qualities Christ looks for in the Church.

The wife gives up her own name and takes on her husband's: she merges her life with his. She recognizes him as her head, and looks to him as her support, protector and guide. She devotes her whole life to his happiness and to carrying out his purposes in her love for him. She naturally looks to her husband to protect her from injury, insult and want. She hangs her happiness on him and expects that he will protect her and he is bound to do it. Their reputation and interests become one. What affects her character or reputation affects his.

NEED: SECURITY—CARED FOR, PROTECTED, LOVED.

PRINCIPLES: Power of submission(no manipulation). Faith—Trust in God-ordained leadership. Declared dependence.

RESPONSIBILITY: INSPIRE

ABILITIES: Insight—spiritual ability to perceive the true-heart purpose, motives, attitudes, emotional desires, intents, goals and aims of the inner person of the authority.

Awareness—spiritual ability to recognize the external faults, defects, errors, flaws and imperfections of actions and words of the authority.

Her ability to perceive can be used to hurt or heal. Her awareness of what he COULD be can help or hinder. He, like any other mortal, may fail. She must let her husband have freedom to have "feet of clay." Let him have freedom to fall short of what he ought to be. Hers is not to be a conditional love—with strings attached, but to love with the same kind of love with which Christ loves his Church.

A WOMAN finds fulfillment in BEING— her POSITION(Vine and Branches)

God's answer to the Babylonian pattern lies in the express teaching of Scripture concerning the responsibilities and privileges of the wife and husband as a human pattern of the Divine order.

BABYLONIAN PATTERN

Next is an outline of the direct OPPOSITE model to God's perfect order; that which Babylon, as a demonic master-spirit, seeks to impose on every home and family it seeks to control and destroy:

(NIMROD The King DIES)

AUTHORITY CUT OFF: The husband in some way dies (divorces, is fired, quits, voted out).

SYMPTOMS

WITHDRAWS from hurt, being put down, despised.

REFUGE—seeks fulfillment in drugs, drink, work, sports, media, sex, money-making, travel, cars, etc.

Opts out of RESPONSIBILITY.

DEMANDS or attempts CONTROL in ungodly, childish or violent ways: TANTRUMS ("I'm going out so don't expect me home tonight!") TEMPER (wife or child abuse: verbal, sexual or physical) and THREATS (kill self, children or wife).

The LIE: "She/They (those under authority—wife, deacons, employees) DO NOT REALLY LOVE YOU, ADMIRE you or APPRECIATE you:"

"Why did you ever take on this RESPONSIBILITY (marriage, church, job) when all they are trying to do is use you. Show kindness to her/them and all you get is hurt and rejection."

"There are OTHER PLACES/people/women you can become involved with who really do appreciate and respect you as a man. If those under your authority are not going to give it to you, then just GO SOMEWHERE ELSE (place/job/world—suicide)."

RESPONSE: "If that's the way they feel, then I'll just step back and let them do whatever they want to do; who needs this responsibility?"

RESULT: Pulls out—becomes a "little boy."

Throws tantrums that prove it.
Becomes childISH not childLIKE.
Attempts to regain control elsewhere.

SEMIRAMIS The Queen—(Controls The Son/Husband/Lover)

OPEN TO DECEPTION

SYMPTOMS: Control—"digs in," hangs on; feels loss of security and protection; does whatever needed to attempt to maintain that base of security.

MANIPULATION—takes control of institution while allowing God-appointed leader to appear so.

THE LIE: "He/They act and react to emotional pressure and responsibility JUST LIKE A LITTLE BOY."

"What you need is someone you can really respect. People don't KNOW LIKE I DO all his/their failures and faults and weaknesses. They have never seen his/their moods and tantrums. If they knew what I did they would never submit to or trust his/their leadership."

"You know more than he/they do about this; YOU ARE MORE QUALIFIED to run this; FOR HIS OWN GOOD you need to take more control and give some subtle direction to this thing (family/church/business) before it all falls apart."

RESULT: Assumes unprotected control and leadership. Becomes independent from authority. Target for demonic deception. Transfers control pattern onto children.

CHILD (Tammuz the Son)

Greatest impress of pattern on the FIRST-BORN SON:
When mother is *DOMINANT:* SON pressured towards a HITLER. *POSSESSIVE:* HOMOSEXUAL. *POLITICAL:* PRESIDENT. *RELIGIOUS:* MESSIAH.

NOTE: The Babylonian pattern will always resist or fight any attempt of the son to assume a true adult male leadership. Attempts made include continual use of baby names, dislike of maturity signs (choosing own clothes, food, marriage partner, growing a beard, earning own income, etc.) Second- and third-born sons are affected also but in more complex ways.

MANIPULATION Techniques

Babylon manipulates by standard kingdom of darkness techniques involving false guilt, criticism, railing, cynicism and belittling; the opposite of a childlike spirit. There are two main methods:

(1) *MORAL DISAPPROVAL:*

(a) *FALSE GUILT:* Making son/husband feel guilty by not conforming to mother's expectations or desires.

(b) *NAGGING:* Continual vocal pressure to conform.

(c) *HINTING:* The opposite of a childlike request. Use of guilt ("other wives all have this") and devious SUGGESTION ("is this the road that runs by the shopping mall?") instead of frank and honest request.

(d) *OPEN CRITICISM:* "The trouble with you is . . ."

(2) *CYNICISM:* Using the power of perception to destroy instead of support and encouragement. "I suppose you think that you can be like . . . Well, if they only knew what I know . . ."

(a) *SEX* used as a weapon for manipulation or to gain power.

(b) *GOADING* him to anger, "Well, go on. Go on! Just show me."

EFFECTS ON THE DAUGHTER

SEXUAL AFFECTION OF THE HUSBAND properly belonging to wife is transferred to DAUGHTER; (The Electra Complex). The dad begins to become sexually involved with his daughter. The daughter is pressured to become sexually involved with dad.

(a) Leads to rocketing *INCEST*—majority of child abuse from relatives.

(b) Incest opens the door to *PROSTITUTION* (significant number of child prostitutes come from incestuous homes).

(c) Mother's *EXAMPLE OF SENSUAL CONTROL* techniques on father damage future relationships of daughter relating to men.

(d) Taught, by example, *MANIPULATION* techniques for future husband/home/family and reestablishes the pattern in the next generation.

(e) Lays foundations of radical and anti-God *FEMINIST* movements.

(f) Husband-hatred and weak or absent father pressures daughter towards *LESBIANISM.*

(g) Rebellion principles establish further search for spiritual power in *WITCHCRAFT and OCCULT.*

This results in the comprehensive biblical description: "Babylon . . . the mother of harlots and all the abominations of the earth" (Rev. 17:5, see also Is. 47:1-15).

BREAKING THE PATTERN

How can a family or an individual in such a family affected by the Babylonian pattern pull out? By a solid commitment in faith to Christ; by a determination, affirmation, and whole-hearted commitment to the Father's commandments; and by taking, in prayer and authority, a determined stand against the Babylonian pattern and all its demonic implications. This would mean first, to consecrate one's whole life to the Lord Jesus Christ; second, to apply your heart and mind to God's Word; and third, to deal with any demonic patterns of bondage. The Babylonian pattern, like most of the lusts and bondages associated with the kingdom of darkness, is *not just a psychological, sociological or practical problem; it is a DEMONIC ATTACK.* It cannot be simply dealt with by just "counsel" or "advice" or even a Christian "marriage seminar." Christian ministers who have taught on the family have lost their families. Christian psychologists who know the dimensions of the problem may themselves become a part of it. And Christian counselors who have given excellent and sound biblical advice to others on marriage have lost *their* marriages. Babylon is an active master-spirit, Satan's own idea of his bride, and Babylon hates the church with everything in her command (Rev. 17:6). The only weapons we have are those that are simple, old, and absolutely powerful; faith, love, and devotion "like a little child" to the Lord Jesus.

MEN

REASSUME Leadership. "Do you want to be whole?" Then begin to assume responsibility again for your decisions. To avoid it is to default on God's Word. Each surrender is a loss of leadership. Take responsibility for your wrong, and repent. Admit your true guilt to God and to your family. Begin to live like a man of God.

If you are a son still living at home, begin to demonstrate some MATURITY in your education, friendships and job. A mother's thing is to make a son feel guilty if he doesn't become what she wants him to be. It is always harder for such a son to leave his mother. False guilt needs to be given to God for deliverance.

WOMEN

Go out of your way to SUBMIT. Biblical submission is not the act of a coward. It can be rather an act of the highest courage. The submission called for in Scripture is exactly parallel to that of becoming a Christian—an intelligent, careful, deliberate surrender to Christ. And that submission is a thing of the SPIRIT and the INNER HEART-ATTITUDE. There are many women who behave outwardly and physically like doormats to a demented husbands's childish rages and dangerous tempers. But their inner spirit is proud, challenging and unbroken. When men lose their tempers they act like fools and little boys; and pushing patience to a breaking point is the Babylonian pattern. A wife can learn the right buttons to push to "get his goat" and any bad mother can teach her 13-year-old daughter to do it too. Common ploys like continual talking, putting him down with destructive criticism or cynicism, is almost a guarantee that he will start to lose it.

CHILDREN

(1) *HONOR* your father and mother. Go out of your way to speak positively of them to others and encouragingly to them.

(2) *BUILD UP* your dad's leadership in the home. MEN (who are to LEAD) will admire. WOMEN (who are to inspire) will love.

(3) *LOVE FREES*—"There is no fear in love; but perfect love casts out all fear" (I Jn. 4:18a). HATE (indifference) and selfishness binds.

(4) *TRUST* is a vital thing. A threatened man holds BACK. A threatened woman holds ON. Restored trust in each other comes from restored faith in Christ at work in each life.

BIBLIOGRAPHY OF SOURCES AND CONTACTS

Abusers, The: Gary Fisher (Mott Media. 1975)

A/F PRODUCTIONS: Box 9000, Tacoma, WA 98424

Battle For The Public Schools: Humanism's Threat To Our Children: Tim LaHaye (Fleming Revell Old Tappan, N.J.)

BOB LARSON Ministries (*Rock Music & Media:* Box 26480, Denver, Colorado 80236)

CENTRUM Ministries: P.O. Box 29069, Hollywood, CA 90029

Child Abuse In The Classroom: Phyllis Schlafly, (Pere Marquette Press P.O. Box 495, Alton, Illinois 62002)

Child Abuse Self-Help: Jim Haskins, (Addison-Wesley)

Children Through The Ages: Barbara Kaye Greenleaf, (McGraw-Hill)

Children Without Childhood: Marie Winn, (Pantheon)

CITIZENS FOR EXCELLENCE IN EDUCATION (CEE): Box 3200, Costa Mesa, CA 92628

Coping With Abuse In Family; Wesley Monfalcone, (Westminster)

Communicating A Christian World-View In The Classroom; Robert L. Simonds (NACE Box 3200, Costa Mesa, CA 92628)

COVENANT HOUSE/UNDER 21; Father Bruce Ritter, 460 West 41 St., New York, N.Y. 10036

Creation In Christ: George Macdonald, (Harold Shaw)

Cry For Help, A: Mary Giffin, M.D. & Carol Felsenthal (Doubleday, 1983)

Cry Out! P.E. Quinn, (Abingdon)

Disappearance Of Childhood: Neil Postman, (Delacorte)

EAGLE FORUM (Phyllis Schlafly); Alton, Illinois 62002

Entertaining Demons Unaware: Gaverluk & Lindsted (S/W Radio Church) P.O. Box 1144, Oklahoma City, OK 73101

Eternity In Their Hearts: Don Richardson, (Regal)

Everlasting Man, The: G. K. Chesterton, (Dodd-Mead)

FAMILY LIFE ACTION COALITION: 217 E. Main, Genoa, Illinois 60135

Family Violence: Richard J. Gelles, (Sage Publ.)

Father-Daughter Rape: Elizabeth Ward, (Woman's Press)
Fighting The Traffic In Young Girls or War On The White Slave Trade—The Greatest Crime In the World's History: Ernest A. Bell (G.S. Ball, 1910)
FORERUNNER, The: P.O. Box 1799, Gainsville, FL 32602
Four Archetypes: C.G. Jung (Princeton University Press, 1969)
Four Arguments For The Elimination Of Television: Jerry Mander, (Morrow-Quill)
FOUNDATION FOR AMERICAN CHRISTIAN EDUCATION: P.O. Box 27035, San Francisco, CA 94127
FOUNDATION FOR SEXUALLY EXPLOITED CHILDREN: (Lloyd Martin & Jill Haddad:) (M.H. Capp, Box 3584, Bakersfield, CA 93385)
Freedom Of Religious Expression In Public High Schools: John W. Whitehead (Crossway Books, Westchester, IL)
GENTLE TOUCH Ministries (Music & Media) Box 590, Orchard Park, N.Y. 14127
Guide To The Christian School: Robert Billings (New Century Foundation, Washington, D.C.)
Home Education & Constitutional Liberties: John W. Whitehead and Wendell R. Bird (Crossway Books, Westchester, IL)
Homegrown Kids; Homespun Schools: Raymond & Dorothy Moore (Word Books, Waco, TX)
Hours With The Bible: Cunningham, Geikie, (Cassell)
How To Stop The Porno Plague: Neil Gallagher, (Bethany House, 6020 Auto Club Rd., Minneapolis, MN 55438, 1977)
Images Of Childhood: Anita Schorsch, (Mayflower)
In Defense Of The Family: Rita Kramer, (Basic Books)
INSTITUTE IN BASIC YOUTH CONFLICTS (Bill Gothard) Box 1, Oak Brook, Illinois
Interpreters Dictionary Of The Bible: George Buttrick, Ed. (Abingdon)
Kiss Daddy Goodnight: Louise Armstrong, (Pocket Books, N.Y. 1978)
LAST DAYS NEWSLETTER: Ed. Melody Green (LDM)
LIVING ALTERNATIVES: Box 4600, Tyler, TX 75712
Mediaspeak: Donna Woolfolk Cross, (Mentor)
Megatrends: John Naisbitt, (Warner Books)

MEL GABLERS, The: P.O. Box 7518, Longview, TX 75607
NATIONAL ASSOCIATION OF CHRISTIAN EDUCATORS
(NACE): Box 3200 Costa Mesa, CA 92628
NATIONAL RUNAWAY SWITCHBOARD: 800 621-4000:
TX 800 392-3352; IL 800 972-6004 or 800 231-6946
NATIONAL FUND FOR RUNAWAY CHILDREN: 1511 K.
St. Suite 805, Dept. P, Washington, D.C.
Our Endangered Children: Vance Packard (Little-Brown)
PAUL & LISA INC.: Box 588, Westbrook, CT 06498
Private Zone: Frances Davee, (Chas. Franklin)
PRO-FAMILY FORUM: P.O. Box 8907, Fort Worth, Texas
76112
*Protecting Your Child: The Christian Society For The Protection
of Children* (Little Ones Books)
Religion Of The Hebrews: J. P. Peters, (Atheneum Press)
Revival: Winkie Pratney, (Whitaker House, Springdale, PA 15144,
1983)
Rock: Bob Larson, (Tyndale, Wheaton, IL 1982)
Rock 'n Roll Babylon: Gary Heman, (Perigee)
RUTHERFORD INSTITUTE: John W. Whitehead (Christian
Legal Foundation; P.O. Box 510, Manassas, VA 22119)
Sex Education In The Public Schools: David Pratte (1822 High-
land Dr. NW, Cullman, Alabama 35055, 1982)
*Sex Through The Looking-Glass: The Dynamics of Human Sex-
uality from a Biblical Viewpoint:* Lambert T. Dolphin and Carroll
E. Gallivan; (Good News Publishers, Westchester, Ill. 60153,
1968)
Stealing Of America, The: John W. Whitehead, (Crossway Books,
Westchester, Illinois 60153, 1983)
Stolen Children: John Edward Gill, (Penguin 1981)
Suicide: David Wilkerson, (Dave Wilkerson Publications, Route
1, Box 80, Lindale, TX 75771, 1978)
Siecus Circle, The: A Humanist Revolution (Sex Ed.); Claire
Chambers (Western Islands Publ., Belmont, Mass.)
Time For Anger, A: The Myth of Neutrality: Franky Schaeffer,
(Crossway Books, 1983)
Textbooks On Trial ("Are Textbooks Harming Your Kids?") James
Hefley

TRUTH ABOUT ROCK: (The Peters) Box 9222, St. Paul, MN 55109

Two Babylons, The: Alexander Hislop, (Loizeux Bros., Neptune, N.J. 07753, 2nd Ed., 1959)

Violence In The Family: Strauss & Steinmetz (Harper & Row)

We Can Combat Child Abuse: Shirley J. O'Brien (U. Arizona, Tucson, AZ 85721, Coll. Agric. Co-Op. Extn. Service. 1982)

We Have A Secret: Lloyd Martin & Jill Haddad, (M. H. Capp & Co., Box 3584, Bakersfield, CA 93385)

What If I Say No?: Martin & Haddad (M. H. Capp & Co. op. cit.)

What You Should Know About Suicide: Bill Blackburn, (Word Books, Waco, Texas 76796, 1982)

When God Was A Woman: Merlin Stone, (Harvest/Harcourt Brace Jovanovich Ltd., 1976)

Woman's Encyclopaedia Of Myths & Secrets: Barbara Walker

YOUTHLETTER: Ed. Jim Reapsom, (Evangelical Ministries)

Special thanks to Dr. Herb Titus of CBN University for legal research and material on child abuse; John Cooney and the N.Z. Grapevine Staff for allowing me to ransack their files; Dana and Bob Rhodes for the books; and Carol Venable of Huntington House, who hunted down more material for me than I thought humanly possible.

MORE FAITH-BUILDING BOOKS
FROM HUNTINGTON HOUSE

America Betrayed, by Marlin Maddoux. This hard-hitting book exposes the forces in our country which seek to destroy the family, the schools and our values. This book details exactly how the news media manipulates your mind. Marlin Maddoux is the host of the popular, national radio talk show "Point of View."

A Reasonable Reason to Wait, by Jacob Aranza, is a frank definitive discussion on premarital sex—from the biblical viewpoint. God speaks specifically about premarital sex according to the author. The Bible also provides a healing message for those who have already been sexually involved before marriage. This book is must reading for every young person—and also for parents—who really want to know the biblical truth on this important subject.

Backward Masking Unmasked, by Jacob Aranza. Rock 'n' roll music affects tens of millions of young people and adults in America and around the world. This music is laced with lyrics exalting drugs, the occult, immorality, homosexuality, violence and rebellion. But there is a more sinister danger in this music according to the author. It's called "backward masking." Numerous rock groups employ this mind-influencing technique in their recordings. Teenagers by the millions—who spend hours each day listening to rock music—aren't even aware the messages are there. The author clearly exposes these dangers.

Backward Masking Unmasked, (cassette tape) by Jacob Aranza. Hear actual satanic messages and judge for yourself.

Beast, by Dan Betzer. This is the story of the rise to power of the future world dictator—the antichrist. This novel plots a dark web of intrigue which begins with the suicide-death of Adolf Hitler who believed he had been chosen to be the world dictator. Yet, in his last days, he spoke of "the man who will come after me." Several decades later that man, Jacque Catroux, head of the European economic system, appears on the world scene. He had been born the day Hitler died, conceived by the seed of Lucifer himself. In articulate prose, the author describes the "disappearance" of the Christians from the earth; the horror and hopelessness which followed that event; and the bitter agony of life on earth after all moral and spiritual restraints are removed.

Globalism: America's Demise, by William Bowen, Jr. The Globalists—some of the most powerful people on earth—have plans to totally eliminate God, the family, and the United States as we know it today. Globalism is the vehicle the humanists are using to implement their secular humanistic philosophy to bring about their one-world government. The four goals of Globalism are *A ONE-WORLD GOVERNMENT *A NEW WORLD RELIGION *A NEW ECONOMIC SYSTEM *A NEW RACE OF PEOPLE FOR THE NEW WORLD ORDER. This book clearly alerts Christians to what the Globalists have planned for them.

God's Timetable for the 1980's, by David Webber. This book presents the end-time scenario as revealed in God's Word. It deals with a wide spectrum of subjects including the dangers of the New Age Movement, end-time weather changes, outer space, robots and biocomputers in prophecy. According to the author, the mysterious number 666 is occurring more and more frequently in world communications, banking and business. This number will one day polarize the computer code marks and identification numbering systems of the Antichrist, he says.

More Rock, Country & Backward Making Unmasked by Jacob Aranza. Aranza's first book *Backward Masking Unmasked* was a national bestseller. It clearly exposed the backward satanic messages included in a lot of rock and roll music. Now, in the sequel, Aranza gives a great deal of new information on backward messages. Also, for the first time in Christian literature, he takes a hard look at the content, meaning and dangers of country music. "Rock, though filled with satanism, sex and drugs . . . has a hard time keeping up with the cheatin', drinkin' and one-night stands that continue to dominate country music," the author says.

Murdered Heiress . . . Living Witness, by Dr. Petti Wagner. The victim of a sinister kidnapping and murder plot, the Lord miraculously gave her life back to her. Dr. Wagner—heiress to a large fortune—was kidnapped, tortured, beaten, electrocuted and died. A doctor signed her death certificate, yet she lives today!

Natalie, The Miracle Child by Barry and Cathy Beaver. This is the heartwarming, inspirational story of little Natalie Beaver—God's miracle child—who was born with virtually no chance to live—until God intervened! When she was born her internal organs were outside her body. The doctors said she would never survive. Yet, God performed a miracle and Natalie is healed today. Now, as a pre-teen, she is a gifted singer and sings the praises of a miracle-working God.

Rest From the Quest, by Elissa Lindsey McClain. This is the candid account of a former New Ager who spent the first 29 years of her life in the New Age Movement, the occult and Eastern mysticism. This is an incredible inside look at what really goes on in the New Age Movement.

Take Him to the Streets, by Jonathan Gainsbrugh. Well-known author David Wilkerson says this book is " . . . immensely helpful . . . " and " . . . should be read . . . by all Christians who yearn to win lost people to Christ, particulary through street ministry. Effective ministry techniques are detailed in this how-to book on street preaching. Carefully read and applied, this book will help you reach other people as you *Take Him to the Streets.*

The Agony of Deception, by Ron Rigsbee. This is the story of a young man who became a woman through surgery and now, through the grace of God, is a man again. Share this heartwarming story of a young man as he struggles through the deception of an altered lifestyle only to find hope and deliverance in the grace of God.

The Divine Connection, by Dr. Donald Whitaker. This is a Christian guide of life extension. It specifies biblical principles of how to feel better and live longer and shows you how to experience Divine health, a happier life, relief from stress, a better appearance, a healthier outlook on life, a zest for living and a sound emotional life.

The Hidden Dangers of the Rainbow, by Constance Cumbey. A national #1 bestseller, this is a vivid expose' of the New Age

Movement which is dedicated to wiping out Christianity and establishing a one-world order. This movement—a vast network of tens of thousands of occultic and other organizations—meets the test of prophecy concerning the Antichrist.

The Hidden Dangers of the Rainbow Tape, by Constance Cumbey. Mrs. Cumbey, a trial lawyer from Detroit, Michigan, gives inside information on the New Age Movement in this teaching tape.

The Miracle of Touching, by Dr. John Hornbrook. Most everyone enjoys the special attention that a loving touch brings. Throughout the chapters of this encouraging book the author explains what touching others through love — under the careful guidance of the Lord Jesus Christ — can accomplish. Dr. Hornbrook urges Christians to reach out and touch someone — family members, friends, prisoners — and do it to the glory of God, physically, emotionally and spiritually.

The Twisted Cross, by Joseph Carr. One of the most important works of our decade, *The Twisted Cross* clearly documents the occult and demonic influence of Adolf Hitler and the Third Reich which led to the Holocaust killing of more than six million Jews. The author even gives the specifics of the bizarre way in which Hitler actually became demon-possessed.

Who Will Rise Up? by Jed Smock. This is the incredible — and sometimes hilarious — story of Jed Smock, who with his wife Cindy, has preached the uncompromising gospel on the malls and lawns of hundreds of university campuses throughout this land. They have been mocked, rocked, stoned, mobbed, beaten, jailed, cursed and ridiculed by the students. Yet this former university professor and his wife have seen the miracle-working power of God transform thousands of lives on university campuses.

Yes, send me the following books:

____ copy (copies) of **America Betrayed!** @ $5.95 =____

____ copy (copies) of **A Reasonable Reason To Wait** @ $4.95 =____

____ copy (copies) of **Backward Masking Unmasked** @ $4.95 =____

____ copy (copies) of **Backward Masking Unmasked Cassette Tape** @ $5.95 =____

____ copy (copies) of **Beast** @ $5.95 =____

____ copy (copies) of **Devil Take The Youngest** @ $6.95 =____

____ copy (copies) of **Globalism: America's Demise** @ $6.95 =____

____ copy (copies) of **God's Timetable For The 1980's** @ $5.95 =____

____ copy (copies) of **More Rock, Country & Backward Masking Unmasked** @ $5.95 =____

____ copy (copies) of **Murdered Heiress . . . Living Witness** @ $5.95 =____

____ copy (copies) of **Natalie** @ $4.95 =____

____ copy (copies) of **Rest From The Quest** @ $5.95 =____

____ copy (copies) of **Take Him to the Streets** @ $6.95 =____

____ copy (copies) of **The Agony Of Deception** @ $6.95 =____

____ copy (copies) of **The Divine Connection** @ $4.95 =____

____ copy (copies) of **The Hidden Dangers Of The Rainbow** @ $5.95 =____

____ copy (copies) of **The Hidden Dangers Of The Rainbow Seminar Tapes** @ $13.50 =____

____ copy (copies) of **The Miracle of Touching** @ $5.95 =____

____ copy (copies) of **The Twisted Cross** @ $7.95 =____

____ copy (copies) of **Who Will Rise Up?** @ $5.95 =____

AT BOOKSTORES EVERYWHERE or order direct from: Huntington House, Inc., P.O. Box 53788, Lafayette, LA 70505.

Send check/money order or for faster service VISA/Mastercard orders call toll-free 1-800-572-8213. Add: Freight and handling, $1.00 for the first book ordered, 50¢ for each additional book.

Enclosed is $ _____ including Postage.

Name _____

Address _____

City _____ State and Zip _____